The Potter's Rib

MENTORING FOR PASTORAL FORMATION

The Potter's Rib

MENTORING FOR PASTORAL FORMATION

BRIAN A. WILLIAMS

REGENT COLLEGE PUBLISHING
Vancouver, British Columbia

Published 2005 by Regent College Publishing
5800 University Boulevard, Vancouver, BC V6T 2E4 Canada
Web: www.regentpublishing.com
E-mail: info@regentpublishing.com

This publication was made possible by a grant from the Lilly
Endowment Inc. <www.lillyendowment.org>

Views expressed in works published by Regent College Publishing
are those of the author and do not necessarily represent the
official position of Regent College <www.regent-college.edu>.

Cover photograph by Bruce Jeffrey

Library and Archives Canada Cataloguing in Publication Data

Williams, Brian A., 1971–
The potter's rib : mentoring for pastoral formation / Brian A.
Williams.

ISBN 1-57383-267-7

1. Spiritual direction. 2. Pastoral theology. 3. Mentoring
in church work—Study and teaching. 4. Clergy—Office. I.
Title.

BV4020.W54 2005   253'.071

C2004-905718-9

CONTENTS

ACKNOWLEDGEMENTS

The financial support of the Lilly Endowment Incorporated of Indianapolis, Indiana is gratefully acknowledged. Without the Endowment's generous support this project would not have been commenced or completed. The Board of Governors of Regent College, Vancouver, is also to be thanked for their oversight and support of this initiative.

I would be making an egregious error in a book on mentoring were I not to acknowledge and extend my gratitude to those who over the years have mentored me both formally and informally, those who took me seriously and with either keen eye or fertile imagination saw evidence of the Spirit. I have not the space to thank each one for their individual contribution to my spiritual and intellectual formation.

Though I do not approach their depth of heart or breadth of mind, the following individuals certainly have given me, as Henry Zylstra would say, more to be Christian with, more to be a theologian with, and more to be a pastor with. They graciously stoked my fires and at times wisely cooled them. I only regret I did not listen more closely, observe more keenly, or ask questions more often while I was with these theological pastors and pastoral theologians. So to Paul Mehrens, Mark Moore, J. K. Jones, J. I.

Packer, and Jonathan Mills, I extend a special debt of gratitude. Along with many others, I have been a beneficiary of their love of Christ and his church.

To those who spoke into this project at significant moments along the way, I extend my gratitude as well. Their words of encouragement often extended my vision, and their words of caution drew it back. Special thanks to Don Lewis, who invited me to work on this project, to Barbara Mutch, who helped give it shape, and to Darrell Johnson, whose encouragement kept me working on it late in the day (and night). My thanks also to those who responded to particular questions and conundrums: Thena Ayres, Brent Fearon, Stan Grenz, Bruce Hindmarsh, Jim Houston, Edward Lee, Pete Molloy, Eugene Peterson, Charles Ringma, David Roadcup, and Sarah Tweedale.

In the case of Phil Reilly, the good-natured Scot who was my research assistant and constant companion during this project, I can only say what he already knows: that without him this text would not have been completed. Phil patiently endured many early mornings, late nights, and a few all-nights during the preparation and production of this book. He put his shoulder to the work alongside mine and pushed it forward—often when I did not know where it was going. He contributed substantially to the pieces on biblical mentors, Catherine of Siena and Dietrich Bonhoeffer, and to the section devoted to practical "tools." For your friendship and your hospitality, I am in your debt.

My deepest gratitude is reserved for my wife, Kim, and my daughter, Ilia. From Kim's ambitious creativity and ministering sensitivity, and from Ilia's wide-eyed exuberance and her love for people, I continually learn what it means to be a person, a husband, a father, and a pastor.

INTRODUCTION

What is pastoral ministry to look like in the twenty-first century? Who is a twenty-first century pastor to be? How is he or she to be educated and prepared in a culture that studiously marginalizes pastors to the unobtrusive fringe?

The book you now hold in your hands and the practice to which you are being invited is one small attempt to respond to those questions. Specifically, it ruminates on the latter question—what is an appropriate, theologically determined way of pastoral formation and preparation for ministry? To answer that we momentarily turn our eyes away from the clamor and banter of our current age, and look instead to those wise practitioners of pastoral ministry among the people of God who have sought to faithfully mediate God's good news to others. What we find are persons who, while they faithfully served their current generation in Israel or the church, also served future generations by preparing other persons to take their place and carry on the task of ministry. As the Spirit called people to their side, they shared the practical tasks of ministry with them. They modeled for them humble service to God's people. They reflected with them on the theological truths that determined who they were and what they did: creation and covenant, sin and grace, Christ and cross, resurrection and ascension. They prayed, worshipped, and sought the will of the Lord together with them. In this way, their successors were formed and prepared for service.

In this text we consider what it might look like to reinvigorate that practice. Following a modern trend, we have described it as "mentoring for pastoral formation," but it might very well go by any number of other names. It borrows from the classical discipline of spiritual direction or spiritual friendship and from the common practice of apprenticeship, yet it is focused on a particular vocation, on the one hand, and, on the other, it is primarily concerned with the formation of a person called by a personal God to serve other persons in the midst of a sin-distorted world. Therefore, pastors must develop both their skills and their spirits. Both of these are developed most comprehensively when the young pastor is set into the thick practice of ministry alongside a more experienced pastor who offers the new pastor a *place* to do ministry and to be a pastor and, more importantly, the *space* to reflect on who she or he is and what he or she is doing.

We have designed this text to be read by both the "pastor-mentor" and, for lack of a better term, the "pastor-mentee." At times it will be specifically addressed to one or the other and at times to both. However, mentoring for pastoral formation, as we understand it, is so similar to what pastors do anyway, and the practice of being mentored—of reflecting on our spirit and pastoral work with another person—is so crucial for any pastor, that each part of the text could be equally relevant to both mentor and mentee.

Our journey begins in the first three chapters with a consideration of what is required for pastoral formation and how it might be accomplished through the practice of mentoring. In chapter four, we look at the possible hazards of mentoring thrown in our path by our culture, our fallen nature, and by some of our common pastoral habits. After reflecting on the actual relationship between mentor and mentee in chapters five and six, we deliberately turn into the history of God's people in chapters seven and eight in order to enlarge our pastoral imaginations and open ourselves to be mentored by other pastors who offer us wisdom born from their own rich and variegated journeys of pastoral preparation and pastoral mentoring. Finally, in chapter nine, we offer a few practical tools that could be used to give shape and form to the mentoring relationship.

Mentoring for pastoral formation requires intentionality, time, and discipline on the part of both mentor and mentee, but the effort, to be sure, reaps a seven-fold harvest. So now we invite you to come alongside Gregory of Nazianzus, Augustine, Catherine of Siena, the apostle Paul, George Herbert, Søren Kierkegaard, and others, as together we consider the rich practice of mentoring for pastoral formation and preparation for service to church and world.

CHAPTER 1

GREGORY OF NAZIANZUS
AND THE FLIGHT OF PASTORS

Who is prepared to respond to the call to pastoral ministry in Christ's church? "No one, if he will listen to my judgment and accept my advice! This is of all things most to be feared, this is the extremest of dangers in the eyes of everyone who understands the magnitude of success and the utter ruin of failure!"[1] Thus exclaimed a new pastor in the fourth century, defending his escape from the church and the bishop who—in what he labeled an act of "noble tyranny"—had forcefully ordained him a priest. Unprepared, he had neither sought ordination nor found it a welcome imposition—and so he fled the city when it broke upon him and ran to the solace of friends in a nearby monastic community in order to reflect upon the high calling and daunting requirements of pastoral ministry.

His retreat, however, lasted only seven months. When he returned fully ready to serve the ordaining congregation of Nazianzus, in what today is central Turkey, he did so under a palpable cloud of mistrust and suspicion. His first sermon, on Easter, A.D. 362, in this predominantly Christian city on the pinnacle of the church year, echoed into an unexpectedly empty cathedral. This young priest had provoked the anger of people wounded by his sudden flight. As the son of the bishop who ordained him, he was expected to aid and eventually succeed his aging father.

Thus, the thirty-year-old Gregory of Nazianzus began his role as theologian and pastor. Eventually known—along with his friend, Basil of Caesarea, and Basil's brother, Gregory of Nyssa—as one of the three Cappadocian Fathers, the great defenders of Nicene Trinitarian orthodoxy, he entered the pastoral vocation on a dead run in the opposite direction, only too aware of his overwhelming inadequacy to meet its demands. Gregory was one of the church's most creative and influential theologians—he was called "the Great" by the Ecumenical Council of Ephesus and "the Theologian" by the Council of Chalcedon, a title the Eastern Orthodox tradition reserves only for Gregory and the apostle John.

Yet the lucid and sobering questions which rang in his heart reverberate in the heart of every would-be pastor or priest, and set before us our task of pastoral formation: Who is prepared to take up this task, and how are they made ready? "I had much toilsome consideration to discover my duty," Gregory wrote, "being set in the midst between two fears." These two fears, which so exercised his spirit, were, in short, disobedience to God's call, on the one hand, and rashness about the nature of pastoral ministry, on the other. Gregory was fearful of presumption because he knew that with the call to ministry came a responsibility to care for souls for whom he would someday be asked to give account. On the other hand, with the cultural establishment of Christianity in the fourth century, he knew that the call also came with the temptation to pride, power, and worldliness.

> Pray, mark how accurately and justly I hold the balance between the fears, neither desiring an office not given to me, nor rejecting it when given. The one course marks the rash, the other the disobedient, both the undisciplined. My position lies between those who are too bold, or too timid; more timid than

those who rush at every position, more bold than those who avoid them all.[1]

Fear of presumption and inadequacy drove him away, and fear of disobedience to God's call drove him back.

Born around A.D. 330 to Bishop Gregory and his devout wife, Nonna, Gregory lacked neither privilege nor education. He was educated in philosophy and rhetoric at Caesarea by Carterius, later tutor of St. John Chryosostom. Here, he began an intimate and lifelong friendship with Basil. After Caesarea, he studied at Alexandria,[3] and then for many years at Athens,[4] alongside Basil and the future Emperor, Julian (later, The Apostate). Though Gregory's academic attainments opened to him the possibility of a distinguished career as a lawyer or professor, his yearnings were for the monastic life of contemplation. In his struggle to discern his future path he consulted—as was his custom—his beloved friend, Basil. They resolved in common to quit the world for the service of God alone and so established a monastery together in Pontus, near Nazianzus.

After two or three years Gregory reluctantly returned to Nazianzus. Upon his arrival, his aging father, in need of his son's support and with the approval of the people of the diocese, forced ordination upon him sometime around Christmas, 361. Alarmed, Gregory fled back to Pontus to Basil's monastic community in order to take due consideration of the tasks to which he was being called. Ten years later in 371, when Basil himself appointed Gregory bishop of Sasima, he again fled from the responsibilities of his office. In all, Gregory fled four times during his life—each time at the beginning of new ecclesial ventures—until he finally took up the pastoral care of the small Christian community at Constantinople when he became their bishop in 379.[5]

With each new pastoral calling the disparity between the great demands of the task and his own meager resources to meet the task induced Gregory to flee: "A man must himself be cleansed, before cleansing others," he said, "himself become wise, that he may make others wise; become light, and then give light: draw near to God, and so bring others near; be hallowed, then hallow them; be possessed of hands to lead others by the hand, of wisdom to give advice." When will someone be ready to do such weighty things? Gregory asks, then answers: "Not even extreme old age would be too long a limit to assign. For hoary hairs combined with prudence are better than inexperienced youth, well-reasoned hesitation than inconsiderate haste . . . Who can mould, as clay-figures are modeled in a single day, the defender of the truth?"[6]

Flight from ordination and the pastoral ministry, however, is not a chapter in Gregory's story alone. Ambrose of Milan, so influential in Augustine's conversion, fled from his unexpected ordination in 373 and hid in a friend's house. Upon being elected pope in February 590, another Gregory—known as Gregory the Great—vigorously protested his election and fled for a time in order to consider the demands of the calling. Augustine wept at his forced ordination at Hippo, in North Africa, for it meant the end of his contemplative life among friends and a plunge into the demanding ecclesial affairs of the church. Before he took office, he pleaded with his bishop for time to prepare for his new task: "Do you truly love the Church itself, to which you wish me to minister? I am sure you love both me and the Church, but you consider me fit, whereas I myself know better."[7] Likewise, Cyprian, Evagrius of Pontus, John Chrysostom, Basil, and numerous others fled for a time to prepare their hearts and minds for ministry.

Scripture, too, presents us with a host of people who either fled or resisted God's call to ministry. "I will be a poor spokesman," protests Moses. "I am too young," says Jeremiah. "My mouth is unclean," cries Isaiah. "I dislike this calling," declares the subject of the most famous flight, Jonah, with whom Gregory directly identifies himself. And though he did not flee, what was the journey of formation like for Jesus? Or for the apostles or Paul? When we examine history and Scripture, we see that the call to ministry induces a legitimate and warranted desire to pause and consider both the nature of the calling and the inadequate resources one brings.

Among modern pastors, flight from one's calling is also common, but not always for the sake of formation. Many pastors take emotional, spiritual, mental, or geographical flights in response to burnout, boredom, moral failure, or loss of faith. It is all too apparent that many who do not fly early for the sake of preparation fly later in either internal or external abandonment of their calling. Whereas Jonah flew because his calling was beneath him, Gregory flew because his was far beyond him. Choosing not to follow Jonah's flight to Tarshish, Gregory observes that "God alone of all things cannot be escaped from or contended with; if He wills to seize and bring them under His hand, He outstrips the swift, He outwits the wise, He overthrows the strong, He abases the lofty, He subdues rashness, He represses power."[8]

We stand today before Gregory's questions: Who is the man or woman prepared to take up this role? How does formation for pastoral ministry take place? What is required to walk between presumption and obedience? How is the Spirit shaping us for ministry? What does it mean for us to be ministers and how do we do it well? Where do we look for models to inform our "pastoral imagination"? And do we respond to the inquirer with the answers of *ordination, graduation,* or *conversion?* With but a moment's reflection we know that even these are inadequate—necessary, perhaps, but not sufficient. First, it is not simply a question of ordination. As Gregory knew, that is comparatively easy, for though most of us seek it rather than endure it, we know well that ordination is not the same as pastoral formation. Though an individual denomination's ecclesiastical requirements may be important—where to study, where to intern, what exams to pass—and though they represent the church's attempt to take responsibility for preparing and equipping those it calls to be pastors, these requirements are not the sum of formation.

Secondly, as most pastors know—or as most come to find out one way or another—it is also one matter to learn to exegete a text, construct and deliver a sermon, or organize a worship service—that is, to do what a pastor does—and quite another matter to become a pastor. Becoming a pastor is not necessarily coterminous with receiving the title "Master of Divinity" or the license to marry and bury. This the highly educated Gregory also knew, for despite having received an almost unparalleled education, he felt that he was unprepared. Nor, finally, is pastoral preparation a question of conversion, for not all receive the call to pastoral ministry subsequent to their call to come to Christ. The one follows the other and is dependent upon it, but not as a matter of course or right.

Nor, as Gregory also knew, is becoming a pastor a question of individual effort or isolated struggle, despite what internal wrangling between spirit and Spirit may go on. Protestantism is full of *sola*s as shorthand summaries of Christian doctrine. We seem to like them: *sola gratia, sola fidei, sola scriptura, solus Christus.* However, one *sola* that has never been part of the Christian tradition—Roman, Protestant, or Orthodox—is *sola pastor.* Preparation for pastoral ministry, therefore, is not a matter of graduation, ordination, conversion, or individual will. Instead, it is a matter of *calling* and *formation* in the company of others.

THE JOURNEY OF PASTORAL FORMATION

It is often the case that more people are doing the tasks of ministry than are becoming pastors. To borrow an image common to both Jewish and Christian heritage, we might appropriately describe the formation of a pastor as a long and arduous journey, one not lightly or carelessly undertaken. As John Chrysostom, the austere fourth-century preacher, warns in his *Treatise Concerning the Christian Priesthood*: "Anyone who is about to enter upon this walk of life needs to explore it thoroughly beforehand and only then to undertake this ministry. And why? Because if he studies the difficulties beforehand he will at any rate have the advantage of not being taken by surprise when they crop up."[9] Formation as a pastor is less like a speedy, climate-controlled flight from San Francisco to Miami and more like a hike from Schenectady, New York to Vernon, British Columbia, with detours through Muskogee, Eureka, and Moose Jaw, and stops at the Corn Palace and the Giant Ukrainian Easter Egg. A journey from Ai to Jordan, Cairo to Jerusalem, Joppa to Nineveh, Tarsus to Rome. The pastoral journey usually neither begins nor ends somewhere glamorous, but requires the full and deliberate attention of the traveler to a particular place and its people. Along the way we meet other travelers ready with wise words hewn out of experience, and we meet former travelers who have settled for the succor of Camel Lights and a truck stop's scorched coffee. On this journey, however, the traveler must learn—and learn early—to attend not only to their knowing and doing, but also to their being, for the temptation to flee from the journey to the sedentary truck stop can be great at times, and only through the grace of the Spirit, the company of others, and a due diligence to our personal and spiritual formation are we able to endure and flourish as pastors.

Many voices of other pastor-travelers who have walked this way before us hearken us to attend to our preparation for the journey. Integrity, credibility, and faithfulness as a pastor depend on a congruence between life and doctrine, spirit and Spirit, Christ-words and a Christ-life. We not only know and proclaim the truth, but in order to do so we must live the truth, and if we might coin a verb, we must *parabolize* the truth. We must become living parables to others of life in the Kingdom. Our spiritual formation is the soil in which grow the skills of pastoral ministry—preaching, teaching, counseling. Without a rich soil, even the most skillfully planted seeds wither in the heat. So witness and testify a chorus of pastors who have endeavored in their own way and in their own time to be faithful parables of the truth to others. Consider the following charges from these fellow-pastors who walked ahead of us from Schenectady to Vernon, Thagaste to Hippo, Africa to Olney:

> It is a poor affair to be a stage-player in divinity, to be able to hold a congregation by the ears, by furnishing them with an hour's amusement, if this be all. But the man who is what he professes to be, who knows what he speaks of, in whom the truth lives and dwells, who has not received the Gospel from books, or by hearers only, but in the school of the great Teacher, acquires a discernment, a taste, a tenderness, and a humility which enable him to console the distressed and open the hearts of the prejudiced . . . So study the Word of God and the workings of your own heart.[10]
>
> —John Newton, "Letter to a Young Minister," 1750

> Pastors should not assume that "when they have read the fathers or schoolmen, a minister is made and the thing done. The greatest and hardest part is within."[11]
>
> —George Herbert, *The Country Parson*, 1630

> Take heed to yourselves, lest you be void of that saving grace of God which you offer to others, and be strangers to the effectual working of that gospel which you preach; and lest, while you proclaim to the world the necessity of a Savior, your own hearts should neglect him, and you should miss an interest in him and his saving benefits. Take heed to yourselves, lest you perish, while you call upon others to take heed of perishing; and lest you famish yourselves while you prepare food for them.[12]
>
> —Richard Baxter, *Reformed Pastor*, 1655

> I tell you, therefore, that is it better to walk by the counsel of a humble and unschooled person with a holy and upright conscience than by that of a well-read but proud scholar with great knowledge. For one cannot share what one does not have inside oneself.
>
> —Catherine of Siena, 1370

No one ventures to teach any art unless he has learned it after deep thought. With what rashness, then, would the pastoral office be undertaken by the unfit, seeing that the government of souls is the art of arts![13]

—Gregory the Great, *Pastoral Care,* 590

First and foremost, I beg your wise holiness to consider that there is nothing in this life, and especially in our own day, more easy and pleasant and acceptable to men than the office of bishop or priest or deacon, if its duties be discharged in a mechanical or syncophantic way; but nothing more worthless and deplorable and meet for chastisement in the sight of God; and on the other hand, that there is nothing in this life and especially in our own day, more difficult, toilsome, and hazardous than the office of bishop, priest, or deacon; but nothing more blessed in the sight of God, if our service be in accordance with our captain's orders.[14]

—Augustine, to his bishop,
upon his surprise ordination, 391

Theological education and pastoral formation and preparation must always ensure that no pastor or student is exempt from the formative process into which they attempt to direct others.[15]

A blurry perception of the pastoral vocation and confusion concerning what ministry is seems to be fairly common—and can lead to disastrous consequences, as evidenced by the wreckage of homes, parishes, and lives led off course by blind pastors following erroneous vocational coordinates. Competing visions, explanations, expectations, and job requirements for pastoral ministry are handed to us from a myriad of sources. Our culture, former pastors, professors, authors, parents, friends, and parishioners all speak into our pastoral identity and, welcome or not, subtly inform our understanding of what we have been called to, shaping the way we think and act. Becoming clear about the nature of the pastoral call is imperative, because we live into those implicit visions we harbor and into the explicit visions we esteem and nurture in our mind's eye. Critical to the process of becoming a pastor is to move beyond the stereotyped images of ministry we encounter and perpetuate.

Uncertainty about the nature of pastoral ministry leaves open a vacuum which others are often too ready to fill with a pantheon of images. Our culture and, unfortunately, our denominations are often full of industrious Ephesian silversmiths, like Demetrius, who are working in the employ of the therapeutic, consumptive culture. They are ready to howl us down if ever we stand in the theatre to point out the folly of the world and the foolish wisdom of Christ, declaring, "the gods made by human hands are no gods at all." It is bad for business when pastors do that. It is not comfortable when pastors do that. Trades lose their good name, and great cultural goddesses are in danger of being discredited. It is not affirming when pastors suggest that our culture's economy of values has no gold to back up its currency, when they suggest that the objects our societies love in common are fading, flickering, insubstantial images. It is not tolerable when pastors intolerant of sin speak words of "grace" and "conversion."

Unless the pastor's vision is clear, however, and unless his or her bearings are taken from the horizon of creation, cross, and Kingdom come and coming, she or he is in danger of rolling like the waves of the sea, blown and tossed by the winds of ego, prestige, and acclamation. One safeguard, as we have already mentioned, is to learn from pastors who have sailed these waters before, made charts of the area, and can provide us with the coordinates to sail between Scylla and Charybdis without wrecking on the one or being sucked into the other. Though we each have to sail these waters ourselves, to do so without a mentor is folly indeed.

SØREN KIERKEGAARD AND THE PASTOR'S CALLING

One of our most faithful iconoclastic sea captains is Søren Kierkegaard, a prescient Christian thinker, himself unlicensed to preach in his own Church of Denmark. His calling was not to preach in a pulpit, but to minister to generations of readers through theological and philosophical texts. In many of his works his desire was to hold up a kind of mirror to those stumbling around in a drunken stupor who had forgotten that they had forgotten who they were and how they were created to be. His vocation was to lead them to a clearer picture of themselves before the triune God of grace and compel them to cast their dimming visions aside in order to gaze at the unseemly sight of him who alone is truly human and who offers the clear vision of sobriety—that lucid sobriety of the apostle Peter on Pentecost, caught up with the other apostles in a state of Spirit-drunk sobriety from which they never recovered.[16]

In a small essay called "Of the Difference between a Genius and an Apostle" Kierkegaard hauls up for consideration the vocation and identity of pastors: what is the sine qua non of pastors, that without which they are not pastors? How are we to understand our vocation in the midst of this culture, which wants us as functionaries and managers and sociological anomalies? As is usual, Kierkegaard stands with Jeremiah denouncing false prophets. He is the faithful friend whose wounds bring healing and the possibility of life. He can be hard to read, primarily because once he grabs hold of you by the scruff of your neck he does not turn you loose until you have come to see the tragi-comic folly of your previously unexamined assumptions and behavior. This small essay plays harmony to Paul's melody in 1 Corinthians 1–2 (cruciform foolishness confounds Greek wisdom) and Galatians 3 (the Christian's life is hid with Christ in God), and has everything to do with pastoral identity. The reader need simply substitute "pastor" for "Apostle." In an attempt to help pastors become clear about their calling, he distinguishes three essential differences between the pastor and the genius, that pinnacle of Romantic individualism so highly esteemed in his culture and ours. His intent is not to slight those who, like himself, are inordinately gifted intellectually; indeed, he would draw them into the service of faith. Rather, his desire is to remind pastors that the task to which they have been called is driven not by their personality, but by the Person who called them. He offers us three observations to consider:

Whereas a genius is born, a pastor is called.

The pastor's identity is wholly determined by his or her call from Christ and commission by the church, rather than by innate intelligence, charm, education, or wit. He who called them hands them their task. Alternatively, the genius is dependent on no external force for his or her identity or purpose, but is self-made, self-determined, and self-satisfied:

> A genius and an apostle are qualitatively different . . . Genius is what it is of itself, i.e. through that which it is in itself; an Apostle is what he is by his divine authority . . . An Apostle is not born; an Apostle is called and appointed by God, receiving a mission from Him . . . As a result of this call he does not become more intelligent, does not receive more imagination, a greater acuteness of mind and so on; on the contrary, he remains himself and by that paradoxical fact he is sent on a particular mission by God.[17]

Whereas a genius is solitary, a pastor is sent to others.

The pastor is commissioned with a task: to mediate the ministry of Christ to others through the Holy Spirit, to preach divine grace to people, to teach them how to pray, to witness to Christ's kingdom, to bind up the broken, work for justice, and lead people to spiritual maturity and acts of service. Though long, this section is worth quoting at length:

> The doctrine communicated to the apostle is not a task which he is given to ponder over, it is not given him for his own sake; he is, on the contrary, on a mission and has to proclaim the doctrine . . . Just as a man, sent into the town with a letter, has nothing to do with its contents, but has only to deliver it . . . so, too, an Apostle really has only to be faithful in his service, and

to carry out his task . . . Genius lives in itself; and might live withdrawn and self-satisfied . . . It is modest of the nightingale not to require any one to listen to it; but it is also proud of the nightingale not to care whether any one listens to it or not.[18]

Whereas the authority of the genius is self-derived, that of the pastor is derived from another.

The pastor calls people to Christ and points people to Christ as the only Priest who serves in the heavenly temple. No cult of personality therefore is acceptable in ministry. The genius, whose authority depends on his or her intellectual acumen and eloquent reasoning, speaks for no one else:

An Apostle is what he is through having divine authority. . . St. Paul must not appeal to his cleverness, for in that case he is a fool . . . No he must appeal to his divine authority . . . One not infrequently hears priests, bona fide, in all learned simplicity, prostituting Christianity. They talk in exalted terms of St. Paul's brilliance and profundity, of his beautiful similes and so on—that is mere aestheticism. If St. Paul is to be regarded as a genius, then things look black for him . . . This kind of thoughtless eloquence is quite as likely to praise St. Paul as a stylist and an artist in words or, better still, since it is after all well known that he was also engaged in a craft, as a tent-maker whose masterly work surpassed that of all upholsterers before and since . . . As a genius St. Paul cannot be compared with either Plato or Shakespeare, as a coiner of beautiful similes he comes pretty low down on the scale, as a stylist his name is quite obscure—and as an upholsterer: well, I frankly admit I have no idea how to place him . . . Christ taught therefore with authority. To ask whether Christ is profound is blasphemy, and is an attempt (whether conscious or not) to destroy Him surreptitiously; for the question conceals a doubt concerning his authority.[19]

BIBLICAL IMAGES OF THE PASTOR

Whereas pastors may be psychiatrists, social workers, or counselors, they are none of these first. They are these insofar as they serve to mediate the ministry of Christ, who called and sent them. In Colossians 1 Paul explains the aim of his ministry to be "that we may present every person mature in Christ," and in Ephesians 4, that the body of Christ may be built up "until we all reach unity in the faith and in the knowledge of the Son of God and become mature." Because this is God's will and desire, as Ray Anderson suggests, "All ministry is first of all God's ministry. Every act of God, even that of creation, is the ministry of God." Therefore, he continues, "Whether we realize it or not, every act of ministry reveals something of God," whether sermon, lesson, wedding service, or "any other word or act that people might construe as carrying God's blessing, warning, or judgment."[20] Thus the pastoral ministry is an extension of and a participation in God's ministry to the world through Christ and the Spirit who effect this gathering and maturing of the people of God.

The authors of Scripture offer us an enormous variety of images and metaphors to clarify our vision and inform our pastoral imagination. If anything, they remind us that ministry is a manifold thing, requiring many forms of service. Pastors are *slaves* of Christ and *servants* of the new covenant. They are *stewards* of the Gospel on behalf of Christ and *helmsmen* who lead congregations. Like *nursing mothers* they tenderly care for spiritual children, and like *physicians* they work to heal the spiritually sick. They are compared to *farmers* who labor to produce crops, to *builders* who depend upon a solid foundation, and to *day laborers* who diligently ply their craft. They are expected to be patient and gentle *teachers* of the truth, faithful *exemplars* of Christ, and diligent *preachers* of God's grace. Pastors are *priests* offering Christ to people and people to Christ, *ambassadors* announcing an urgent message, and *prophets* identifying the perversion of the human heart. Finally, they are *shepherds* tending to the flock of the Good Shepherd.

But despite having Scripture's numerous images of the pastoral vocation before us, or the manifold examples of pastors from the history of the church behind us, we must each answer the following questions within ourselves: How do *I* work toward clarity of *my* pastoral vision? How do *I* learn to live into any one of these images of pastoral ministry? What do *I* require for the formation of *my* pastoral identity? How might *I* faithfully follow the examples of those who have pastored Christ's flock before me?

FOUR AREAS OF PASTORAL FORMATION AND PREPARATION

To begin to answer that question, we return to Gregory of Nazianzus. Much less well known than his five orations on Christology and the Trinity, but no less historically influential for that matter, is the small text on pastoral ministry that Gregory wrote during his initial flight to Basil's monastery. In this work, he balances rigorous castigation of the priestly presumption and flippancy he witnessed around him with his desire to be obedient to the divine call to ministry. He was ashamed of many of his fellow-priests, he admits, who were "pitiable as regards piety, and unfortunate in their dignity." He charged that many of these priests, in their desire to curry favor, became "ventriloquists and chatterers, who serve their own pleasures by words uttered from the earth," and in their desire to "gain the special good will of the multitude" they ruined themselves and the souls taken in by them.[21] The ease with which they succumbed to the temptations of pride and self-aggrandizement alarmed Gregory, while their moral and spiritual laxity kept him from responding to the call to ministry. This he was determined to avoid, knowing that the consequences of such folly would extend far beyond his own person. If he were led astray by false images and motivations, others would follow him off the path to their own destruction.

Referred to either as his *Second Oration*, or *In Defense of his Flight to Pontus*, this small text decisively influenced both John

Chrysostom's fifth-century magisterial *Treatise Concerning the Christian Priesthood*, as well as Gregory the Great's sixth-century text, *Book of Pastoral Rule*, which became the primary text on pastoral care in the church for a thousand years.[22] Each of these texts, written by pastors for pastors, sets forth the responsibilities of ministry in the form of *apologias* for their author's hesitancy to take up the priestly office.

In this text, Gregory offered his congregation in Nazianzus an *apologia* for his vacillation in the face of ordination; to subsequent generations he offers the ripe fruit of pastoral wisdom, which grew from his reflections on the indigenous pressures and necessitous qualities of the faithful minister of the gospel. Throughout his text, he canvasses four main fields necessary for formation and preparation—areas that he had to explore before he could commit himself unfeignedly to the pastoral care of others. Gregory's text was not the last, but it was certainly one of the first such reflections on pastoral ministry. His intention was not to set the bar for pastoral ministry unbiblically high, but to give the young pastor every reason to resist entering the ministry until the desire to be obedient drove them to do so. His concern was the Spirit's deep and gracious conversion of the pastor.

Even though he wrote more than 1600 years ago, Gregory's four-fold emphasis is still a useful guide for pastors, no matter their age or time in ministry, their unique struggles or particular situations. These four areas are: moral, spiritual, and personal formation; pastoral calling, images, and imagination; theological reflection and deliberation; and practical pastoral skills.

Moral, Spiritual, and Personal Formation

Along with every other text in the classical tradition of pastoral theology, Gregory centers on the call to spiritual and moral formation included in the call to ministry. Pastors can hardly call others to the way of holiness and sanctification without first having walked that way themselves. Having been called to set an

28

example for others in life, faith, speech, and purity, he counsels that the pastor "should be of such virtue, so simple and modest, and in a word so heavenly, that the gospel should make its way, no less by their character than by their preaching."[23] Both Gregory's era and his own thought was taken up with the grand struggle between flesh and Spirit, leading to the widespread desire to flee the worldly life for the sanctuary of contemplation in the monastery. This desire for intimate, undisturbed communion with God apart from the distracting demands of society is a common theme among the church fathers and mothers. However, the call to holiness and purity of heart is not the invention of an age overly marked by Greek dualism, and thus conveniently inapplicable or irrelevant to ourselves. Ministry begins with and is shaped by the heart of the pastor.

When Gregory turns to consider the necessary formation of the pastor's heart and spirit before God he finds himself utterly unworthy and unqualified. The person who would be pastor "must himself be cleansed, before cleansing others: himself become wise, that he may make others wise; become light, and then give light: draw near to God, and so bring others near; be hallowed, then hallow them; be possessed of hands to lead others by the hand, of wisdom to give advice."[24] "With these thoughts," he declares,

> I am occupied night and day: they waste my marrow, and feed upon my flesh, and will not allow me to be confident or to look up . . . They make me consider, not the position of a prelate, or the guidance and direction of others, which is far beyond my powers; but how I myself am to escape the wrath to come, and to scrape off from myself somewhat the rust of vice.[25]

Gregory was extremely aware of the weakness of his own heart, and the speed and ease with which he could be led astray. How could he or anyone meet the requirements for ministers set down in Scripture? He was sorely exercised by the recognition that in himself "vice is something attractive and ready at hand, and that nothing is so easy as to become evil, even without any one to lead us on to it; while the attainment of virtue is rare and difficult, even where there is much to attract and encourage us."[26] The wise pastor who would lead others, he counsels, cannot afford willful blindness, lest he or she take with them into the yawning ditch of error the souls entrusted to their care of whom they will be held accountable.[27]

Gregory allows the pastor no space to relax content with what spiritual and moral formation they have attained, because though relative to others it may be great, relative to what they are called to it is but the first step of a long and never-ending journey into Christlikeness. Looking forward rather than back, he encourages the pastor to

> dwell upon the loss of what is still beyond him, rather than the gain of what he has attained, and consider that which is beneath his feet a step to that which comes next: and not think it a great gain to excel ordinary people, but a loss to fall short of what we ought to be: and to measure his success by the commandment and not by his neighbours.[28]

It is difficult to unlock the door to our heart and allow words to search us and reflect back and forth within us. Much easier is it to read over lines of Scripture or lines of Gregory and leave them resting on the topsoil of our minds rather allow them to plow deep within us and begin nourishing the kind of fruit we produce. But Gregory, with David, implores the Lord to search his heart and see if there is any wicked way within him that needs to be rooted out. In a searching paragraph reminiscent of the psalmist's piercing reflections, Gregory asks how he could dare to clothe himself "with the garb and name of priest" before he has offered to God his contrite spirit as a living and holy sacrifice, before my hands had been consecrated by holy works;

before my eyes had been accustomed to gaze safely upon created things, with wonder only for the Creator, and without injury to the creature;

before my ear had been sufficiently opened to the instruction of the Lord, and He had opened mine ear to hear without heaviness, and had set a golden earring with precious sardius, that is, a wise man's word in an obedient ear;

before my mouth had been opened to draw in the Spirit, and opened wide to be filled with the spirit of speaking mysteries and doctrines; and my lips bound, to use the words of wisdom, by divine knowledge, and, as I would add, loosed in due season:

before my tongue had been filled with exultation, and become an instrument of Divine melody, awaking with glory, awaking right early, and laboring till it cleave to my jaws:

before my feet had been set upon the rock, made like hart's feet, and my footsteps directed in a godly fashion so that they should not well-nigh slip, nor slip at all;

before all my members had become instruments of righteousness, and all mortality had been put off, and swallowed up of life, and had yielded to the Spirit?[29]

Pastoral Calling, Images, and Imagination

The pastor's moral and spiritual formation, however, are not alone sufficient. He or she must be clear about the nature of pastoral ministry. Gregory muses that even if someone "is free from vice, and has reached the greatest heights of virtue: I do not see what knowledge or power would justify him in venturing upon this office."[30] Would-be pastors must also understand their unique responsibility to God and their unique relationship with other people. To that end pastors must examine the dominant images that animate their ministry, which they hold in their mind's eye and attempt to indwell. Gregory's age was no less replete with

31

dizzying distractions, false images, and cultural incursions into churches than our own: "Everyone rushes hither and thither in confusion," he says, as if "everything has reverted to the original state of things before the [order of the] world."

His lament over the state of the ministry and the culture of his day is a deterrent to modern romanticizing about some never-existing golden age of the church. He pastored under the short rule of his former classmate, Julian the Apostate, who attempted to undermine through public and widespread ridicule Christianity's privileged position. He labored against the long reach of such popular heresies as Arianism, Sabellianism, and tritheism that sought to undermine people's faith in Christ as the Son of God, and he pastored alongside priests who had grossly misunderstood their calling or willfully substituted their own more convenient images for those given in Scripture. He laments that such priests "intrude into the most sacred offices . . . lay claim to the sanctuary, and push and thrust around the holy table, as if they thought this order to be a means of livelihood, instead of a pattern of virtue, or an absolute authority, instead of a ministry of which we must give account"[31]—we might say they reduced their "calling" to a "job," a choice of career rather than a response to God.

The two images that for Gregory summarized the role of the pastor were the pastor as a "physician of souls" and the pastor as "shepherd of the flock." The former in particular echoes through dozens of writings on the pastoral vocation throughout the church's history. Gregory writes that "the guiding of man, the most variable and manifold of creatures, seems to me in very deed to be the *art of arts* and *science of sciences.*"[32] Gregory thus bequeaths two phrases to the history of pastoral care, usually given in their Latin translations: ministry as the *cura animarum*, the cure or watchful care of souls, and ministry as the *ars artium*, the art of arts, the most demanding task that could be given to man or woman. A medical physician, in comparison, is concerned with the health of a body destined to perish, whereas the pastor is concerned with the health and eternal life of the soul, in turn glorious and devious, fallen and in need of healing and restoration through Christ.

Similar to a medical doctor, the discerning pastor must be concerned with "the diagnosis and cure of our habits, passions, lives, wills, and whatever else is within us, by banishing from our compound nature everything brutal and fierce, and introducing and establishing in their stead what is gentle and dear to God." Considering pastoring as the art of arts, he says that "the scope of our art is to provide the soul with wings, to rescue it from the world and give it to God, and to watch over that which is in His image, if it abides, to take it by the hand, if it is in danger, to restore it, if ruined, to make Christ to dwell in the heart by the Spirit: and, in short, to deify, and bestow heavenly bliss upon, one who belongs to the heavenly host."[33] The pastor is responsible to "treat" each one entrusted to his or her care, and "to guide them according to the methods of a pastoral care which is right and just, and worthy of our true Shepherd." "The scope of the pastoral art," as one commentator summarizes, "the goal of the physician of souls, is to contend on behalf of God and thereby to lead people back to God."[34]

As we have seen and as we know, Scripture offers numerous images of pastoral ministry that might inform our "pastoral imagination," or, as some have called it, our "priestly consciousness." The point is that we must examine our images to see if they comport first with those offered in Scripture and, secondly, with those from the history of pastoral care in the church. Gregory testified what we know to be true, the "errant imagination robs us in great measure of reality," or in turn leads us back into reality. We seek to learn from other wise pastors, recorded both in Scripture and history, who have gone before us, not in order to duplicate their methods, but to indwell the pastoral vocation as faithfully in our day as they did in theirs, and to allow them to enlarge our pastoral imaginations. Like them, we may adopt new images not found specifically in the pages of Scripture, but which nonetheless present themselves faithful to biblical concepts and stories. Clarity about one's vision and calling, however, does not necessarily lighten the task. In fact, it gives it a weight and importance it does not have for those determined to serve self- or culture-generated images. To inform his image of the pastoral vocation, Gregory turns first to Christ, the "Shepherd of shepherds," then to Paul, and, in consecutive chapters, to Hosea, Micah, Joel, Malachi, Jeremiah, Ezekiel, and other prophets.

Finally, Gregory knows that the calling to ministry is not necessarily easily discerned. He, of all people, is sensitive to the need for prayerful questioning of and reflection upon the work of the Spirit who draws people into the service of the church. Not only must we be clear about the nature of ministry, but we also must discern whether we have been called and equipped to do it. Gregory turned to his friend, Basil, and to the church in Nazianzus for confirmation that he indeed was being led to ministry. His desire to be obedient finally overcame his personal hesitations.

> I resort once again to history, and on considering the men of best repute in ancient days, . . . I discover that some readily complied with the call, others deprecated the gift, and that neither those who drew back were blamed for timidity, nor those who came forward for eagerness. The former stood in awe of the greatness of the ministry, the latter trustfully obeyed Him Who called them. Aaron was eager, but Moses resisted, Isaiah readily submitted, but Jeremiah was afraid of his youth, and did not venture to prophesy until he had received from God a promise and power beyond his years . . . By these arguments I charmed myself and by degrees my soul relaxed and became ductile . . . the testimonies of God, to which I had entrusted my whole life, were my counselors. Therefore I was not rebellious . . . but I fell down and humbled myself under the mighty hand of God . . . I withdrew for a little while, till I had considered myself and consoled my grief: but now I am commissioned to exalt Him in the congregation of the people, and praise Him in the seat of the elders.[35]

Theological Reflection and Deliberation

The third area upon which the pastoral preparation and formation depends was, for Gregory, the first of its actual duties, that is, theological competency and an accurate distribution of the Word of God to souls entrusted to the pastor's care. The pastor has no other role than to lead people back to God and "give wings to the soul." To fulfill that role, and in order not to lead people somewhere other than to God, the pastor's words and actions must be biblically and theologically determined at their very core. Considering the doctrines about which the pastor must be clear, Gregory offers a summary of the gospel. He lists "the truth of our original constitution, and final restoration, the types of the truth, the covenants, the first and second coming of Christ, His incarnation, sufferings and dissolution, with the resurrection, the last day, the judgment and recompense . . . to crown all, with what we are to think of the original and blessed Trinity."[36] Again, in defense of his flight, he insists "this involves a very great risk to those who are charged with the illumination of others."[37]

Theological sloppiness or laziness only too easily confirms people in their dogmatic error and leaves them bound by erroneous and unexamined notions of God and by the false dogma of others. Gregory knew firsthand the deleterious consequences of theological error both to the unity of the church and the salvation of persons. The Trinitarian heresies of his own day had shipwrecked the faith of many and led them not to the God who is Father, Son, and Spirit, but to a God whose name was filled with empty terms and deceptive identities. It had led people not to God as he truly is, but to "god" as they wished him to be and thought he ought to be. Therefore the pastor must be a theologian, one who reads and thinks from Scripture and to Scripture in a disciplined and habitual way. In a later oration on being a theologian, Gregory cautions us against thinking that theological matters are so "cheap and low" that they do not require the full attention of our spirit and mind. He argues that not everyone is automatically ready to preach or teach, but only those "who have been previously purified in soul and body, or at the very least are being purified," and to whom "the subject is of real concern, and not they who make it a matter of pleasant gossip, like any other thing, after the races, or the theater, or a concert, or a dinner, or still lower employments."[38]

Gregory describes four kinds of people to whom the theological pastor must respond. In doing so he insists they must invoke the aid of the Spirit by whom alone they will be able "to perceive, to expound, or to embrace the truth in regard to God,":

1. The ultra-conservatives, who refuse to learn or receive correction:

the more fervent they are in the faith, the more hostile are they to what is said, supposing that a submissive spirit indicates, not piety, but treason to the truth, and therefore they would sacrifice anything rather than their private convictions, and the accustomed doctrines in which they have been educated.[39]

2. The theologically misinformed:

Accordingly, to impress the truth upon a soul when it is still fresh, like wax not yet subjected to the seal, is an easier task than inscribing pious doctrine on the top of inscriptions—I mean wrong doctrines and dogmas—with the result that the former are confused and thrown into disorder by the latter . . . a soul to be written upon should be free from the inscription of harmful doctrines, or the deeply cut marks of vice: otherwise the pious inscriber would have a twofold task, the erasure of the former impressions and the substitution of others which are more excellent, and more worthy to abide.[40]

3. The ignorant but arrogant:

what is to be said of those who, from vain glory or arrogance, speak unrighteousness against the most High, arming them-selves with the insolence of Jannes and Jambres, not against

Moses, but against the truth, and rising in opposition to sound doctrine? Or who through ignorance and, its consequence, temerity, rush headlong against every form of doctrine in swinish fashion, and trample under foot the fair pearls of the truth?[41]

4. The bitter relativist who refuses to believe truth is possible:

What again of those who come with no private idea, or form of words, better or worse, in regard to God, but listen to all kinds of doctrines and teachers, with the intention of selecting from all what is best and safest, in reliance upon no better judges of the truth than themselves? They are, in consequence, borne and turned about hither and thither by one plausible idea after another, and, after being deluged and trodden down by all kinds of doctrine, and having rung the changes on a long succession of teachers and formulae, which they throw to the winds as readily as dust, their ears and minds at last are wearied out, and, O what folly! they become equally disgusted with all forms of doctrine, and assume the wretched character of deriding and despising our faith as unstable and unsound; passing in their ignorance from the teachers to the doctrine: as if anyone whose eyes were diseased, or whose ears had been injured, were to complain of the sun for being dim and not shining, or of sounds for being inharmonious and feeble.[42]

Knowing that we very often live from our ideas and images, both inchoate and articulate, the careful pastor will endeavor to assist each person according to his or her needs and abilities. Living and pastoring theologically, therefore, is an act of love on behalf of the pastor for his or her congregation. Theological deliberation, that theological reflection oriented to and resulting in action, is fundamental for pastors, who have been charged with helping others see and hear and walk and talk truthfully. The individual and the community depend upon their ability to do so. The ability of the pastor to respond in theologically appropriate ways to the multiple needs of a community is chief among Gregory's concerns, and requires not only competent theological reflection and deliberation, but also proficiency in the practical skills of preaching, teaching, counseling, and any other practice through which the Word is made known and knowable in the concrete situation of others.

Practical Pastoral Skills

In following Gregory's pursuit of vocational holiness and faithfulness we have considered the need for moral and spiritual formation, the need for discernment of our call and clarification of the call to ministry, and the need for careful theological reflection and deliberation. Finally, Gregory's fervent attention is directed to the more immediate and practical task of ministry, the "great skill required" to shape our gospel words and actions in a form appropriate to the exceedingly diverse stages of spiritual and intellectual maturity found in any believing community. We might say, how to bring The Story to bear on the individual stories people bring with them, or how to help them recognize that their stories are caught up in the drama of a much larger cosmic Story of creation, Christ, and church. This is ultimately a practical task rooted in a reflective task, and includes the pastor's skill in both public and private ministry: preaching, teaching, counseling, encouraging, equipping, and the like. A pastor must not only know what to say, but how to say it and when to say it.

Gregory is one with Paul in this. Within any ecclesial communities are "those who are in habit babes, and so to say, new-made," who need to be fed "with the milk of the most simple and elementary doctrines" in order that they not be "overwhelmed and oppressed" with theological food beyond their ability to digest. Likewise, communities include those whose "senses have been sufficiently exercised to discern truth and falsehood," who require mature wisdom, "the higher and more solid food." Gregory warns that if these are "made to drink milk, and fed on the vegetable diet of invalids, they . . . would not be strengthened according to Christ, nor make that laudable increase" in spiritual maturity which the Word desires to produce.[43] This complex task, the person-specific shape of ministry, becomes Gregory's refrain:

> As then the same medicine and the same food are not in every case administered to men's bodies, but a difference is made according to their degree of health or infirmity; so also are souls treated with varying instruction and guidance.[44]

> To me indeed it seems no slight task, and one requiring no little spiritual power, to give in due season to each his portion of the word.[45]

> How difficult it is to discuss such important questions, especially before a large audience, composed of every age and condition, and needing like an instrument of many strings, to be played upon in various ways; or to find any form of words able to edify them all, and illuminate them with the light of knowledge.[46]

Not only does this require a general proficiency in both theological reflection and practical skills, it also demands that pastors be surprised neither by grace nor by sin in people's lives. In particular, it means they must know well the people of their church and the social context of their ministry, as there is no ministry abstracted or protected from the thick existence of persons, families, and neighborhoods. Gregory extols the apostle Paul as model pastor in this regard. Through several paragraphs he chronicles Paul's manifold ministry and adaptable message, noting that "at one time he feeds with milk, at another he handles mysteries; at one time he condescends, at another he raises to his own level; at one time he threatens a rod, at another he offers the spirit of meekness; at one time he is haughty toward the lofty, at another lowly toward the lowly. Now he is least of the apostles, now he offers a proof of Christ speaking in him."[47] Likewise the pastor, charged with the *cura animarum*, the care of souls entrusted to him or her, must be able to change the unchanging message of the gospel according to context, persons, and needs in order to speak gospel words of healing and restoration that can be heard and accepted. As Gregory testifies,

> men and women, young and old, rich and poor, the sanguine and despondent, the sick and whole, rulers and ruled, the wise and ignorant, the cowardly and courageous, the wrathful and meek, the successful and failing, do not require the same instruction and encouragement.[48]

> . . . Some are led by doctrine, others trained by example; some need the spur, others the curb; some are sluggish and hard to rouse to the good, and must be stirred up by being smitten with the word; others are immoderately fervent in spirit, with impulses difficult to restrain, like thoroughbred colts, who run wide of the turning post, and to improve them the word must have a restraining and checking influence.[49]

> . . . Some are benefited by praise, others by blame, both being applied in season; while if out of season, or unreasonable, they are injurious; some are set right by encouragement, others by rebuke; some, when taken to task in public, others, when privately corrected.[50]

CONCLUSION

Gregory comes alongside other pastors, points to these four large fields that require formation and cultivation, and says, "Start walking here. Begin exploring here, and there, and over there. Begin sketching in a rough map. Start making trails between the areas, because what happens in one area directly determines what happens in another. Though the areas are ultimately uncanvassable, and new paths will always need to be forged, you should wear your shoes out becoming intimately familiar with them. The paths should be dirt and rock from all your constant walking. That is, have you made paths from the study to the street? Do you know the path from the prayer-bench to the pulpit? If walking those paths seems like climbing up sheer rock, find someone to point out the fingerholds and ledges you cannot yet see. Look for the cairns set up by those who traveled this way before. For in the walking to and fro along these trails a pastor is formed. You may need to practice walking between two particular fields more often than others, or you may be less experienced exploring one field or another, but still you must begin."

Despite the eloquence and influence of his own writing, Gregory knew that texts such as his were insufficient in themselves to train pastors in the art of pastoral care and ministry: "To set before you the distinction between all these things, and give you a perfectly exact view of them . . . is quite impossible, even for one in the highest degree qualified by care and skill." Instead, much like the physician of bodies, "actual experience and practice" are required to form the "physician of souls."[51] Gregory seems to make two points here. The first is that pastoral preparation and formation is possible, which should be encouraging to many of us. Knowledge, maturity, and wisdom are realizable goals. His second is that certain kinds of repeated action are required to move there: the practices of disciplined reflection upon our life and doctrine, of making theologically determined decisions, and of diligently preparing one's heart and mind before God alone and in the company of others.

CHAPTER 2

PASTORAL *SAPIENCE* AND PASTORAL *HABITUS*

When we invite Gregory or any one of the great cloud of pastoral witnesses to mentor us in our understanding of the person and the practice of the pastoral ministry, we invite them to question us about our ministries and our preparation for ministry. To read them is to accept W. H. Auden's famous question, "Have you been read by any good books lately?" Their questions are not likely to be the questions our contemporaries ask, and that is one of their strengths. They do not inquire about the size of our church or the last conference we attended. Neither do they inquire about our academic pedigree, nor our denomination, nor, unfortunately for many of us, the size of our personal library, or even if their collected works fill our bookshelves.

When George Herbert, the seventeenth-century Anglican pastor and poet, comments on "the parson's library," for instance, he suggests that the primary resource for pastoral ministry, besides Scripture, is not in fact a set of theological dictionaries or commentaries, nor his own Anglican Book of Common Prayer, nor the leadership and ministry magazines that monthly fill our mailboxes. Instead, the "parson's library is a holy life," precisely because the parson knows his own sin and temptation, his own perpetual repentance, and his own attempt to live into the grace of God and to worship in spirit and truth. From his experience he is able, like a master librarian, to draw down now this volume and now that volume full of stories of God's grace in his own life in order to share them with others. When we open ourselves to be "read" by Herbert, he asks whether our primary source for ministry is our informed head or our transformed heart, and what bearing the one has upon the other.

When Herbert does turn to Scripture, that place where the parson "sucks and lives," he insists again that a "holy life" is the first requirement for its proper study and understanding. In other words, he found that faith, obedience, and understanding are mutually generating, and asks us whether we have discovered the same. His second suggestion is prayer, his third a synthetic collation of Scripture with Scripture. Finally, acknowledging "God in all ages hath had his servants, to whom he hath revealed his truth" he invites the church fathers and other commentators to speak, "that there may be a traffic in knowledge between the servants of God for the planting both of love and humility."

When we allow ourselves and our ministries to be read by those pastors in the classical tradition of pastoral ministry, their first concern is always the coherence of the pastor's life, prayer, and worship with his or her doctrine and actions. We might refer to this as pastoral *sapience*, which is the *wisdom* that slowly emerges as the Spirit brings each area of pastoral life into congruity with one another and with the gospel. Pastoral wisdom, long in coming, embraces pastors' spiritual formation and contemplation of God, their discursive theological reasoning about God and the church, their affections and love of God, as well as their pastoral ministry in response to God. This wisdom is nourished by a cohesive integration of pastoral, scriptural, historical, systematic, social and practical studies. It saturates the whole of a pastor's life and cannot be parceled out to one discipline or another. Moreover, it cannot be generated through the imposition of a ready-made technique. The practices and habits that bend one towards wisdom resist formula and passive disinterest.

Anticipating the objection of those unaccustomed or disinclined to the sacrifices necessary to advance in any skill or craft, Gregory draws an analogy from their delightful pastimes to the "chief good" of wisdom:

> Well, dancing and flute-playing require to be taught and learnt, a process which takes time, and much toil in the sweat of the brow, and sometimes the payment of fees, and entreaties for initiation, and long absence from home, and all else which must be done and borne for the acquisition of experience: but as for wisdom, which is chief of all things, and holds in her embrace everything which is good, so that even God himself prefers this title to all the names which He is called; are we to suppose that it is a matter of such slight consequence, and so accessible, that we need but wish, and we would be wise?[1]

Different theologians and eras have pointed to one or another path to wisdom, from intellectual contemplation, to reformation of the affections, to the necessity of concrete praxis. All, however, have learned from the wisdom tradition embodied in the book of Proverbs, which tirelessly extols the extravagant value of wisdom over silver, gold, or jewels, or may we improvise and say, over career, reputation, publishing, or large crowds: "nothing you desire can compare with her." In wisdom we find the integration and congruity of "every good path," that is, of all other virtues and worthwhile pursuits. Proverbs 2 promises that the wise will understand *righteousness, justice,* and *equity,* which are virtues necessary for governing the public life of the community; the wise will find pleasure in *knowledge,* a guard in *understanding,* and a watchman in *discretion,* which are the virtues necessary for governing the private life of the individual. Likewise, Proverbs 8 associates wisdom with truth, right, noble things, prudence, insight, and sound counsel. Blessed indeed, therefore, is the person, and so also the pastor, who "finds wisdom, and . . . gets understanding . . . for they will be life for your soul and adornment for your neck." Lest we be discouraged by our lack of these things, however, we should recall that wisdom offers herself to the simple, the foolish, and to those who "lack sense," would they but seek her and treasure her above all else.

In his *Soliloquies*, Augustine declared that to obtain wisdom he desired to know that which he did not know: "God and the soul," nothing else. "I love nothing but God and the soul, and I know neither."[2] His *Confessions* thus appear to be a sustained exploration of these two subjects: the possibility and actuality of knowing God through confessing God's involvement in the whole of his life, and the possibility and actuality of knowing God in himself as he had revealed himself in creation and the incarnation. "May I know you, who knows me. May I 'know as I also am known' (1 Cor 13:12)."[3] The outcome of this double knowledge of God and human creatures, including his own self, was wisdom.

John Calvin follows Augustine's lead when he declares, in the well-known opening lines of his *Institutes of the Christian Religion*, "Nearly all the wisdom we possess, that is to say, true and sound wisdom, consists of two parts: the knowledge of God and of ourselves." And these two parts, he argues, are mutually connected by many bonds. We cannot begin to contemplate ourselves without immediately being aroused and led by the hand to seek God, in whom we live and move and have our being. So also, Calvin insists, no one "achieves a clear knowledge of himself unless he has first looked upon God's face, and then descends from contemplating him to scrutinize himself."[4] Both of these theologian-pastors imply that every bit of human knowledge and action is open to the action and definition of God.

Augustine also drew a very helpful and influential distinction between *scientia* and *sapientia*. *Scientia*, the obvious ancestor of our word "science," refers to rational knowledge of individual things, while *sapientia*, wisdom, refers to the "spiritual truth" which affects every area of one's life.[5] Extending Augustine's fourth-century discussion into the twenty-first century, Eugene Peterson alerts careful pastors to the importance of the distinction between "wisdom" words and "scientific" words in the proclamation of the gospel:

> There is a great chasm in our Western world in the way words are used . . . It is the split between words that *describe* the world and reality from as much distance as possible through generalities and abstractions, and words that *express* the world and reality by entering it, participating in it by metaphor and command. Describing words can be set under the Latin term *scientia*, expressing words under the term *sapientia*—or in English, science and wisdom. Science is information stored in the head that can be used impersonally; wisdom is intelligence that comes from the heart, which can only be lived personally in relationships.[6]

Sapientia is delight in the grace of God, love and worship, gratitude. *Sapience* is practical and personal, for it turns the believer outwards to God and to other people. Science threatens to depersonalize knowledge in order to make it precise, exact, and manageable. Wisdom personalizes exegetical, historical, and theological knowledge in order to live it faithfully. Understanding with *sapience* tries to grasp the unity, breadth, and depth of the world revealed to us in Scripture, and to receive with thanksgiving and reverence the wonderful, stubborn, complex people God brings into our lives. *Scientia* threatens to construct a system of propositions in order to explain the world and manage it. It lays a high stress on specialized skills of analysis, sophistication about methods of exegesis, and strategies for management and achieving results. Wisdom has to do with speaking words of creation into the *tohu wabohu* of someone else's life, words that through the Spirit give life.

If wisdom is a knowledge and vision of the unchanging God who provides order and boundary to our world, attended by the congruence of our souls, our thoughts, and our action to God, and if that sapiential knowledge allows us to peacefully and graciously respond to the chaos of immediacy, then the flutter and busyness of our lives and ministries may represent a lack of pastoral wisdom. Our question is how to cultivate, nurture, and practice Christian pastoral wisdom. We might borrow another phrase and call the practice of wisdom the formation of a pastoral *habitus,* a disposition or posture of the soul, the mind, the affections, and the intellect, which shapes our life before God and with others. A pastoral *habitus* includes an affective disposition that, as Augustine said, leads one to love God in another person, "either because God is actually present in him, or in order that God may be in him. This is true love."[7] Now pastors are famous for their habits—jangling change and clearing their throat during sermons, tapping fingers and doodling during board meetings, but a pastoral *habitus* refers to more than simply what we or our parishioners recognize as habits. *Habitus* refers to our "habitual way of being," which includes the cognitive, affective, imaginative, and behavioral aspects of who we are. A pastoral *habitus* is thus a way of being that integrates, or at least brings into dialogue, the four large areas of concern Gregory emphasized in his *apologia.*

Dialogue of this sort, however, can be very difficult to foster during the normal course of academic studies. In school we are usually taught to speak in *scientia* but not necessarily in *sapientia.* The classroom is not conducive to *sapientia.* Ed Farley, in his now classic text, *Theologia: The Fragmentation and Unity of Theological Education,* suggests that when theological studies were separated into four distinct disciplines in the eighteenth century—generally those of biblical studies, church history, systematic theology, and practical ministry—the result was a loss of sapiential theology, or theological wisdom as the unifying goal that gave coherence and direction to each of the disciplines.

If not the mere academic diversification of the disciplines, which may have been necessary, then certainly the excessive professionalization of the disciplines has contributed to their artificial and unhelpful separation. Integration, which does not happen as a matter of course, has been largely left to the student or pastor to attempt on their own, at some time after graduation. "Systematic theology," now a discipline that attracts a certain type of student or pastor, is not all that the church has traditionally meant by "theology."

For instance, it would be somewhat hard to classify the writings of the sixteenth-century reformer, theologian, and pastor, John Calvin. You do not have to agree with everything Calvin wrote to recognize that in his *Institutes of the Christian Religion* and other writings, he is a biblical exegete, then worship leader, then theologian, teacher, rhetorician, pastor, pietist, polemicist, and historian. The point is that he brought all these into dialogue in himself and in his work for the edification of the church. To read him is to begin to understand what the older divines meant when they distinguished *scientia* from *sapientia*. For Calvin, theology indeed had to lead to doxology; doxology in turn nourished theology. Theology included for Calvin the cultivation of the disposition of one's soul, rather than the mere encyclopedic accumulation of technical skills or theological and exegetical facts.

Pastors, who mediate the Word's ministry through their words, have to be careful with their use of language and knowledge. Knowledge that is not put to use or is not transformed into wisdom passes through like any other unusable waste. Knowledge is what students know very well, though. We stockpile it. We snack on it. We acquire ancient languages. We learn to exegete. We practice preaching. We discover Arius and Arminius, Irenaeus and Teresa, Gunkel and Harnack, Hooker and Bultmann. And it is hard to avoid the conclusion that knowledge is what we are expected to dispense to people in our ministries. As we were taught, so we teach.

Learning to theologize, however, is different than learning a compendium of theological, exegetical, and historical answers, or learning how to construct a sermon. A theologian may in fact know many details and theories and data about the Bible and the historical tradition, but that does not describe how a theologian thinks. *Theology* is fine as a noun, and it refers to a number of things: etymologically, talk about God; historically, the church's talk about God and the things of God; systematically, the attempt to demonstrate the coherence and truthfulness of talk about God; exegetically, the Bible's talk about God. But while pastors need to know theology as a noun, it is just as important for them to know theology as a verb, as something they must learn to do, and do spontaneously—extemporaneously theologizing.

Ellen Charry reminds us in her book, *By the Renewing of Our Minds*, that Christian doctrines and biblical studies have an end beyond themselves in the cultivation of wisdom. Combining the Greek word for human excellence, *arete*, and the Greek word for begetting, *geneo*, she argues, coining her own word, that Christian doctrine should be "aretegenic," generating the Christian virtues of faith, hope, and love in both pastor and parishioners.[8] The information we acquire and pass on should in-form people and aid them in the renewing and restoration of their hearts and minds in conformity to Christ. This was St. John's declared purpose in writing his gospel—"These are written so that you may believe that Jesus is the Christ, the Son of God, and that by believing you may have life in his name"[9]—belief and life in his name, not simply knowledge of what he did and who he claimed to be. This is John as pastor. The question we still must ask ourselves, however, is how pastors begin to move from knowledge to wisdom, from dispensing information to helping people become disciples who think and live in new ways.

PASTORAL MINISTRY AS CRAFT TO BE LEARNED

In response to that question, the theologian Stanley Hauerwas has written extensively on the benefit of approaching Christian living and thinking as crafts to be learned from other more skilled practitioners. In community with others we practice how to be Christians, and, derivatively, how to be Christlike pastors. This is not to discount the Spirit's quickening work in our lives, but to take into account that the Spirit sets us into a historical community from whom we learn how to be. The following classic selection from Hauerwas is lengthy, but offers an excellent description of what is required to cultivate a pastoral *habitus*. He offers the example of learning how to lay bricks, a craft that cannot be mastered simply by hearing or reading how to do it.

> To learn to lay brick, it is not sufficient for you to be told how to do it; you must learn to mix the mortar, build scaffolds, joint, and so on. Moreover, it is not enough to be told how to hold a trowel, how to spread mortar, or how to frog the mortar. In order to lay brick you must hour after hour, day after day, lay brick.
>
> Of course, learning to lay brick involves learning not only myriad skills, but also a language that forms, and is formed by those skills. Thus, for example, you have to become familiar with what a trowel is and how it is to be used, as well as mortar, which bricklayers usually call "mud." Thus "frogging mud" means creating a trench in the mortar so that when the brick is placed in the mortar, a vacuum is created that almost makes the brick lay itself. Such language is not just incidental to becoming a bricklayer but is intrinsic to the practice. You cannot learn to lay brick without learning to talk "right."
>
> The language embodies the history of the craft of bricklaying. So when you learn to be a bricklayer you are not learning a craft *de novo* but rather being initiated into a history. For example, bricks have different names . . . to denote different qualities that make a difference about how one lays them. These differences are often discovered by apprentices being confronted with new challenges, making mistakes, and then being taught how to do the work by the more experienced. All of this indicates that to lay brick you must be initiated into the craft of bricklaying by a master craftsman . . . Often the best teachers in a craft do not

necessarily produce the best work, but they help us understand what kind of work is best.[10]

The pastoral craft is what we need to learn, from pastors whose relation is immediate to us and from pastors whose relation is mediated by texts that carry their words and stories to us. We learn from others who represent faithful and embodied attempts to live into their callings. The fourth-century Gregory concurs with the twentieth-century Hauerwas:

> We are aware that it is better to offer our own reins to others more skilful than ourselves, rather than, while inexperienced, to guide the course of others; and *better to give a kindly hearing than to stir an untrained tongue*; and after a discussion of these points with advisers who are, I fancy, of no mean worth, and who, at any rate, wish us well, we prefer to learn those canons of speech and action which we did not know, rather than undertake to teach them in our ignorance. For it is delightful to have the reasoning of the aged come to one even until the depth of old age, able, as it is, to aid a soul new to piety. Accordingly, to undertake the training of others before being sufficiently trained oneself, and to learn, as men say, the potter's art on a wine-jar, that is, to practice ourselves in piety at the expense of others' souls seems to me to be excessive folly or excessive rashness—folly, if we are not even aware of our own ignorance; rashness, if in spite of this knowledge we venture on the task.[11]

The nineteenth-century Anglican, Bishop Fraser of Manchester, agrees with both Hauerwas and Gregory:

> If incumbents give a title to a young curate, it seems to be that the incumbent is just as much bound to teach the curate how to do the work to which he is called as a joiner would be to teach an apprentice his trade.[12]

CHAPTER 3

MENTORING FOR PASTORAL FORMATION

The excerpts from Hauerwas, Gregory, and Fraser introduce us to the relationship that is at the heart of this text: that between a person who is new to the craft of pastoral ministry and a person more experienced and practiced in the art. Throughout the history of the church various means have been employed to prepare persons for ministry. Historically the preparation of ecclesial leaders was accomplished through monasteries, cathedral schools, universities, and, finally, in seminaries, Bible colleges, and training institutes. Depending on the era, the responsibility fell to bishops, abbots, deans, professors, or local priests. Augustine, Cyprian, Origen, Basil, Benedict, Calvin, Bucer, and the Puritan pastors John Newton, Wesley, and the like were each involved in preparing young pastors for ministry. Lest we overstate our case, however, it is clear that not every era of the church's history, nor every place the church was found, took as much responsibility for this task as others—but this failing was at their loss.

Though the question as to "how" someone might best prepare for service to the church has been variously answered, depending largely on when and where the question was asked and to whom the question was put, one practice that has been a constant in some form or another throughout the history of the people of God, whether in Israel or the church, is the practice to which you are now being invited to participate, that is, *mentoring for pastoral formation and preparation.* Mentoring for pastoral formation, as we are considering it, is preceded by the venerable tradition of spiritual direction and spiritual friendship, though unlike these it is focused on preparation for a particular vocation. Therefore, besides borrowing from the practice of spiritual direction, it also learns from the practice of apprenticeship and from the more recent developments of Clinical Pastoral Education (CPE) and seminary programs for Supervised Ministry Internships.

Informal or spontaneous, disciplined or unintentional, it is a practice that attempts to encourage and facilitate the dialogue that leads to pastoral *sapience* and the formation of a pastoral *habitus* by bringing a less experienced pastor into relationship with a more experienced pastor so that the two might work alongside each other in a common ministry and consider the task of ministry with one another. In his text, *Duties of the Clergy,* St. Ambrose counsels young clergy to follow the examples of Joshua with Moses, Elisha with Elijah, and Timothy with Paul, for "Familiarity with good men is very advantageous to all, especially to the young . . . It is a very good thing to unite oneself to a good man. It is also very useful for the young to follow the guidance of great and wise men. For he who lives in company with wise men is wise himself."[1] Even after the rise of the university in the thirteenth and fourteenth centuries—with its unique way of knowing and educating, where, it has been rather convincingly argued, for the first time knowing was separated from being and doing—some form of pastoral apprenticeship or mentoring remained normative in many parts of the church until at least the eighteenth century.

However, for various sociological and ecclesiastical reasons, this historically confirmed and theologically grounded practice of pastoral preparation has not been the norm for many seminary students or would-be pastors during the past two hundred years. Many of the methods or institutions for training clergy have been shaped and determined by sociological and cultural factors rather than theological factors; that is, they developed and adapted according to the changing needs and models of the dominant cultures within which they were embedded. The environmental factors which contributed to a culture of hospitality and the cultivation of pastoral friendship have largely been displaced by the desire for efficiency and controlled standardization. That most preparation for pastoral ministry takes place exclusively in the seminary or university instead of in partnership with a church or a more experienced pastor is more an accident of history than the result of careful theological deliberation.

Mentoring for pastoral formation, on the other hand, can refer to the diverse array of formal relationships and informal friendships in which older or more experienced pastors, priests, or ministers offer their eyes, ears, voice, and hands to younger or less experienced pastors in order to help them explore the overlapping contours of who they are in Christ and what they are called to do for Christ. This is the overlap of their *being* and their *thinking* under the indigenous pressures, responsibilities, and tasks of *doing* pastoral ministry—when they intentionally participate in the ongoing formation, preparation, and education of fellow pastors at uniquely critical moments in their lives, when they are learning how to do and to be and to think, drawing patterns and forming habits that they will carry with them into every church or place of ministry in which they serve. As most pastors will attest, though our preparation and formation formally begins in seminary, it certainly does not end there. Nor, as their churches can attest, should it end there. The purpose of pastoral mentoring is to introduce the agenda of this lifelong journey and to commence attending to it. Careful support of new ministers both in seminary and immediately following is crucial to continue this process of formation and maturation for ministry.

FROM ACADEMY TO SANCTUARY

The transition from the seminar room to the elder's meeting, or from the library to the pulpit, or from debating theories of epistemology to speaking salutary words of grace is difficult. It may be more difficult for some than others, but it requires thoughtful consideration by anyone. As students we are comfortable with and have likely become relatively adept at a certain way of learning, constructing, and presenting knowledge. For several years we have trained our minds to think in a particular way. The knowledge and skills learned in seminary are fundamental. However, we have to learn how to shape and use that knowledge and those skills in new ways with each person we counsel or pray with or teach.

We may have come to enjoy heady theological discussions and contentious debate. We may wake in the morning with visions of Isaiah or St. Theresa dancing in our heads and drift to sleep with Jeremiah or G. K. Chesterton barking in our ears. We have tried to keep pace with distance runners like Barth and stopped to marvel with poets like Hopkins and Dillard. For some, Amos, Dorothy Day, Micah, or Gustavo Gutierrez played Virgil and helped us to look and see the in-breaking of the new creation and the promise of a new exodus. These people have been our companions in seminary and will likely continue to be our companions in ministry. These have been our mentors, and they may become the companions and mentors of our parishioners. However, to become such they must be introduced, and the introduction requires some thought on behalf of the mutual friend. This is simply to say that exegesis alone does not a sermon make, nor theological argument a word of pastoral care, nor an informed parishioner necessarily an inwardly formed disciple.

The first few years of ministry are a critical time because new pastors are forced to clarify their convictions and beliefs and articulate them to people for whom it is not merely an academic matter. "What do I really believe and why?" "What is fundamental and what peripheral?" "When I stand in the pulpit on Sunday, or sit with a skeptic on Monday, do I have words of life and truth to speak?" This can be a decisive time when mind and spirit are quickened by the sheer facticity of the immediate situation. "And now I have to speak and act." No one asks for a thesis or essay—even though we may give it to them sometimes. They ask for words that speak God's grace and God's grandeur, words that open up space for them to repent and pray, worship and act. Words and actions that form the unformed and fill the unfilled, that speak and enact creation into chaos.

It is a critical time because it can throw into sharp relief our lack of experience and lack of skills. We fail. We flounder. And we do not drown only because there are others present to pull us out of the waters, dry us off, and send us out for another swim. That is not an excuse for laziness or lack of care on the part of the mentee. It is simply a reality of inexperience. When Karl Barth returned to preach at his first parish of Safenwil after a twenty year absence and a radical theological shift, he confessed to those still present: "I can see now that I did not preach the gospel clearly enough to you during the time when I was your pastor. Since then I have often thought with some trepidation of those who were perhaps led astray or scandalized by what I said at the time, or of the dead who have passed on and did not hear, at any rate from me, what by human reckoning they ought to have heard."[2] And we can identify with this pastor and learn from his experience and his words, and we learn from the experiences and words of pastors who have intentionally or unintentionally mentored us. And we give thanks that the church does not rest on our shoulders nor live by our words. And we give thanks that the Spirit speaks through many more vessels than us. And then we try to speak again. And then we try to act again in a new way.

In his sixteenth-century text, *Laws of Ecclesiastical Polity*, whose chapter on the church was mandatory reading for all Oxford students until the early twentieth century, the Anglican Richard Hooker responded to Puritan charges that Anglican ministers were not sufficiently qualified when they took office. Hooker acknowledged the disparity between pastors of his own day and those of previous generations. In the past, he says, the chief study of pastors was "the exercise of piety . . . whereas their scope was obedience, ours is skill; their endeavor was reformation of life, our virtue nothing but to hear gladly the reproof of vice; they in the practice of their religion wearied chiefly their knees and hands, we especially our ears and tongues." However, he insists, maturity, wisdom, and skill come with time, as young pastors learn to live into their calling: "If want of learning and skill to preach did frustrate their vocation, ministers ordained before they be grown unto that maturity should receive new ordination whensoever it chances that study and industry doth make them afterwards more able to perform the office—what conceit can be more absurd?"[3]

As we have said, in these formative years, the course is plotted along which the pastor will likely travel for some time. In the sixth century, St. Benedict constantly reminded the priests entrusted to his care that their end depended upon their beginning. We cannot simply decide one morning ten or fifteen years after graduation to reinvent ourselves as the humble and wise pastor we always envisioned. We have to become that person. And we become that person by making decisions today, and in particular, at the beginning of our time in ministry. It is in these years at the end of seminary and the beginning of pastoral ministry that our formation will in fact occur, that patterns will be cut, and that ways of being will be determined.

The question we must consider, however, given that we cannot opt into or out of formation, is whether we will allow our formation to stumble along haphazardly, unintentionally, and unreflectively, influenced by implicit and unobserved visions. If we are not intentional about our formation, we will be more vulnerable to the tacit and sometimes forceful shaping brought about by our socialization into a denominational ethos, a cultural or economic class, or various other group-sanctioned ways of being. Who do we want to become as pastors? To what is the Holy Spirit drawing our attention at this critical moment? The question we put to ourselves must not be, "What can I get away with not examining?" or, "What habits and dispositions and practices can I leave undisclosed?" Instead, we need to ask, "What do I need to root out now, early in my life of ministry?" Arrogance? Pride? Sexual indulgences? Inferiority? Anger? Prejudice? Social blindness? Gender prejudice? Busyness? We take with us into ministry all that we are, all the patterns of thinking and being that we have developed over the course of our lives.

GIFTS OF *PLACE* AND *SPACE*

The need for this has not gone entirely unnoticed by the theological academy. Mentoring for pastoral formation still occurs, or is at least attempted, in the current structure of our seminaries. Many seminaries and Bible colleges, in at least the last thirty years or so, have developed required programs of "supervised ministry internships," which attempt to make formal provision for the kind of mentoring for pastoral formation we are considering here. These internships usually take place near the end of a student's course of academic study, when a student is invited to participate in the ongoing life of a particular ministering and worshipping community. The details of the respective programs differ. Some are part-time programs, concurrent with academic studies, some are full-time and require a temporary hiatus from school. Many require extensive training and preparation of the mentor, a few do not. Often the details divide along ecclesial lines, whether Roman Catholic, Protestant, or Orthodox. However they differ in details, structure, tradition, theology, or setting, though, two common characteristics endure: these are the gift of *place* and the gift of *space,* and they reflect older forms of mentoring for pastoral formation. These gifts are given from the ecclesial community to the student-pastor it has invited to participate in its ongoing life of ministry. The seminary or Bible college does not have the resources to give these gifts. The seminary has its own unique gifts, of course, but these cannot replace those given by the localized ecclesial community.

What do we mean by gifts of *place* and *space*? The student-pastor is given a *place* to participate in the ongoing ministry of a localized community, and they are given *space* to reflect on their ministry in regular conversations with a mentor-pastor and with other persons in the community who have been organized into some sort of "lay support team." The *place* is important because it allows the mentee to participate in a wide-range of ministries in the life of the church. It provides them a place to practice the art of pastoring and serving a community. We need to do this. We need to learn how to get in on what God is already doing in this place, among these people, at this time. That should be the assumption of the student-pastor: "God is at work here, and I am getting in on that work for a short period of time, so where can I serve and what can I learn about myself and the body of Christ?" In their future ministry the young pastor will be called upon to serve the church in a variety of ways. Thus in their mentored practice of ministry the community can provide a place for them to practice speaking the gospel in public and private, and step into the bustling and the quotidian rhythm of church life. This usually includes participation in any of the following:

- *Worship:* preaching, praying, leading the liturgy or music, serving the Lord's Supper, planning various forms of services;

- *Pastoral and church administration:* planning meetings, organizing volunteers, maintaining a budget, advertising, deciding who is going to fix the hot water heater this month;

- *Christian education and formation:* planning and writing curriculum for adults, youth, and children; recruiting, training, equipping, and supporting teachers;

- *Pastoral care and counseling:* both formal and informal, for both youths and adults, in situations of grief and joy;

- *Outreach to those beyond the church walls:* planning and executing appropriate forms of evangelism and nurture, invitation and instruction;

- *Social and community concerns and needs:* caring for the weak, vulnerable, and needy in our communities and making space for them in the life of the church.

Though student-pastors should participate in a wide variety of ministries, there will often be particular areas where they would like more practice and experience. These could be areas where they feel weak, or areas in which they are strong and will likely minister after graduation. Mentoring for pastoral formation is not intended to domesticate or root out the passion and energy of seminarians with the tools of "real world" committees, visitations, programs, and junior high sleepovers, but rather to assist in the cultivation of their calling and knowing and being in the midst of all these.

The *space* to reflect upon that ministry and upon their own formation in ministry is even more important. For it is there, in the space created for reflection, conversation, and deliberation that learning and formation occurs. Experience alone does not teach us much. It only teaches if it is followed by reflection and deliberation—looking back and looking forward. The primary purpose of the "supervised ministry internship" is not simply to provide a place for a student or new pastor to gain "experience," though that is important. The primary purpose is formation and preparation, made possible through disciplined reflection with a mentor.

Why do young pastors need another set of eyes, another set of ears, another mouth, and another set of hands for their own development? Well, our own eyes are remarkably dull when it comes to self-examination. We can become astonishingly adept at looking at but not recognizing both our strengths

61

and weaknesses. We suffer from spiritual glaucoma, theological stigmatism, relational blindness, and vocational occlusion. We cannot see and therefore cannot know ourselves clearly. But when we are sitting across from a friend who holds up a mirror for us and asks us to look, or offers to describe for us what she sees with her eyes, it becomes much more difficult to look away, much easier to see who we have become.

That said, the thought of a mentor should not conjure up images of that Grade Six Sunday school teacher who all too willingly catalogued our personal vices week by week. Mentoring pastors are pastoral mentors, meaning they are radically *for* us. They are radically *with* us. They too have been called to serve the church as we have been called. They too, along with us, are dedicated to helping people become persons in Christ, helping people to see, hear, obey, and live before the one Creator, Reconciler, and Redeemer who has called us his people. The mentor will probably be one of the most significant persons in the education and formation of the mentee. In our lives we have but a few people who really listen to us, or who genuinely care about our well-being and life as persons and as pastors and commit themselves to us. Neither seminary professors nor fellow seminarians will likely serve as personal a role in the preparation of pastors. This is one reason it is imperative that the seminary and church understand themselves as partners together taking responsibility for the formation and preparation of pastors and leaders for the church as Christ's Body.

When Roman Catholics and Protestants founded seminaries in the sixteenth century, they took their names from the seedbeds where plants and trees were cultivated before they were hardy enough to be transplanted into their final location. Seminaries, in turn, were places where the church took responsibility to cultivate those persons called by the Spirit and the church to pastoral ministry. This was not intended to imply that the "seeds" needed to be protected in climate-controlled greenhouses attended by the artificial light of the heat lamp and the artificial rain of the sprinkler head, safe from inclement weather. It did imply that they had been set aside for a particular task that required cultivation rather than the free reign of their natural inclinations. The appropriateness of this metaphor becomes even clearer when we consider that mentoring pastors water what others have planted before them, and which after them will produce a bountiful harvest and benefit for many other people and communities.

CHAPTER 4

MENTORING AGAINST
THE STREAM

However beneficial the relationship or the results of mentoring for pastoral wisdom and preparation for ministry, we must be aware that it still takes place under the influence of the culture into which pastors are set and the patterns of sin that uniquely mark each of the persons involved. While we look forward to the rich experience of mentoring, we must also remain vigilant to the forces and influences that carry the potential to impede the relationship. Therefore, in this chapter we turn to consider a few of these possible hindrances.

AGAINST THE STREAM OF POPULAR CULTURE

"Mentoring" is a concept and a practice whose coinage has been rather devalued in recent days. Economists tell us that one way to devalue a currency is to flood the market with counterfeit currency—cheap imitations that lack the gold necessary to give it substance. The contemporary "mentoring" scene is like a cultural deluge, in fact, that threatens to carry us into the tributaries of stoic self-mastery, therapeutic self-actualization, or heroic self-accomplishment.[1] Riding this torrent are a bevy of carnivalesque vessels racing full-throttle, piloted by scores of self-described Life-Coaches, Power-Mentors, Wellness Counselors, and Self-Help Technicians. Each of these ships promise a more rationally refined technique or a more effective method to rescue those of us floundering in the cataracts and to help us into their cruise boats of successful and satisfying lifestyles. This commercialization of mentoring is but the latest lucrative offshoot from the tree of religious and therapeutic free enterprise. And it is a tree heavy with fruit pleasing to the eye. "Ye shall be as gods," it promises—if you follow these three steps, five stages, nine secrets, six routines, and all in seven days. Then you can have the poised, successful, fulfilled self you have always wanted.

But that seems to be exactly the problem—the self and the self's obsession with the self, and the self's self-determined and self-directed self-will. The "self" has become so large that we can no longer see past our selves to know where and who we are. We can hardly see others, and we certainly cannot see the grandeur of creation or the crashing-in of the eschaton. Emotionally and spiritually starved, we are only offered our selves for nourishment. But in the end we can never cannibalistically consume enough of the self to be satisfied, because the self alone is not satisfying.

Enter Will Barrett, the courteous protagonist of Walker Percy's novel, *The Second Coming*, who "lived in the most Christian nation in the world, the U.S.A., in the most Christian part of that nation, the South, in the most Christian state in the South, North Carolina, in the most Christian town in North Carolina." His route to the soporific suburbs led him along Wall Street and into a marriage lined with old money. Successful, he lived in a lovely home with a lovely view, "surrounded by good cheerful folk, family and friends, and merry golfers." Despite this geographic and material affluence, within twenty pages of the opening, he sits in his garage dizzy from listless apathy, a loaded 1941 German Lugar in his right hand, contemplating suicide. Percy tells us that from the seat of his Mercedes he looks to a patch of sunlight under the bumper of his deceased wife's Rolls Royce, sees a cat and has one of many "revelations:"

> There was the cat. Sitting there in the sun with its needs satisfied, for whom one place was the same as any other place as long as it was sunny . . . The cat was exactly a hundred percent cat, no more no less. As for Will Barrett, as for people nowadays—they were never a hundred percent themselves. They occupied places uneasily and more or less successfully. More likely they were forty-seven percent themselves . . . All too often these days they were two percent themselves, specters who hardly occupied a place at all. How can the great suck of self ever hope to be a fat cat dozing in the sun? . . . a person nowadays is two percent himself. How to restore the ninety-eight percent?[2]

And a host somewhere answers, "buy this DVD, follow these four steps . . . "

Though an oft-asked question, few of us are willing to hear the answer that calls for death to the self, even if this death leads to life. Several of Percy's characters are concretions of Christ's warning that whoever grasps after his life will lose it, but whoever surrenders his life will gain it in abundance. Commenting on Barrett and other tragi-comic characters in his novels, Percy notes that they typify an age trying to achieve life through disordered means:

> It is the century of the love of death. I am not talking just about Verdun or the Holocaust or Dresden or Hiroshima. I am talking about a subtler form of death, a death in life, of people who seem to be living lives which are good by all sociological standards and yet seem to be more dead than alive. Whenever you have a hundred thousand psychotherapists talking about being life-affirming, and a million books about life enrichment, you can be sure there is a lot of death around.

For Will Barrett, everywhere he looked—at his family, friends, and neighbors—he saw death. When he looked in his own heart he saw death. The prospect of living out his life stalked by death was so painful, this modern man literally ran away from home, crawled into a cave in the woods, and sat in pitch darkness, waiting for death. More accurately, he sat there threatening God with suicide. But typically, he no sooner takes up his desperate vigil than he comes down with a toothache, which comically and pathetically draws him out of the cave. In his search for the other ninety-eight percent, however, Barrett's eyes are eventually opened. But there are many people offering to restore that ninety-eight percent, and all through a little video available for just three easy payments of $19.99 that will unlock our human potential.

James Houston, in his giant-slaying book, *The Mentored Life,* observes that the promise of "a harmonious personality, constant serenity, and balance in mental health" is not new. It was promised by the Stoic philosophers, among many others, in the face of the disintegration of their world, when the grand narrative of the Roman Empire was collapsing around them. As Seneca writes in a letter to his young friend, Lucilius: "Take joy only in that which comes from what is your own. What do I mean by what is your own? I mean you yourself and your own best part."[3] In hostile, uncertain times, the promise of self-control and self-mastery through self-actualization is seductive, and modern, secular therapists and lifestyle coaches profit from it.

Unfortunately, enticing programs like these are available not only in the "marketplace," where parishioners spend most of their time, but also in the corridors of Christendom, where we want to do our best for the kingdom. Programs for developing pastors and church leaders sometimes, though certainly not always, differ really very little. We are offered new ways to gratify our selves, even if the mediums are different. Swap a few words around. Cut out "business" and "executive," paste in "church" and "leader." Cut out "the opposite sex," paste in "volunteers" and "seekers."

Cut out "bank account," paste in "building program." And leave in words like "quick," "proven," "manage," "career," "effective," "influential." This is why books like *Fund-Raising Sermons That Work* and *Guaranteed Church Growth* find an audience. We should be careful, however, lest we let our mind's eye wander far from our own hearts to settle on certain Faustian preachers and Promethean pastors we have known. Every pastor at some time or another comes to know these temptations.

The culture of self-actualization, whether within our churches or without, seems to be characterized by at least these two things: rational techniques for the sake of speedy progress, and self-mastery for the sake of self-sufficiency and an attractive lifestyle leading to self-fulfillment. It looks to "mentoring" and "coaching" often for a quick and manageable technique to help individuals gain at least a modest and respectable degree of prestige and comfort.

Mentoring for *pastoral* formation, however, looks rather different from this, or at least it should—not that it leads people into failure, self-doubt, and indolence. The fundamental difference is that mentoring for pastoral formation is not a technique, and it is not oriented to improving one's self as usually understood. It is oriented to neither power nor prestige, nor even "success," and it certainly cannot be practiced hastily. Instead, it is grounded in a deepening friendship, and turned toward the work of the Spirit, which leads us to put on Christ and die to self in preparation for service to church and world.

First, mentoring is not about the imposition of a technique or logarithm that two participants can apply in order to produce a desired or expected result. It is much more spontaneous, unpredictable, and unrefined than that. In his classic text, *The Four Loves*, C. S. Lewis describes "friendship" in such a way that we may consider mentoring for pastoral formation a genre within this larger category of human relations:

> Lovers are normally face to face, absorbed in each other; Friends, side by side, absorbed in some common interest . . . Friendship

arises when two or more of the companions discover that they
have in common some insight or interest or even taste which the
others do not share . . . It is when two such persons discover one
another, when, whether with immense difficulties and semi-
articulate fumblings or with what would seem to us amazing
and elliptical speed, they share their vision . . . *Do you see the
same truth?*—Or at least, Do you care about the same truth?[4]

Similarly, mentor and mentee covenant together to look in the
same direction, to look for the same truth and share with the other
what they see.

Mentoring for pastoral formation is not a hasty affair, either.
Persons are neither formed nor re-formed hastily. Maturity cannot
be accelerated like an atom in a cyclotron. Hasty mentoring is
depersonalized mentoring because it meets its time schedule only
by abstracting from the quite particular and complex faith and
vocational journey of the individual person. The formation of
wisdom is appropriately compared to the waiting and watching
associated with childbirth. Consider Hannah, Sarah, Elizabeth,
and Anna and Simeon, who, in patient expectation of birth,
were forced to wait far beyond the standard nine months. As
they experienced the disparity between human and divine time,
wisdom was gestating and being born within them.

Patience is that first characteristic of charity we owe one another
in the ecclesial community. It keeps us from undue expectations of
ourselves or of others, which lead to frustration and the defensive
posturing of arrogance. It keeps us from sabotaging the good we
may do when our minds are tranquil rather than impetuous: "In
its agitated state the impatient mind acts as if it did not know what
it was doing, only to feel regret later when it realizes what it has
done," observes the sixth-century Pope Gregory the Great.[5]

Instead, a mentoring friendship may not too inappropriately
be compared to the patient watchfulness and attentive calm that
characterizes those tree-like creatures, the Ents, who cared for the
forest in J.R.R. Tolkien's book, *The Two Towers*. To everything

and everyone they give their deliberate and sturdy consideration. Remember reading descriptions of Treebeard and the others? Their eyes were but the sparkling surfaces of deep reservoirs filled up with ages of memory and long, slow, steady thinking. "I don't know," the hobbit, Pippin, mused, "but it felt as if something that grew in the ground . . . was considering you with the same slow care that it had given to its own inside affairs for endless years." Our habits and ways of being and thinking are set deep within us, dug out over twenty, thirty, forty years. Digging new channels of thought and new avenues of response and reaction cost not a little toil and consume not a little time. This requires the slow care of inside affairs that is of the essence of substantive formation.

Second, mentoring for pastoral formation is not about turning in on the self and the self's self-generated visions and desires for the sake of self-fulfillment. Instead it turns us outward to Christ whose ministry we mediate, and inward to the formation of our hearts in the image of Christ. It orients us not to visions of ecclesiastical sugarplums dancing in our heads, but rather to the concrete labor of the Holy Spirit in our life and the life of others. It aids us to reflect on what the Spirit has been doing in our lives, is doing now, and is drawing us to in the future. There is a profound de-centering of the self in the self, and a re-centering in Christ and the Spirit. When the apostle Paul defends his life and calling as a pastor in Second Corinthians, he declares:

> For what we proclaim is not ourselves, but Jesus Christ as Lord, with ourselves as your servants for Jesus' sake. (4:5)

> Not that we are sufficient in ourselves to claim anything as coming from us, but our sufficiency is from God, who has made us competent to be ministers of a new covenant. (3:5–6)

Therefore, we are ambassadors for Christ, God making his appeal through us. (5:20)

For we who live are always being given over to death for Jesus' sake, so that the life of Jesus also may be manifested in our mortal flesh. (4:11)

Mentoring for pastoral formation turns us outward not only to Christ and the Spirit, but also outward to church and world. Paul's joy was never solitary. He rejoiced in the faith of the churches and labored to pour his own life out for their sake, for their maturity, for their life in Christ. "Indeed, the whole purpose of [Ephesians] is an illustration of the social character of Christian mentoring as beneficial socially; for what is 'personal' is shared with 'the Other.'"[6] The practice of mentoring finds its mandate in Paul's explanation of his ministry: "We proclaim him, admonishing and teaching everyone with all wisdom, so that we may present everyone perfect in Christ. To this end I labor, struggling with all his energy, which so powerfully works in me."

Mentoring itself is part of this practice of admonishing and teaching for the sake of maturity, and not only for the maturity of the single mentee, but through that mentee for a whole host of other people whom the mentor will never know. That is the glory of the communion of saints. We labor on behalf of those whose faces we will never see and whose names we will never hear.

AGAINST THE STREAM OF OUR FALLEN NATURES

Mentoring for pastoral formation not only attempts to move against the wan flow of our self-indulging culture, but it also moves against, or at least attempts to take account of, the deeper tempestuous flow of our fallen and ever-falling sinful natures. "My sinful desires are my weight, and they carry me where they will,"[7] said Augustine, and, as we know, the inertial weight of our fallen natures often carries us away from other persons in one way or another. If we cannot physically get away from others, we either veil ourselves from them and stringently restrict access, or we encroach upon them, "thingify" them, and treat them accordingly, handing them pre-written roles for our own drama.

We owe to Martin Buber the well-known distinction between an "I-Thou" relationship, in which two persons mutually address and respond to each other, and an "I-It" relationship where one or both depersonalize and commodify the other for the sake of some sort of self-satisfying gain, whether financial, emotional, sexual, or vocational. Either pulling back from the other or harnessing them as a means to my end entails a despairing abandonment of *personal* communion. "Despair" is the proper word because though we have been created to know and love the other, we cannot concurrently honor their personhood and achieve our desires, so we sacrifice the former and violate our natures—which leads to the despair of disorder. Recognizing this in himself and others Augustine surmised, "there is nothing so social by nature, so unsocial by its corruption, as this race."[8]

We prove ourselves wise, however, when we recognize that every relationship is marked by these Babel-like effects of sin. It bears upon the mentoring friendship in a particular way. We are concerned with pastoral formation, fundamental to which is moral and spiritual formation, which are matters of the heart. And who can bear to examine their own heart, let alone draw it out willingly to reveal it to someone else with all its duplicitous misgivings? "In this journey of our earthly life," says Augustine, "each one carries his own heart, and each heart is closed to every other."[9] Attention to the "heart" is unavoidable in this relationship, however. While it differs from classical spiritual direction, which focuses primarily on matters of the heart, we cannot here pretend that this is not a central concern of our pastoral ministry as whole persons.

In both the Old and New Testaments, the "heart" denotes the whole of who and how we are—our desires, passions, and affections. It is the seat of our wisdom and understanding, and the source of our actions and speech. The "heart" comprehends the complex inner reality of God's human creation—is it too much to say that a person *is* their heart? When God addresses our hearts, he addresses us at our most transparent, exposed depth. When our hearts are made new—a heart of flesh given for a heart of stone— we are made new. The change is not tangential to the person. No more fundamental or subterranean level is imaginable. When C. S. Lewis laments the emergence of "men without chests" in *The Abolition of Man,* he means people without the character of heart capable of adequately directing their heads and their loins—both of which follow the leading of the heart.

A cascade of texts demonstrates the frequency with which the heart is a metaphor for the whole person before God.

From the heart come words and thoughts:

"What proceeds out of the mouth comes from the heart. This is what defiles a person." (Mt 15:18)

"The good draw what is good out of the good treasure in their heart. The wicked draw evil from the evil in their hearts. Words flow out of what fills the heart." (Lk 6:45)

The heart is in need of cleansing:

"The heart is more devious than anything else and desperately sick. Who can understand it?" (Jer 17:9)

God restores the person by reforming their heart:

"Deep within them I will plant my Law, writing it upon their hearts." (Jer 31:33)

"A new heart I will give you, and a new spirit I will put within you; and I will take out of your flesh the heart of stone and give you a heart of flesh." (Ez 36:26)

God addresses and indwells the heart:

"The love of God has been poured into our hearts by the Holy Spirit." (Rom 5:5)"God has sent the spirit of his Son into our hearts." (Gal 4:6).

"May the Lord direct your hearts in the love of God." (2 Thes 3:5)

God examines the heart:

"You probe my heart, Oh Lord, and examine me at night. You test me." (Ps 17:3)

"Search me, O God, and know my heart! Try me and know my thoughts." (Ps 139:23)

Robert Meye summarizes this biblical picture of the heart: "The heart is a place of belief in God and a place of resistance to God, a place of openness and place of hardness. It is a place of offering to God and a place of sinning against God. It is a place where the bounty of God is poured out and a place where we are known for what we are. The language of the heart describes the character of a person."[10] Likewise, Gregory of Nazianzus reminds us "the whole of our treatment and exertion is concerned with the hidden man of the heart, and our warfare is directed against that adversary and foe within us, who uses ourselves as his weapons against ourselves."[11] Thus the "heart formation" of the pastor is essential. His or her own "heart formation" will provide a reference point for discernment in ministry, as each proposes to lead in the "heart formation" of the body of Christ entrusted to his or her care.

While we acknowledge that only the Spirit truly knows the heart, as the mentee comes to trust the mentor, she will be enabled to open her heart and consider it together with the Spirit and mentor.

Not only do we note the difficulty of baring our hearts, but, to a slightly lesser degree, we ask, who can bear to watch a sermon of himself on video, let alone watch it with someone else who might critique its form or substance? Death to self, indeed, for our selves are occasionally such fragile constructs that criticism of a sermon, lesson, or pastoral conversation can strike like criticism of who I am as a person. What we do is part of who we are—and preaching, teaching, counseling, praying is what seminarians are supposed to be able to do. That was the point of those years of study, dozens of classes, thousands of dollars, prayers, spiritual retreats, seminars, and ordination boards. At the end we are expected to be efficient, articulate communicators of the gospel, shrewd exegetes of modern culture, faithful students of Scripture. Therefore, when something we have done or have said is questioned or critiqued, it may cause us to call into question who we are and the direction we thought we were heading.

Therefore, we may very well find ourselves resistant to the practice of mentoring and being mentored. Through subtle and not so subtle means we may attempt to bend mentoring under the pressure of our will –for autonomy or our will for self-preservation. Many of our classical theologians have suggested that the root of sin is *superbia*, or pride. So the temptation to sin is a temptation to prideful autonomy. And autonomy in turn is the pretentious claim to self-definition that spurns the claim of both God and others. Our presumptive *perception* of what others might think and our presumptive *perception* of what God might think of us may inform our idolatrous self-creation, but we cannot suffer their *actual* voices to speak into our hearts. To do so would be to surrender our claim to autonomy. So we protect our creation. We drag it away from the presence of others. We hedge it in and set about imitating it as best we can. We try to live into our own external projections of ourselves as persons and pastors. We can reflect upon our persons, and do stand in a sort of internal relation with ourselves. We can think about who we are, and we can even maintain a dialogue with ourselves. But the prideful claim to autonomy insists that no one else be invited into our dialogue. It assumes we have undistorted epistemic access to our selves, that is, that our self-perception is infallible and without need of another.

In the mentoring friendship a request is made for another person to graciously help us drag that carefully protected image of ourselves as persons and as pastors out into the open so that together we might consider its truthfulness. Walking around it and looking it over with someone else involves both *mortification* and *vivification*, to use Reformation language—a dying for the sake of living. Those parts that must die must be left to do so if the living and life-giving parts are to flourish. Dietrich Bonhoeffer rightly described the practice of confession of the heart as the profoundest kind of mortification. But given our cultivated instinct for self-preservation, we all too easily avoid confession and any practice that might resemble confession, because it includes a dying to self, even though that self may be less than who we really are.

Thomas Merton, who participated in the spiritual supervision and mentoring of Roman Catholic priests for several decades, observes what we might expect, that some novitiate priests

> are not pleased with the available director because he does not flatter their self-esteem or cater to their illusions about themselves. In other words, they want a director who will confirm their hope of finding pleasure in themselves and in their virtues, rather than one who will strip them of their self-love and show them how to get free from preoccupation with themselves and their own petty concerns, to give themselves to God and to the Church.[12]

Instead of entering openly into a mentoring friendship, we usually protect our self-created images in one of two ways, both of which are derivative of the demand for self-determination—either we fashion a hesitant self that can do no right, that can hear nothing but criticism, that eagerly molds itself to any word of counsel; or we fashion a demonstrative self that can do no wrong, hear no criticism, or heed any word of counsel. Whereas Paul says, "For if anyone thinks he is something, when he is nothing, he deceives himself," we also say, "if anyone thinks he is nothing, when he is something, he likewise deceives himself."

The various ways we relate to people are usually so deeply ingrained in us that we are unaware of them. Learning to recognize those ingrained patterns, however, and either sanding or polishing them as needed, is an important task for any minister. The mentoring friendship provides a safe place to become aware of these habitual ways of being towards people, and to begin to practice new ways of being. There is often a direct correlation between how the mentor and mentee relate to one another and how each relates to other persons within or outside of the church. This correlation very often extends to or extends from how each relates to God as well. We enter into the mentoring friendship acknowledging from the start that we are sinners, fallen and saved by God's grace, whom he has brought together for a time to talk and pray about the important things—Father, Son, Holy Spirit, creation, redemption, Pentecost, prayer, ministry, worship.

THE HESITANT MENTOR

As mentors, we are sometimes hesitant to offer ourselves to a pastor-mentee because of our genuine sense of inadequacy. So we refrain from offering critical observations. We refrain from confronting the mentee. We abdicate our responsibility to spur them on to spiritual maturity and works of service. Our hesitation may also result from fear that our own personal and pastoral weaknesses or failures may be exposed. What if the mentee becomes aware of the incongruities in our lives, and our own lack of spiritual and theological formation? The pains and insecurities we secretly harbor entice us to ease away from the mentee and pray our retreat goes unnoticed. But this may indicate a certain presumption on our part, namely, that at some time in the past, we reached the terminus of our own formation as persons and pastors, instead of remembering that, along with the mentee, our formation is always "on the way."

As mentors we may not infrequently feel threatened by our mentee's apparently formidable abilities. They may be extremely effective communicators. They may possess refined personal and practical skills and convey at least the appearance of spiritual depth. Their body of theological or exegetical knowledge may be broader than ours, or may at least be more current than ours (whatever advantage that might be for a discipline rooted in millennia). The mentee may in fact be a better organizer and recruiter (if so, you should probably hire them). And they may very well be able to bring helpful suggestions or observations based on current pastoral literature. Their Greek and Hebrew may be sharper, and they may even make a richer pot of coffee or tell a better story. But one thing they lack: experience in the diligent practice of pastoral ministry. It is that experience alone that engenders the subtlety and understanding that our vocation requires: an understanding of people, an understanding of place, an integration of knowledge, practice, and prayer, and experience in the drama of stodgy sin and surprising grace that plays on the stages of the human heart. This does not give the mentor an "edge" over the mentee; instead it opens up a way to love the mentee and to nurture the church through him or her.

THE DEMONSTRATIVE MENTOR

As mentors, rather than withdrawing ourselves and our images of ourselves from mentees, our other option is to thrust ourselves or our pastoral images forward as the primary model that the mentee ought to follow. The demonstrative mentor thus sets about trying to reproduce or duplicate herself in the lives of her mentees, inculcating and encouraging a kind of *imitatio mentoris* that quickly shifts the focus of the conversations from the mentee to the mentor as advice-giving teacher and sower of pithy maxims and morals for the mentee to gather up as he can. It is always gratifying to our ego to have a disciple, to think about duplicating ourselves in someone else. But one of us is probably enough. If the wise God of the universe did not see fit to make two of any one of us, then we might think better of any attempt to do it ourselves. For when our "disciples" fail us, or find cumbersome the tailor-made suit of armor we foisted upon them, and when instead they pick up a sling and some rocks, and in doing so far surpass us, we best be cautious lest we find ourselves flinging javelins from the recesses of a dark mood. If the Corinthians were not baptized into Apollos or Paul, but rather Christ, then neither are our mentees baptized into us. They have been baptized into Christ and called to mediate his ministry in his Spirit, however that may look. Christ in David Tanner in Austin, Texas looks very different from Christ in Doris Chao in Hong Kong, China or Christ in Jimmy Krane in Cape Town, South Africa.

In his perspicacious little book, *Life Together*, written while principal of the underground seminary in Finkenwalde, Germany, Dietrich Bonhoeffer joyfully concedes

> God did not make others as I would have made them . . . God does not want me to mold others into the image that seems good to me, that is, into my own image. Instead, in their freedom from me God made other people in God's own image. I can never know in advance how God's image should appear in others. That image always takes on a completely new and unique form whose origin is found solely in God's free and sovereign act of creation. To me that form may seem strange, even ungodly. But God creates every person in the image of God's Son, the Crucified, and this image, likewise, certainly looked strange and ungodly to me before I grasped it.[13]

MENTEES

As a new pastor in a mentoring relationship, you, too, may assume one or the other of these postures—of the hesitant or demonstrative mentee. Both you and your mentor need to remain alert to this possibility, paying particular attention to your personal motives and dispositions. Becoming aware of points of resistance and defenses that may hinder the mentoring friendship is an important part of learning both how to mentor and how to be mentored. Therefore it is important to be made aware of these issues and to reflect on which posture we are more likely to adopt in the mentoring friendship. It would be most helpful if you discussed this openly with your mentor during the first or second meeting. Both you and your mentor must commit to work toward being vulnerable and transparent with one another and resist the temptation to *appear* other than you are. To try to *appear* is a mistake, as it is always the manifestation of a desire *to conceal*. As the mentee, you should ask your mentor to challenge you if they sense that you are not being vulnerable , since this can become a hindrance to both the mentoring friendship and your ministry. As Randy Reese and Keith Anderson describe in their book, *Spiritual Mentoring*, "The mentoree must also remember that submissiveness to the process of spiritual mentoring is primarily a submissiveness to the Holy Spirit, not a wooden, mindless obedience to a mentor. The mentor is a voice that guides but not a voice that dictates."[14]

THE HESITANT MENTEE

The posture of the hesitant mentee may be the result of a diffident, melancholic personality, or it may be the effect of a previously destabilizing experience in either his professional or personal life. On the other hand, the hesitant mentee may experience enervating doubts about her academic preparation, pastoral abilities, or calling to ministry. Anxiety about the adequate "performance" of ministry makes the mentee hesitant to do anything outside of the mentor's clear direction or pre-approval. The mentor's opinion and decisions become determinative in everything. Immature dependence of this sort reveals itself through the desire for magical solutions that exonerate one from taking necessary responsibility.

Another characteristic of the hesitant mentee is an excessive need for the mentor's affirmation. We all need affirmation and encouragement, but the hesitant mentee orients his ministry towards it. As a result, he becomes overly sensitive, and either interprets criticism as rejection, or absorbs the criticism and compounds it with his own self-deprecating observations. Another way of inducing affirmation is for the mentee to make the mentor feel that he is being too hard on himself. To avoid criticism altogether, the mentee may eschew difficult tasks: "that didn't show up on my spiritual gifts analysis"; "I haven't had that class yet;" "I haven't been able to read that book"; "I'm really not very good at . . . " If something actually does not go well, he may blame the mentor: "I did it like you told me, and it didn't work;" "You didn't give me enough information to be able to do it well." Likewise, the mentee may be reluctant to discuss her ponderous sermon, misspoken words, or awkward attempt at pastoral counseling.

The hesitant mentee may avoid any discussion that leads to the exposure of her moral vices or personal insecurities—particularly if she feels that she is not being called to ministry—and so nudge conversations away from herself toward any neutral harbor that presents itself, such as family, politics, current events, or our classes. Or, the mentee may focus attention on the personal life of his mentor by asking about her family, background, or future. If the mentor notices a consistent pattern of avoiding personal or threatening areas, it would be wise to bring it to the mentee's attention in order to assist the mentee in digging up the roots of his or her avoidance. Pastors who are too dependent on the praise and accolades of others may be tempted to shift their ministry from speaking gospel words to speaking pleasing words.

As another diversionary technique, the hesitant mentee may introduce a controversial theological or ecclesiastical question in order to fill the time with the mentor's explanation and so actively resist revealing his heart. On the other hand, the mentee may fail to bring questions or reflections about significant ministry events and so passively resist formation. Likewise, the noble tasks of planning and organizing the next ministry event, or the ignoble temptation to bring up inter-staff conflict, can become welcome harbors in which some mentees may hide. A mentee may repeatedly plan events or meetings that conflict with the scheduled time to meet with his mentor, or he may show up late, need to leave early, or simply fail to show up at all. The hesitant mentee may excuse her inadequate preparation for the meeting on the basis of academic pressures, claiming that she is doing the best she can "under the circumstances." Or, when the discussion turns to the cultivation of the interior life, the mentee may cobble together a description from scraps of pious-sounding, second-hand jargon.

Although the mentors need to confront these various attempts to geld the mentoring friendship, they do not need to practice a hermeneutic of suspicion towards mentees and deconstruct every authentic attempt to articulate heart and mind. Nor should mentors suspect a sincere theological disagreement to be the result of some unresolved psychological or spiritual tension. Mentors should help their mentees see that duplicity in the relationship is ultimately disadvantageous, since it inhibits his or her formation and preparation for future ministry, when these unresolved issues will continue to manifest themselves, possibly with more deleterious consequences.

THE DEMONSTRATIVE MENTEE

The demonstrative mentee, in turn, is a reformer, who is confident, self-sufficient, and accustomed to trusting his or her own judgments. The challenge for demonstrative mentees is to heed the exhortation of James 1:19 to be "quick to listen" and "slow to speak." Demonstrative mentees will need to scrupulously practice being "quick to listen": quick to listen and learn about the ecclesial and social community, quick to listen to what God is doing and where they can get in on it, quick to hear their mentors' suggestions and observations. And they will need to practice being "slow to speak": slow to dismiss their mentors' experience and wisdom, claiming "all these I have known since I was a boy"; slow to criticize lest they start straining gnats and hunting down specks; slow to implement their emergency procedure for resuscitating a church's spiritual health; slow to defend their condescension and gracelessness—before they find themselves praying along with the self-assured liturgist, "God, I thank you that I am not like all other men . . . "; slow to put their theological knowledge on parade; and slow to make their mentors feel guilty about offering critical observations. The biblical words for this are patience and humility.[15]

Because both the mentor and the mentee are trying to understand themselves theologically rather than simply moralistically or psychologically, it will be important for them to come together by openly acknowledging their sinful conditions and the peculiar ways their sin manifests itself—not for the sake of foreshadowing or excusing future failure or sloppiness, but because genuine conversation depends on it—indeed, genuine ministry depends on it. The apostle Paul consistently refused to address people moralistically, plotting people on a graph somewhere between good and bad, or psychologically, plotting people somewhere between healthy and unhealthy, or balanced and unbalanced, or happy and sad. Rather, he addressed them as sinners who were out of relation with God, regardless of their mental state of mind— this is one element of the offense of the gospel. It does not ask if you feel like or look like a sinner. It says Christ has come for you because you are a sinner, and your sin manifests itself in myriad ways both subtle and stark.

This must inform not only our pastoral ministry in general, but the mentoring friendship in particular. When we fail to see others theologically, we can foist upon them a heap of unrealizable expectations, and then respond accordingly when they fail to meet them. When we fail to see that sin is not a lack of knowledge but rather a sin-bent disposition, we resort to all sorts of inadequate means to correct it. Commenting on the usual disparity between a pastor's understanding of people and the people's self-understanding, Eugene Peterson comments, "if the pastor rigorously defines people as fellow sinners, he or she will be prepared to share grief, shortcomings, pain, failure, and have plenty of time left over to watch for the signs of God's grace operating in this wilderness, and then fill the air with praises for what he discovers."[16] Dietrich Bonhoeffer considered the confession that we are mutual sinners set in grace as the final breakthrough to true community. A pious community, in contrast, "permits no one to be a sinner" and is "unimaginably horrified if a real sinner suddenly turns up among the pious."[17] Pastors in a mentoring friendship, however, are not so horrified, but know the presence of sin to be an opportunity for the presence of grace.

AGAINST THE STREAM OF ECCLESIAL CULTURE

The Pastor

As we have seen—and might have expected—mentoring for pastoral formation calls to the dock the contemporary culture of mentoring for self-actualization and cross-examines its fundamental assumptions and testimonies about its model for true humanity. We are little surprised as well when alerted that we will need to maintain a vigil against the intrusion of our cultivated habits of sin-induced self-preservation and isolation. However, mentoring also runs against the stream of some of our most comfortable ministerial roles, and counter to some of our church's expectations.

Most pastors do not have to be talked into doing the work of mentoring. A pastor who must be convinced to invite a younger pastor into a mentoring friendship usually already has a waiting room full of tasks elbowing for attention and cannot imagine opening the door to anyone or anything else. What they may fail to realize, however, is that the kind of mentoring we are considering requires but a small adaptation of what we already do as pastors. Privately, we talk with people, anticipating the descent of the Dove upon our conversation. We pray with people. We speak gospel words of grace into sin-bent lives. We look for evidence of God at work where least expected. Personal and intimate, this side of our ministry complements our public acts of preaching and teaching, leading and training.

And both of these are necessary. It is necessary for the pastor to be biblically and theologically competent, to be able to articulate the gospel, to be able to lead others into ministry. But the public side of our ministry can grow so large that it encroaches upon the private. Praised for our salutary preaching or teaching, we can begin to assume the mantle not of a prophet but of a spiritual fixer, an answer-woman or answer-man, a spiritual guru doling out advice to needy souls. And then the personal side of our ministry gets swallowed up by the public side. Private conversations do not cease—people still come for prayer and counsel—but we take the form appropriate to our public ministry and apply it to our private, dispensing ready-made sermons and pre-fabricated devotionals like perforated communion wafers. Convenient. Uniform. Tasteless. Colorless. Unimaginative.

It is likely that as pastors we do in fact have a significant amount of experience with people, and possibly even with interns or mentees. Our experience probably serves us well and allows us to be comfortable with all sorts of people. Being with people is part of our calling, right? Yes and no. Praying with this angry mother is our calling. Listening to this abused wife is our calling. Standing with that juvenile at court is our calling. Dining with this family in their home is our calling. However, when our public kerygmatic ministry of proclamation begins to invade our private ministry of pastoral care, when we are tempted to pull out pre-cut timbers for custom-order projects, then Jacob Firet warns, "our pride whispers to us that we can tell at a glance what is going on, that we need not be open to learning, because without any effort we can discern in the new situation or person what we have experienced before."[18]

The Church

Mentoring for pastoral formation also asks something of the people in our church. It asks them to think about the church theologically rather than sociologically. Sociologically, the church is a voluntaristic society of individuals who meet weekly to hear a twenty-two-minute spiritually edifying discourse delivered by a professionally trained orator. The service has been practiced, i.e., there are no uncomfortable gaps in the performance when an actor forgets their cue. Each ceiling fan is set on the same speed. The cordless microphones have new batteries, and the preacher always remembers to turn it off before she sings the closing hymn. The music is appealing. The speakers never feedback. The children are sufficiently reverent during communion, or at least quiet, which we assume is the same thing.[19] What does the sociological church think about interns? They think they are fine as long as they work with the youth, where they can do little harm, and as long as they do not take up too much of the senior pastor's time.

But mentoring for pastoral formation asks churches to think theologically about their own existence and about their participation in the pastoral formation of the mentee-intern ministering to them and along with them for a limited time. Many churches that invite interns consider themselves "teaching churches," churches that host new pastors and offer them a place to work and grow without the pressure of getting everything right. This is necessary because new pastors have been known to stand in the wrong place during the Eucharist and fumble the words of the liturgy. New pastors (and not only new pastors!) have been known to preach sermons both ponderous and facile. But they are fellow believers, and fellow believers called to mediate Christ's ministry among us. Therefore, the ecclesial body is corporately and individually responsible for their formation and preparation. Whereas their seminary professors and pastor-mentors play lead roles in their development, the members of the church need to understand their supporting roles lest their unexamined expectations give birth to acerbic, condescending, destructive criticism. This involves helping our churches see beyond the immediacy of their own community to develop an ecclesiology that includes all the future people to whom and with whom this particular mentee will minister regardless of denomination or locale. The congregation as "teaching church" understands that time and money set aside for pastoral mentoring is one way it participates in and serves the whole Body of Christ, the church extended in both space and time—the communion of the saints.

The Academy

In a way, mentoring for pastoral formation also moves against the ethos of the academy, whether seminary or secular university. The academy encourages and rewards individual brilliance, and it fosters competition—healthy and unhealthy. It can promote careerism. It honors the "genius." But no one enters pastoral ministry hoping for career advancement or individual fame. It may happen, but in itself is an unworthy goal—like being a play actor in divinity. So mentoring for pastoral formation works to subvert the image of the lone-ranger or CEO pastor and instead cultivate truthful dependence, humility, and teachableness.

CHAPTER 5

PASTOR AS MENTOR

For a Christian, there are, strictly speaking, no chances. A secret Master of the Ceremonies has been at work. Christ, who said to the disciples "Ye have not chosen me, but I have chosen you," can truly say to every group of Christian friends 'You have not chosen one another but I have chosen you for one another.' The Friendship is not a reward for our discrimination and good taste in finding one another out. It is the instrument by which God reveals to each the beauties of all the others. . . . They are like all beauties, derived from Him, and then, in a good Friendship, increased by Him through the friendship itself, so that it is His instrument for creating as well as revealing. . . . It is He, we may dare to hope, who sometimes does, and always should, preside. Let us not reckon without our Host.[1]

—C. S. Lewis, *The Four Loves*

Our first host in the mentoring friendship is God, who invites us to participate in his ministry to the world and who ushers us into a community of others called into fellowship with him. He hosts us in his good creation and provides for our needs. He blesses. He invites. He asks us to share bread and wine at his table. The country pastor, George Herbert, refers to this Host as "quick-ey'd Love," who bids us sit with him despite our protests. Like

89

Herbert's guest, however, we judge our eyes unfit to look upon him, our lips too unclean to receive his food:

> Love took my hand, and smiling did reply,
> Who made the eyes but I?
> Truth Lord, but I have marr'd them; let my shame
> Go where it doth deserve.
> And know you not, says Love, who bore the blame?
> My dear, then I will serve.
> You must sit down, says Love, and taste my meat:
> So I did sit and eat.[2]

Our hospitality to one another can obviously only mirror and reflect the hospitality of this Host, but being welcomed by him, we welcome others. In ministry, he invites us to serve at his banquet, to play host with him and invite others to sit and taste his meat, to be as hospitable with them as he is with us. We invite those in highways and byways, some of whom may apparently be angels, according to the author of Hebrews. So in the mentoring friendship, the pastor and church play host to a student pastor who, like all guests, will usually only be present a short time. Like other hosts and guests they sit together, enjoy each other's company, learn from one another, and share good stories and profound words. But unlike most guests, he or she comes not only to be served but also to take up apron and platter and participate in the church's service to others. In this they are not only cared for, but also learn how to serve alongside their immediate host and the quick-ey'd Host who invites us into his service.

Therefore, education and formation are the primary foci of the younger pastor's participation in the church's life. The mentee is not serving the church simply because it *needed* someone to answer phones, sponsor the Grade Six youth group, or preach at the seven a.m. sunrise service. Plugging quotidian holes and filling ministerial gaps is not the *raison d'etre* of the internship. If, in consultation with the mentor, such tasks are apportioned to the intern (a likely situation in most cases), they should impel the mentee toward the *telos* of their apprenticeship—clarification of their self-understanding as a person in Christ and a pastor to Christ's church, and increased proficiency in the various theological and practical skills which will serve their pastoral ministry.If we accept this *telos* as the goal, and commit to the practice of mentored reflection as the means toward that goal, we have what Aristotle termed the final cause and the efficient cause, yet we lack one thing, the material cause—the object or subject of our reflection. The cognitive and affective development of the mentee, if abstracted from a concrete worshipping community, is not sufficient for pastoral formation—necessary, but not sufficient. Instead, reflection looks for the overlap of *who* people are in Christ with *what* they are doing for Christ. It assumes that who they are is disclosed by what they do, and what they do informs who they are. Such disclosing and in-forming requires the new pastor to be deeply embedded in service to the community. Mentoring for pastoral formation takes place alongside and through the mentee's ministry in the ecclesial community. Mentoring takes place primarily through a series of weekly conversations, between which life and ministry take place. From the ministry that occurs between these conversations, the mentee draws out a few thoughts and experiences for shared reflection and mutual consideration. Then they set out again, taking into the next week of ministry what they observed and learned from the previous week.Under the guidance of the Holy Spirit, mentors plays host to mentees and help them discern those obstacles that slow or inhibit their formation as persons in Christ and as pastors for Christ. Likewise, mentors help mentees discover both the long-term work of the Spirit in their lives and the unique ways they have been gifted and graced for ministry. Standing radically for and with mentees, mentors confront obstacles and encourage gifting, and they do so by offering their eyes to observe, their ears to listen, their voices to speak, and their hands and feet to model—and all of this is made possible by the Spirit who draws them together.

THE OFFER OF EYES

As foolish as it may seem to us or as offensive as it may seem to others, God has chosen not to be God apart from us, but to speak through us, revealing himself through our stuttering speech and our faltering work. While still a country pastor, Karl Barth articulated the dilemma that makes insomniacs of ministers: "As ministers we ought to speak of God. We are human, however, and so cannot speak of God. We ought therefore to recognize both our obligation and our inability and by that very recognition give God the glory."[3] Under his caveat, we determine to do both the public acts of ministry (preaching, leading communal worship, readying people for acts of service) and the private acts (praying with a grieving widower, reading Scripture with a teenager, listening to a distraught parent) well, and to do them better than we did last time. We search for creative and honest words that open up space for people to see, trading in our limping clichés and threadbare phrases now too feeble to carry semantic weight. We endeavor to be mindful caretakers of the arts when we attempt to use drama, music, dance, or literature to inform the imaginations of our embodied parishioners and offer new visions for living before God. We attempt to prepare people to live theologically and to act Christologically in defiance of consumerist economics or soul-destroying technology. We search. We try. We take care. And we ask for help along the way from fellow pastors and believers.

If you are a new pastor, you can offer other pastors some of this help along the way, but you will need the experienced eyes of a mentor to observe three things for you:

- your concrete acts of ministry;

- any passions and patterns that animate or debilitate your work and relationships, so that you can attend to the past and present creative activity of the Spirit in your life;

- the Spirit's subtle work of recreation and transformation in other people's lives.

OBSERVING CONCRETE ACTS OF MINISTRY

It is extremely difficult, if not impossible, to be fully cognizant of ourselves in the middle of an event of ministry like a sermon, a conversation, or service to someone in need. It would be paralyzing if we were, and to some degree we need to lose awareness of ourselves in order to serve the other. The mentoring pastor, therefore, commits to observe the new minister in acts of ministry and attend to the panoply of verbal and explicit communication as well as the ancillary non-verbal and implicit communication. This does not imply that the mentor needs to shadow the mentee, open an account at The Spy Store, or install two-way mirrors and a video surveillance system in order to observe him or her effectively. Neither need it imply the mentor be at every event of ministry in which the mentee participates.

The necessary "observation," in fact, could be either direct or indirect: a) direct observation occurs when the mentor is actually present with the mentee during an "act" of ministry; b) indirect observation includes any of the following: watching a video recording or listening to an audio tape of a sermon, lesson, or conversation; c) reading a written verbatim or reflective description of a particular conversation or event; d) listening to the mentee's oral description of some significant ministry event that occurred since their previous conversation. Most pastoral mentoring friendships set in the context of supervised ministry programs will employ all four of these forms of observation, each of which are described in more detail in the final chapter on "tools" for mentoring.

The mentor has a decisive advantage over preaching or counseling in a classroom "lab" situation in that she can observe the mentee in numerous settings, engaging in various acts of ministry over a protracted period of time. The mentor is thus better qualified to offer the kind of personal review and encouragement that the mentee needs. Likewise, whereas certain intimate moments of ministry are obviously inappropriate for classroom observation and review, mentor and mentee may choose, when appropriate, to participate in private pastoral conversations or acts of ministry together. Not only may the mentee be able to observe the mentor and gain experience in such a setting, but the mentor will also be able to observe the mentee's personal demeanor and pastoral skills.

OBSERVING PASSION AND GIFTS

To "mentoring" we have already attached a number of promising adjectives: pastoral, formative, relational, spiritual, historical, counter-cultural. One apt modifier that may not be readily present is "liberating." We alluded to this earlier, without defining it as such, when we described mentoring for pastoral formation as the practice of assisting a new pastor to be *the person they were created in to be in Christ* and *the pastor they were called to be for Christ*. Paulo Freire, the Latin American educator, suggests that the "liberatory task" is the mentor's fundamental concern. "It is not," he insists, "to encourage the mentor's goals and aspirations and dreams to be reproduced in the mentees," but to allow mentees to fulfill their own calling in their own history.[4] Similarly, in his well-known book, *To Know As We Are Known*, Parker Palmer quotes the first-century desert father, Abba Felix, who suggested that to teach is to create "a space where obedience to the truth is practiced."[5]

"Obedience to the truth" is a strange phrase. We usually think of "recognizing" or "knowing" or "telling" the truth. "Obedience," likewise, usually carries our minds to a whole range of moral and ethical questions. God calls us to be obedient to his Word. Moses commanded the Israelites to be obedient and therefore "Choose Life!" Children are instructed to obey their parents in the Lord. However, as Jonah, the virgin Mary, the apostle Paul, or Gregory of Nazianzus could testify, we can also be obedient or disobedient to a calling. Pastors know the call to vocational obedience from inside. We try to live it. Accepting our calling and sticking to it, however, often requires a Marian surrender: "May it be to me as you have said." Not only must I be obedient to a calling, but *I* must be obedient to the particular ways God has graciously gifted and prepared me for my calling, forging within me unique passions, strengths, interests, and desires. God does not limit himself to his general address to humankind, but particularizes his call to individual persons.

The wise pastoral mentor looks to partner with the Holy Spirit, patiently discerning the possible divine origins of the mentee's passions or abilities and diligently looking to create space for these to flourish to the benefit of the church community. Flannery O'Connor, the Southern short-story writer, speaking to an audience about writing, declared that she wrote because she was good at it:

> There is no excuse for anyone to write fiction for public consumption unless he has been called to do so by the presence of a gift. A gift of any kind is a considerable responsibility. It is a mystery in itself, something gratuitous and wholly undeserved, something whose real uses will probably always be hidden from us.[6]

The presence of a gift, O'Connor asserts, may carry the responsibility of obedience to a call.

Being helped along toward this "obedience to the truth" and recognizing that we may be "called . . . by the presence of a gift" is liberating indeed, for it is predicated on the belief that God has called us as whole persons to mediate his ministry. God's preparation of us began long before his calling came to us. In time, the Holy Spirit particularizes us in all our uniqueness, and we become more of who we were created to be than before. Certainly, the Spirit draws us to participate in Christ, makes us one body and one people in Christ, hides our life with Christ in God, and draws us into one baptism to serve one Lord—we should not forget our communal identity for a moment. However, despite that very real unity, the one Holy Spirit did not reverse Babel through drawing each person or pastor into complete conformity, but through a kind of unity that manifestly affirms and celebrates the Spiritual flourishing of diversity. The mentor, therefore, looks for the particular gifts that the mentee brings into the pastoral ministry as well as those gifts that begin to emerge in the course of ministry.

What keeps us from drawing into service some of our deep passions and interests or recognizing that they may be serviceable to the kingdom? Perhaps these gifts have not yet had opportunity to fully reveal themselves, and so we are not fully aware of them. If so, we have no choice but to rely on the faithful words of our friends, family, and parishioners—or our mentor—to confirm them and provoke us to recognize their legitimate place in our vocation. Other times, though aware of them, we nervously depreciate their possible contribution, unsure of them ourselves. So aware are we of our own duplicitous weakness that the assurances of another's voice and another's eyes often commands more authority than our own.

Liberative mentors will allow their seeing and hearing to be led by a cluster of key questions, the answers to which may provide small clues to their mentees' gifts and calling:

1. When do people seem to hear the gospel and respond to the mentee's ministry? Why do they respond?

2. How does the mentee most naturally relate to other people and minister to them?

3. Does the mentee have a natural rapport with other people that allows him or her to speak truthful words in pastoral counseling or discipleship?

4. What is the mentee's passion in ministry? Where does he or she delight in ministry: teaching, worship, evangelism, youth, children, the elderly, new Christians, non-Christians? Does the mentee particularly enjoy apologetics, dogmatics, hermeneutics, or homiletics?

5. Does the mentee have a passion for the weak and the marginalized, the orphan, widow, and refugee in distress?

6. Do certain interests or concerns recur in the mentee's conversations? Does a passion for truth, beauty, love, justice, comfort, holiness, or some other "good" seem to animate his or her thinking and acting?

7. Do particular theological concerns or questions drive the mentee's thinking: a theology of creation, or worship, or ecclesiology, or justice, or ethics?

8. What does the mentee think the world most needs that the gospel offers? In turn, what does he or she think the church desperately needs that the gospel offers?

9. Is there a particular gift or interest present in the mentee, whether the result of natural talent, nurture, or supernatural spontaneity?

10. What does the mentee seem to enjoy and how could God use what he or she enjoys doing? Music, film, poetry, writing, drama, photography, sports, or visual arts?

Though many different responsibilities and tasks fall to every pastor, and though God promises to work through our weakness, he also promises to care for the church by providing a panoply of gifts to his people—and not every gift is given to every believer. Our passions and strengths may be a clue to our calling, and to how in fact we might best serve the church and flourish as persons. Part of the mentor's role is to help the mentee see the Holy Spirit's activity in preparing him or her for ministry. This involves a great confluence of one's natural abilities or interests, education, familial relations, gender, and experiences. What might God have prepared this person to do for the kingdom and how might the mentor become a tool of the Holy Spirit toward that end?

When the apostle Paul exhorts Timothy in 1 Timothy 4:14 not to neglect or despise his gift, his *charismata*, and in 2 Timothy 1:6 to "fan into flame the gift of God, which is in you through the laying on of my hands," he models this important role of the mentor. Paul exhorts Timothy to "be diligent," "give yourself wholly," "watch . . . persevere." We can assume that Timothy knew the nature of this *charismata* and did not need Paul to alert him to it. What he did need was encouragement. Even though the gift was bestowed miraculously through the laying on of hands, through neglect, it could apparently cool like an unattended campfire. In fact Paul's admonition is to "rekindle" and "re-stoke" the gift that lay like glowing embers within him. The Latin Vulgate got it right by translating this *resuscites gratiam Dei*—"resuscitate the gift of God." Mentors will need to be attentive to any gifts that the Spirit may have given to their mentees, which may be in danger of cooling, or which may have never been recognized or fanned into flame for service to the church. If mentors are watchful, they may be able to assist their mentors by diligently adding logs of encouragement to the fire and finding places for their gifts to burn in the church so that that others might benefit from the light and heat.

The Potter's Rib

This liberating role is the distinguishing mark of classical spiritual direction. The director does not attempt to lead the directee according to his or her wishes, but to discern the particular way along which God may be leading the directee. "Let such guides of souls recall that the principal agent, guide and mover of souls is not the director, but the Holy Spirit. They are themselves only instruments to guide souls in the way of perfection by faith and by the law of God according to the spirit that God is giving each one."[7]

A twist on Paul's image of the potter and clay may be helpful. Numerous times, the Lord refers to himself as the master potter, who alone determines the shape and use of the earthen vessels he forms and quickens with life. Extending this metaphor, we might say that the pastor-mentor offers him or herself to be used like a potter's "rib" by Christ and the Spirit—God's two hands, as Irenaeus calls them—as he or she shapes and molds the mentee. The potter's rib is a smooth flat tool made of a piece of either hardwood, plastic, or shell that fits in the palm of the hand. Curved on one side with a straight edge on the other, the rib is used to pull up the cylinder or bowl out of a spinning lump of clay. With the curved side a potter applies pressure both inside and outside the pot to slowly draw it into the desired shape, liberating it, in a way, to be the flower vase or serving dish the potter intends it to be. With the straight side the potter scrapes off excess clay, smoothes the sides, and trims the top. If too much force is applied the rib punctures the pot and sends it spinning off-balance back into a lump. If too little pressure is applied the lump of clay never moves and does not fill out its intended shape. The rib is a tool to help the potter, but the potter retains the privilege of determining its shape, the color of the glaze, and whether it is to be used as bedpan or bridal cup.

John Linnan describes the purpose of pastoral and spiritual mentoring well when he refers to it as rendering the kind of assistance that brings the mentee into a dialogue with God through which "God will shape him or her in that way which more enables this unique person to be in his or her own unique way Christ for this time, this place, this church, and this world"[8]—a jar of clay formed to carry sacred mysteries.

OBSERVING PATTERNS AND HABITS

In the Beginning, a playful retelling of the creation story for children written by Steve Turner, shows how God's creating word takes precedence over all other words, and evokes the creative response of creation:

God said WORLD and the world spun round
God said LIGHT and the light beamed down
God said NIGHT and the sky went black
God said LAND and the sea rolled back
God said LEAF and the shoot pushed through
God said FIN and the first fish grew
God said BEAK and the bright bird soared
God said FUR and the jungle roared;
God said SKIN and the man breathed air
God said RIB and the girl stood there
God said GOOD and the world was great
God said REST and they all slept late. [9]

John Calvin and Karl Barth would readily approve.

Though the first words of Genesis present us a glimpse of the creation story, they do not make known the full identity of the Creator and the purpose of creation. The first Word of creation actually comes in Colossians 1, "For by him all things were created, in heaven and on earth, visible and invisible . . . all things were created through him and for him," and John 1, "In the beginning was the Word . . . All things were made through him, and without him was not any thing made that was made." These texts reveal that the first Word came *in media res*—in the middle of a chaotic, sin-laden time, when the Word through whom all things were created entered creation to recreate it. It is only when that Word is spoken that the creating words previously spoken are clarified and understood. Only with the speaking of that Word into human flesh does the rest of human flesh come to know its true identity

God's call to vocation is similar. It, too, comes as a word *in media res*, and it clarifies and gives coherence to the scattered details of our previously penned stories. God's call comes to Moses, the refugee-murderer in the middle of his new life; to Elisha plowing his field; to Nehemiah hiding out from the Assyrians; to Rahab entertaining foreign men; to Matthew collecting taxes; to Saul, the

Pharisee, crushing blasphemers; to Augustine, the lustful rhetor; to John Newton, the slaver; to the revolutionary Dostoevsky standing blindfolded in a firing line. If our calls are not so dramatic, they differ simply in degree rather than kind and come no less personally than any of these. Though God created us and watched over our growth and development, it is only when his word comes to us that we are able to fully understand who and why we are.

We have just considered the prevenient work of the Spirit in our lives shaping and crafting us as persons and as pastors well before we were given eyes to see or ears to hear what was going on in and around us. But the Spirit does not get to work with pure and pristine clay dug out of the back corner of Eden. The Spirit works with what Augustine calls our "second nature," since our first was overthrown in Adam. Waging war against the gracing Spirit has been the dictator of our second nature, the law of sin and death, whose policies and statutes attempt to circumscribe our every movement. This law acts like a hardening agent, making us less pliable to the deft touch of the Spirit. It manifests itself in our disordered desires, which habituate our wills to distorted ways of being, thinking, and acting that determine our seeing, speaking, and relating. And these we inevitably carry into our ministries— our calling has made us neither genius nor angel.

The human powers of misperception are truly remarkable, however. Not only do we overlook those Spirit-bestowed abilities or experiences given us for the sake of the community, we also see but do not see our habitual practices of vice or selfishness that threaten to hamper if not debilitate our ministry in the community. We see without seeing because our attempts at self-knowledge often resemble looking in those squares of silvery plastic passed off as mirrors in highway rest-stops. Warped and filmed they suggest and conceal more than they reflect and reveal. We return to our cars not only forgetting what we looked like but never really knowing in the first place. And so we stand in front of our traveling companion and ask, "Ok, so tell me, how do I look after sixteen hours in the car?"

The attentive mentor looks for patterns or habits that could hinder the mentee's ministry, that carry the potential for spiritual and personal exhaustion, moral and ministerial failure. This is much more difficult to observe than a sermon or lesson and requires much more trust, humility, and genuine openness from the mentor and the mentee. The mentor does not hold up a perfect mirror to the mentee, as if possessing near godlike powers of perception. Instead, he or she offers a sketch of the mentee, like that of a quick-eyed portrait artist, who in handing the sketch over asks if the lines look familiar. Are they recognizable? Does it seem accurate? Experience, maturity, and wisdom change the lines of our faces, so we sit for drawings again and again.

What we are describing is the ministry of discernment, which recognizes blind spots in someone else's perception of reality and in love helps to clarify that person's vision. This is the artistic labor not only of the mentor, but also of any pastor who desires to accompany people toward spiritual maturity, and it is one that the new pastor learns through the eyes of his or her mentor—graced eyes that lead blind men and women to see, forgiven debtors that forgive debtors, pastoring mentors who have been pastored mentees.

As mentors we are well aware that we received and continue to receive the call of God's Word in the midst of our own muddled stubbornness, and so we strut little pretense when sent to the aid of a brother or sister wandering in a dark wood. The apostle Paul contends for the title of Chief Sinner and decries his own enviable pedigree and laudable endurance record in order to boast in the unlimited patience and unmerited grace of Christ. He challenges the sin of his churches not from a posture of poised self-righteousness but from a posture of sustained forgiven-ness. Mentoring requires that we follow Paul's example here as well. It requires that the mentor's words be like the faithful friend's clean wounds, administered with the promise of sustained first-aid, rather than like the moralists and Pharisee's withering words, delivered in hasty disregard for the other's health.

Following Paul's example, Augustine often predicated the practice of love and the obligation to forgive on the recognition of our common sinfulness and need of grace. Preaching to catechumenates on the Lord's Prayer in Matthew, he implored them to recognize their common plight not only with fellow believers but with enemies as well:

> It is not the human nature in him that is at enmity, but his sin . . . He is as you are; you have a soul, and so has he; you have a body, and so has he. He is of the same substance as you are; you were made both out of the same earth, and quickened by the same Lord. Acknowledge in him then your brother . . . So let your prayer be against the malice of your enemy, that it may die, and he may live.[10]

Hopefully, the mentor and mentee do not consider each other "enemies," but they do regard the other as a fellow forgiven sinner. When confronting the mentee, the mentor speaks as a sinner, and when receiving hard counsel, the mentee hears as a sinner. It is on this basis that any two Christians meet each other.

Despite his awareness of the universal human condition in sin, and particularly his own disposition toward it, Augustine did not retreat to the unloving passivity of self-deprecating tolerance or "unconditional regard." He was far too aware of the noxious consequences of his own sin-bent ways to coddle or ignore them in others. In a letter to a Roman magistrate, Marcellinus, eager to excuse the violence of a murderous mob, Augustine contended that out of love "it is a Christian's duty to consult men's welfare rather than their wishes . . . their advantage and not their pleasure." Our debt and duty of love does not allow us to leave the other person stumbling toward the cliff edge. Augustine names this necessary but difficult task "benevolent severity" or "severe benevolence," literally, good-willed gravity or austerity. In Proverbs 15:31 this is the "life-giving rebuke" that leads to a seat among the wise. To refrain from speaking this word is not love, but a treacherous disregard that confirms the other in their error. Amidst the mentor's many roles this is one. "Salt may sting a wound, but it keeps it from gangrene," explains a rather salty priest in Georges Bernanos's *Diary of a Country Priest.*[11]

Kenneth Pohly describes this experience of grace and judgment in his text on pastoral supervision:

> It is in these terms [grace and judgment] that we experience pastoral supervision. We come under judgment every time we bring a piece of our life experience to another person or group for reflection. To share the events of brokenness, division, hostility, failure, doubt, and indecision which mark our ministry—or even those moments of joy and success to be celebrated—is to lay ourselves open to the criticism of our colleagues as well as God. None of us enjoys having our col-leagues evaluate a sermon we have preached, a situation we have bungled, or communication that has broken down. That can be frightening, anxiety-producing, intimidating; it is certainly an invitation to judgment. It can also be challenging, restorative, exhilarating. It becomes this when grace is experienced as well as judgment.[12]

SPECIFIC AREAS FOR SHARED EXPLORATION

Many of the areas of our lives that require examination are less the result of easily identifiable sins or vices than they are the result of the sin-shaded confluence of personality, gender, familial relations, education, formative experiences, practiced habits, and learned patterns of defense and affirmation. Together these shape who we are. The following series of items highlights the fact that mentoring cannot be done abstractly or impersonally. Generic mentoring and generic churches are both illusions that very quickly break up against the reality of other persons. We cannot worship in a trans-historical church, which bypasses the localized churches we serve. There are only persons created in God's image, and each one of them carry a story and history as complex, intimate, and diverse as our own. The same is true for every person we pass on the street or who sits in the pew or calls us in order to seek counsel for a strained marriage or complain about our management of the toddler's room. Karl Barth considered pastoral ministry, including pastoral mentoring, to be irreducibly bound up with the "concrete participation of the one in the particular past, present, and future of the other, in his particular burdens and afflictions, but above all in his particular promise and hope in the singularity of his existence as created and sustained by God."[13] The particular. The singular. The concrete. This is where God operates and where we have been called.

The following list of items is not intended to serve as an emotional checklist for personal inventory, but rather to stand as signposts to fields open for shared exploration. The more we understand about our motivations, our reactions, and our expectations in ministry, the less likely we will end up imposing our wishes on and meeting our needs through others, and the more likely we will be able to meet their needs by walking with them in the Spirit, praying with them, leading them toward spiritual maturity and acts of service.

Work

Different people have different capacities and energy levels for work. Some of us tend toward passivity and find little meaning in our work, and some of us tend toward compulsive workaholism and try to find meaning through the quantity of our labors. We need to consider what kind of pastoral work we find meaningful and whether we need to alter our perception. Do you trust that the church or ministry will endure without your presence, or do you work as though it depends upon your Herculean efforts? We will naturally have strengths and weaknesses in particular kinds of work. Some of us are more naturally suited to motivating and training people, some to dealing with abstraction and ideas, some to organizing and planning events or ministry teams, some to counseling or teaching. We need to learn to recognize the kinds of work that excite and enliven us, and those that drain and tire us, and also know when to seek the necessary assistance.

Authority

Responding to authority is a delicate matter for many. There are two kinds of authority: one is political or positional authority determined by office or status; the other is natural or epistemic authority determined by knowledge and experience. It is important to recognize how we respond to each. Do you sufficiently respect positional authority, or quickly dismiss it? Do you predicate your ministry upon the esteem of natural authorities? We tend to imitate those we esteem, and in our ministries we can find ourselves performing acts and choosing words that we hope will please or impress someone who is an authority for us. On the other hand, as this text argues, we should indeed learn from and model ourselves after wise authority figures and learn from wisdom born of experience. This question is also relevant for how we respond to church tradition and structure, which we may either prematurely reject as stifling routinization or uncritically submit to as the final word. How can we strike a balance between independent thought and due respect for authority? How do we take care that we do not abuse the authority and power with which we have been entrusted?

Initiating

This relates to our ability to solve problems and exercise leadership without the express direction of an authority figure, be it a professor, mentor, or pastor. This is a matter of coming to understand how much support and structure we need to work well. Do you need a comprehensive structure, or do you need general parameters only? Likewise, some people need more room for creativity and novelty than others, who may become anxious about too little guidance. Some might initiate relationships without difficulty, but find it exceedingly difficult to initiate organization and implementation.

Gender

How does our gender relate to our ministry? How do you relate to persons of the same sex or of the opposite sex? Do you have preconceived roles that you project onto them? Do you allow them to be different than other men or women you have known? What bearing does the fact that you are a woman or a man have upon your pastoral ministry? How does your gender affect your perceptions of God, the church, or your own identity as a person and pastor? Do you seek the affirmation of either men or women in particular? Do you struggle with lust? How might you maintain integrity with persons of the opposite sex? Are there specific policies in place in the church that are designed to assist pastors and parishioners to maintain integrity in this area? Is there a procedure in place for handling cases of indiscretion or accusations of abuse?

Sexual immorality among pastors is not as foreign as we might like to think. Countless families, churches, and ministries have been devastated by the failure of pastors, both men and women, in this area. Rarely the result of a predatory personality, sexual immorality is usually the fruition of small moments of indiscretion and indulgence. Ministry can often be a lonely and alienating vocation, which may lead us to seek out inappropriate but emotionally satisfying relationships with particular persons. Likewise, because pastors often meet people at intimate and vulnerable moments in their lives, they must be especially careful not to abuse their role and violate the integrity of their calling but to direct those persons to the only one who can truly satisfy them, the God who loves them and desires the best for them. Furthermore, because church staff members often work very closely, at times in contexts of significant pressure or joy, bonds of friendship and affection will naturally grow. Each person, however, should be careful to hedge these healthy and necessary bonds so that they do not become a controlling vice.

These issues touch the core of who we are and will be more significant for some than for others. Though the specific policies that will enable one pastor to maintain integrity in this area may be different from those needed by another, no one should delude himself or herself into thinking he or she will not be susceptible to failure in this area, given the right combination of circumstances in one's personal and church life. Gender and *eros* are powerful parts of who we are as persons, and therefore exceptionally prone to sin's distortion and society's corruption. In this area both mentor and mentee should seek frank and forthright honesty.[14]

Time and Discipline

The shape of time is one of the most important disciplines for a pastor to develop. Many are so inundated with tasks and demands they have no time for the central pastoral tasks—prayer, study, preaching, and people. And so we learn to live with the perpetual flutter of a thousand butterflies in our chest and fail to learn the wisdom of sabbath-keeping. The sabbath was given to teach Israel that God, rather than their busy labors, sustained them. In *The Contemplative Pastor,* Eugene Peterson quotes Hilary of Tours, who diagnosed pastoral busyness as "*religiosa sollicitudo pro Deo,* a blasphemous anxiety to do God's work for him." Peterson goes on to comment that we are often busy as pastors because we are vain and want to appear important, or because we are lazy and let others commandeer our schedules, or because we don't believe that the lion's share of the work is the Lord's.[15] However, the health and sanity of the mentee's future pastoral ministry depends on forming patterns of work, rest, play, and prayer while the mold is still soft. Ambrose of Milan, the learned bishop who baptized Augustine, clarifies this point for us in his book *Duties of the Clergy*: "Am I to suppose that he is fit to give me advice who never takes it for himself, or am I to believe that he has time to give to me when he has none for himself? . . . How is there room for [giving] counsel here where there is none for quiet?"[16] Helping the mentee carve out a shape in time is a great gift that the mentor can give to the mentee, to his or her family, and to his or her future place of ministry.

Listening

Listening has to do with how well we are able to hear other opinions rather than our own. How well are you able to focus your eyes, ears, and mind on others? Do you give others space to articulate their thoughts and feelings, or do you fill up the space with your own nervous verbiage? Have you already made a decision before you hear from anyone else? Do you expect the Spirit to speak through other people?

Equipping

Are you able to equip others for ministry and release them to do the work without stepping in to correct or micromanage their efforts—even if you could have done it better? Do you affirm other people and encourage them in their ministries or does your tunnel-vision inhibit you from seeing what others are doing? Can you work with a group or do you need to work alone? Can you find joy and delight in others' ministry and the ways the Spirit is actively in-forming them?

Conflict and Criticism

How do you respond when others dislike and criticize your decisions or disagree with you about a point of theology or ministry? Can you reflect upon your personal involvement in a particular issue and discern when you are zealous for the subject matter and when you are zealous about not losing an argument? What is the relative importance of the issue? How do you love someone who has criticized or hurt you? Conversely, how do you communicate criticism to others?

Stress and Anxiety

People certainly deal with stress and anxiety in various ways, many of which could adversely affect our families, friendships, or ministries. We become impatient, dismissive, and insensitive, or pessimistic and easily distracted, or domineering and legalistic, sloppy, resistant to necessary change, indecisive and despondent, or obsessive. If we know what induces our anxiety, we can more accurately take measures to avoid it. Knowing how we respond to it, we can implore the aid of others to help us diminish its potentially harmful effects and help us avoid seeking solace from inappropriate sources.

Risk

This relates to our willingness to attempt something when the outcome is uncertain or unknown. Such attempts always involve a certain amount of vulnerability that we may or may not be willing to accept. Our self-esteem can be so closely bound up with our success and failure that we can become calculating about the tasks we accept or attempt and studiously avoid what might be difficult. On the other hand we may risk all sorts of unplanned and undisciplined ventures that falter due to our lack of intentionality. Do you attempt only those things at which you know you will succeed? Are you crushed when you feel something has failed? Do you crave challenge or shun it?

Affirmation

Do you need individual affirmation? How intensely do you require success and the acclamation of others to affirm your self-worth? Are you able to affirm others, even at your own expense? Are you able to maturely receive praise or compliments without denying them or lobbying for them? Do you practice self-deprecation in the presence of others to induce their affirmation? Are you able to affirm and encourage others?

Response to Failure

A sense of failure and profound inadequacy is unavoidable in ministry. We are not allowed the certainty of success that a geometric proof or computer program allows. We are about the business of being with peculiar people and helping them learn to pray and worship and live. But we can fail in a number of ways and for a number of reasons. How do you respond? Do you set yourself up for failure from doubt about the efficacy of your genuine effort? Do you attempt too much and so cannot help but fail? Do you learn from failure or become embarrassed? Do you locate the source of failure outside of yourself or do you locate it solely within yourself? It is important for mentors to share their own experiences of failure with their mentees and to help them find legitimate perspective so that they can bring their failures to the cross.

Personal Relations

How do you usually relate to other people? Are you competitive, aggressive, selectively sociable, empathetic, dependent, effusive, shy, restrained, distrustful, frank? How do you communicate with others? Some people communicate indirectly, suggesting rather than telling, and usually expect others to communicate with them in like kind. Others are more direct and forthright communicators who may overstate their case, but usually expect others to address them in the same way. Persuasion and argument come easier to some, evocation and imaging come easier to others.

Integrity

Are you faithful in the small and the large things? Do you disregard bothersome details when they seem to impede more important work? Do you return phone calls and show up on time for meetings? Do you sufficiently respect other people's time to prepare for meetings, including meetings with the mentor?

Decision Making

Are you able to make decisions, or do you rely on other people so you can avoid responsibility or the possibility of failure? Do you make decisions quickly and impulsively, or do you need significant time to contemplate beforehand? How do you respond if you are forced to make a decision quickly, or if others disagree?

Care for the Weak

How do you respond to people who are children, elderly, sick, dying, homeless, addicted, or uneducated? Do you expect to learn from them? Do you anticipate hearing the voice of the Spirit in them? Is it hard to reach out to them and care for them? Conversely, do you only seek out weaker persons to minister to because you feel less threatened by them or because they affirm your sense of usefulness and importance?

Cultural Sensitivity

Are you aware of and comfortable with people from other cultures? Do you take into account their needs and ways of doing ministry? How does culture shape how others hear the gospel? How might ministry in a North American culture differ from ministry in an Asian, African, or South American culture? Do you have some form of prejudice against certain persons or groups of persons that might hinder your sharing of the gospel? Might you need to take a noontime nap on the roof and pray for visions of unsavory farm animals flying down in great white sheets?

This list, while far from comprehensive, is intended to alert both mentor and mentee to potentially fruitful areas for reflection and discussion.

MENTOR OFFERS EYES TO TRAIN MENTEE'S EYES

Mentees ask mentors to lend their vision for a time in order to help mentees hone their ministry skills, detect and affirm their strengths and passions as gifts of God, and be alert to their patterns of weakness and assist them toward responsible decisions. Finally, mentees ask mentors to look with them for the work of the Holy Spirit in the lives of individuals and the church. The Holy Spirit's work can be missed if we do not attentively listen and watch, or if we know not what to look for. The emergence of small buds that mature into ripe Holy Spirit fruit go easily undetected if we do not give our eyes time to focus or if we are too quickly distracted by squawking birds or worm-eaten leaves. Demands and crises distract us from the slow spiritual formation of persons. They distract us from seeing and attending to people spiritually and theologically. People themselves are often unaware the Spirit is busy pruning, grafting, and fertilizing their hearts and minds. But pastors anticipate it and hopefully become adept at detecting the subtle clipping and nurturing that takes place. The experienced, practiced eyes of others can be a great aid in this. The mentee might ask, "Do you see what I see?" or "Have I missed something?" or "How would you see this?" We need help to see the Spirit's dancing flame upon the brow of unlikely pentecostals.

When mentees follow mentors' eyes, they might not see hills full of angels, horses, and chariots of fire like Elisha's nearsighted, phenomenally minded servant saw in 2 Kings 6, but they might see the no less dramatic and equally real presence of the Spirit breaking, blowing, and beckoning within the church. Like that holy army, the imminence of the Spirit and the reality of our situation are hidden by a thin scrim, behind which the tutoring spirit of our age implores us not to look. We are expected to remain attentive to that which is most readily apparent—economics, power, pleasure, status, career, wars and rumors of war. But the one who gives sight to the blind invites us to look up and see what else is there—to see fields ripe for harvest, to see the earth as creation, to see God in Christ, to see the church as Bride and Body, and kingdoms displaced by the Kingdom.

Some of our most helpful guides in the practice of seeing are novelists, poets, architects, and artists who, along with pastors, are called to see into and through the mundane, called to help us see and touch embodied grace and Word. As pastors we do not learn like a painter to look for the lines, contours, textures, and colors that form people and objects, but we do look for Christological, ecclesiological, and eschatological shapes and hues. Together with others, we learn how to practice this sort of theological double-vision, seeing the reality of our church and this or that person inlaid in the world of Scripture and theology. [17]

The writer Flannery O'Connor is among our most helpful guides when it comes to seeing people, for she rattles any attempt to allow our eyes to lull into singular vision. Her stories are inhabited by scores of unlikely pentecostals, ever disturbed and startled by the Spirit. One writer said that reading O'Connor is like being "concussed by grace"—struck with a gracious blow that shocks the reader into lucidity. A devout Roman Catholic, her prescient description of the writer's vocation and vision comports remarkably well with the practice of pastoral seeing. With only a little shift we can transfer her observations about budding authors to emerging pastors:

> Very few people who are supposedly interested in writing are interested in writing well . . . They are interested in being a writer, not in writing . . . It is a good deal easier for most people to state an abstract idea than to describe and thus re-create some object that they actually see. But the world of the fiction writer is full of matter, and this is what the beginning fiction writers are very loath to create. They are concerned primarily with unfleshed ideas and emotions. They are apt to be reformers because they are possessed not by a story but by the bare bones of some abstract notion. They are conscious of problems, not of people, of questions and issues, not of the texture of existence, of case histories and of everything that has a sociological smack, instead of with all those concrete details of life that make actual the mystery of our position on earth. [This Manichean spirit] is also pretty much the modern spirit, and for the sensibility infected with it, fiction is hard to write

because fiction is so much an incarnational art . . . Fiction is about everything human, and we are made of dust, and if you scorn getting yourself dusty, then you shouldn't try to write fiction. It's not a grand enough job for you . . . I'm always highly irritated by people who imply that writing fiction is an escape from reality. It is a plunge into reality and it's very shocking to the system.[18]

Paul, too, encourages discontentment with singular vision, seeing either only Scripture or only the immediacy of circumstance. In Ephesians, for instance, he tutors us to see the Christological and ecclesiological shape of reality. He teaches Ephesian Christians and generations of pastors how to see theologically very real people— walking, talking, smoking, working—and the real church— praying, arguing, worshipping, playing. When John Calvin referred to Scripture as divine spectacles that grant clear vision to dim eyes, this is what he had in mind.

First, Paul beckons the Ephesian church and us (1:15–2:10) to see Jesus the Nazarene through the lens of Psalm 8, and to see him as the second Adam under whose feet everything has again been placed, who stands in place of every first Adam. Paul helps us to see that this second Adam became the perfect covenant partner that neither the first Adam, nor Israel, nor the church could ever be, the one who faithfully took up our alienated and suffering humanity, in all its unnatural isolation from God, and offered it back to God in his life, death and resurrection. At the same time, he offers us the lens of Psalm 110, an enthronement psalm of King David, through which we see Christ as the ascended King sitting at the Father's right hand, reigning over church and cosmos. Secondly, Paul enables us to see the church as the community caught up with Christ in these two movements—that of the New Adam returning to the Father and that of the Eternal King reigning with the Father. Through the indwelling of the Holy Spirit, Paul wants us to see that the church participates now in this new creation and in this powerful kingdom. None of this was readily apparent

115

to those who merely observed the itinerant carpenter's son or the motley church, but Paul coaches believers to look at the crucified Nazarene and see the ascended Lord, at cantankerous Mrs. Smith in the second row and see a new creature, and at our grade eight Sunday School class and see the eschatological church. To the Corinthian church Paul testified, "From now on, therefore, we regard no one according to the flesh."[19]

It is a unique community that lives between the times— between the ascension and the second coming—living in the "meanwhile," straddling both this age and the age to come. As Charles Williams so memorably described it, the beginning of the church is found in a "metaphysical trigonometry . . . at the meeting of two heavenward lines, one drawn from Bethany along the Ascent of Messias, the other from Jerusalem against the Descent of the Paraclete." The subsequent history of the church, according to Williams, is therefore the history of the "operation of the Holy Ghost towards Christ, under the conditions of our humanity."[20] According to Paul, we should regard it in no other way.

Church is the *event*, if you will, where authentic humanity is already emerging as the Spirit moves to reorder disordered lives in the image and likeness of the new Adam. Paul describes the church, every church—your church, even—as the "fullness of Christ," the exact phrase he uses in Colossians to describe the fullness of the Father which dwelt in Christ. So Paul says, "Now, this is who you are; this is who gathers with you to worship; practice looking and living from this vision." Thus the incarnation is the hermeneutical horizon from which we take our bearings for authentic personal and ecclesial identity, while the church is the prophetic sign and parable to the world that God has organized all things around the incarnate and ascended one.[21] Unless we learn to look from Christ to other people and from other people to Christ, our vision will be unduly distorted.

Do we as yet perceive the full reality of creation's restoration? No, obviously not, but Paul's ultimate point in these verses is to open his readers' eyes to see that the very same power which was at work in Christ's resurrection and ascension is at work "in us who believe." Unless we practice seeing the temporal with Paul's eschatological eyes, like Elisha's servant we see only the strong forces of the Arameans battering at the door, or like the Ephesians, the mob of idolatrous silversmiths rousing culture against us, or with a bevy of disillusioned pastors, we become discouraged with our cretin churches, lower our eyes, and forsake our calling. George Herbert counseled himself in *The Country Parson* not to be distracted by appearances and so, in his case, disdain to enter a less than lovely dwelling place, "though he even have to creep into it, and though it smell never so loathsomely . . . God is there also, and those for whom God died."[22] Together mentor and mentee practice this theological double-vision—seeing what is in front of us, seeing who is in front of us, and seeing them both in all their particular physical and spiritual dustiness and their eschatological, pneumatological promise.

The Offer of Ears

Listening is at the heart of mentoring for pastoral formation. Sitting, waiting, ear cocked to hear, ready to receive the stories, thoughts, questions, and confessions that come to us. Of all the virtues and practices we cultivate, this is the primary act of love that precedes and permeates everything else that happens. Why? Because it is only through the disciplined habit of listening that we begin to know another person—and knowing and being known is requisite for any formative friendship. Speech and words are called to perform many acts. They name ships and babies. They make husbands and wives out of people who moments before were not. They provoke passions, reveal truth, and create beauty. They worship and witness, tear down and build up. They shape the way we think, and they carry the thoughts of our hearts and minds to other people. Friendship between companions, lovers, colleagues, or spouses begins with listening and falters when listening ceases. Our speech is who we are in verbal form, and when our speech is dismissed or disdained, then who we are is silenced.

That we can never fully know someone else or enter into his or her internal world is no impediment to our obligation to listen, for neither can we fully know ourselves. And so we should just as soon stop thinking as desist listening. Even being in Christ through the Holy Spirit we remain mysteries to ourselves, Judases to our best intentions. Yet in helping someone else understand who we are, or who we perceive ourselves to be, by carrying our thoughts to them, our own self-understanding inevitably deepens. On the other hand, when we offer to listen to someone else, we create for him or her the same possibility of greater self-knowledge. Therefore, we suggest that the mentor loves and serves the mentee by offering, along with eyes, his or her ears to listen.

The Extended Conversation

Apart from the other person's self-revelation our knowledge of the other is tentative, indeed, as it is grounded on observation and generalized assumptions that are abstracted from previous experiences. We can assume only a few things before we begin to listen. As mentors, we may assume that grace wrangles with sin in the intern, but we do not yet know how this person has been wrenched by sin or how his or her soul has been graced by Christ. We may assume that the mentee is marked by family and culture, bearing inherited and imposed images, but we do not know how she has borne them or rejected them, and at what cost. We may assume a little about her education, but we do not yet know what unique passions or questions animate her thinking. And what can we assume of the mentee's spiritual formation, faith journey, or theological maturity? The many-splendored way the Spirit will speak through them to open our eyes, shore up our hearts, enliven our minds, and enrich our community is entirely beyond our assumptions and expectations, as well.

The incarnation offers a possible parallel. The enfleshed Word is the faithful revelation of God. Christ is both speech and act of God, and in everything he said or did, he was the fullest revelation of the person of the Father. To know God, we first turn not to our speculative assumptions or to common speech about "god," but we turn to Christ, his Word incarnate. "Teaching about Christ begins in silence," waiting for a Word.[23] God says, I am known here in this person, and to see him is to see me, to know him is to know me. Analogously, human speech is ordained to faithfully represent our thoughts and emotions. Our words should seek the kind of fidelity that mark the incarnate Word's faithful revelation of the Father—even though Son and Father enjoy a unity of being far beyond what we share with our own words. Words that manipulate, oppress, deceive, or diminish are untrue and unfaithful words. Likewise, however, rejection or acceptance of the Word means rejection or acceptance of the one who spoke that Word. Analogously, we love people well when we stop our own voice long enough to listen to others and accept their words, even if we disagree or question the content of their words.

Slowly and deliberately, therefore, the mentor listens to the mentee in one extended conversation that continues from week to week. During those weeks mentor and mentee each attempt to speak ordering words of grace into disordered lives, leads fellow-sinners into holy worship and to live as faithful ambassadors of the inbreaking Kingdom—not always an easy task, and one that exposes the paucity of our habitual self-reliance and confirms our need for a listening ear. Most of us will have but a few people over the course of our lives truly listen to us in any kind of sustained manner—maybe a spouse, maybe a friend or two—and even fewer to whom we can unburden the weights of vocational ministry. People are usually less liberal with their ears than with their money—it can be much more costly. The culture in which we live and minister is not conducive to intimate, personal communion. Who has time for it? Who has energy for it?

If the classical tradition of pastoral ministry is to be believed, it is the pastor who must stake out time for listening and, in particular, listening to other believers and pastors. Bonhoeffer, our faithful mentor in many of these matters, insists,

> the first service one owes to others in the community involves listening to them. Just as our love for God begins with listening to God's Word, the beginning of love for other Christians is learning to listen to them. We do God's work for our brothers and sisters when we learn to listen to them. So often Christians, especially preachers, think that their only service is always to have to "offer" something . . . They forget that listening can be a greater service than speaking . . . But Christians who can no longer listen to one another will soon no longer be listening to God either; they will always be prattling even in the presence of God.[24]

Thus pastoral mentors create space to listen to new pastors, both informally and formally. *Informally*, they listen during those casual encounters and conversations when the mentor and mentee pray together, tape up leaky water heaters, plan worship retreats, gulp down cheap church coffee (is there any other?), visit a hospitalized parishioner, and engage in the kind of casual and prayerful conversations about life that fill up a large part of what we do as pastors. These natural and spontaneous moments often catch our verbal sentries off guard. Words flow more freely when our mental editors are not so busy correcting and excising phrases before our mouths publish them. The interning pastor may feel freer in these moments to broach questions considered too homely for the "formal" weekly meetings. However homely they appear, these diminutive questions are often more enduringly needlesome than we expect. Likewise, an offhand comment may reveal far more about the state of our heart or mind than our more deliberately constructed statements will. Unguarded, the heart speaks character-revealing words: sometimes the "old man" speaks, alarming us, and sometimes, the "new man" speaks, alerting us to the work of the Spirit.

Formally, mentor and mentee agree to meet regularly, usually once a week, for slow rumination upon some piece of ministry or question of formation brought to the table by the mentee. It should be noted that only the schedule for the meeting is formalized—the actual conversation is not, but neither is it haphazard. The impetus for determining the focus of these conversations lies largely, though not exclusively, with the mentee. One week she may need to process a significant conversation or ministry event that either failed or succeeded. Another week a sticky pastoral or theological question may demand attention. Occasionally, the conversation may be dignified by the confession of a troubled spirit grappling with temptation, sin, and grace. At other times, both mentor and mentee may be so emotionally and spiritually exhausted that they surrender their time to prayer, speaking and listening to God instead of each other. Though only a general guide, Gregory of Nazianzus's four areas of consideration seem to offer inexhaustible possibilities for these formative conversations if we but bear them in mind: a) personal, moral, spiritual formation; b) pastoral identity and calling; c) theological reflection and deliberation; d) practical skills of pastoral ministry.

The learning of the mentee must ultimately be self-directed, or at least self-motivated. For the most part, mentees must begin to discern their needs and how to meet them. Excessive dependence on the direction of others can result in an inner laxity inimical to pastoral formation and ministry. Diligent attendance to the apprehensive questions that arise from one's own soul is imperative, as is a determined intention to bring those questions and problems in transparent openness, risking being known for the sake of maturity. While not activistic, nothing could be less passive than the mentoring friendship. Pastoral formation does not happen simply because mentor and mentee sit in an office together for an hour once a week shooting words into the breeze. Perfunctory mentoring friendships are pretend relationships, and the business at hand—the formation of a person as a pastor—is too important for such make-believe. This is one reason that the impetus for the weekly meetings remains with the mentee, for then the friendship has a better chance of stalling the advance of the insidious spirit of functionalism, which might tempt the mentor pastor to treat the time together as the imposition of a remote academic institution or ordination committee that ultimately distracts from the immediate demands of ministry and accomplishes little of any substance in itself.

Otium Sanctum

Listening does require self-discipline, for unlike God the Father, who always takes the initiative in speaking, and whose Word carries absolute authority, our own halting attempts to find words that translate our internal conversation into external speech require time, patience, and hope on the part of both speaker and hearer. We require a certain respect and reverence from the other. The appropriate posture for this expectant pastoral listening requires what the Latin fathers referred to as *otium sanctum*, "holy leisure," a quality of spirit traditionally characterized by Mary's receptive posture at the feet of Jesus. It balanced the *onus amoris*, the active "works of love," to which we are also called, traditionally characterized by Martha's service. "Holy leisure" described the soul's contemplative posture in the company of God—precisely what is required when mentor and mentee meet. Together we sit, talk, pray, and listen in the company of God, who also listens and speaks. Augustine and St. Benedict refer to this qualification of spirit as the *vacare Deo*, the vacating or emptying of our spirits before God of the usual clamor and fragmented "prattle" that distract us from listening. When we steady our twitching inclination to do something in the conversation—to speak, to interject, to fix, or to teach—then we are ready to listen and receive the other person.

Otium sanctum, therefore, requires preparation by both persons before they meet. Settling their spirits and tabling the demands of the moment, they think and pray toward their time together out of respect for the other person and the Spirit whom they invite to their conversation. Thus the "holy leisure" of one's spirit does not balance works of love, but it becomes a work of love—and not an easy one—that far outweighs many more obvious acts of service. Paul enjoined the Ephesian Christians to speak only words conducive to the constructive upbuilding of others "according to their needs"; the corollary injunction is that we withhold our words as the other has need.[25] The mentee in particular has need of a listening ear or two. He or she requires that aural space the mentor creates when practicing an *askesis* of speech, a disciplined self-control that invites the mentee to pour into that space his or her story of faith and experiences in ministry. The first *ascetics* were not emaciated desert-dwellers donning passion-punishing hair shirts. They were disciplined Greek athletes training to avoid the physical flabbiness of self-indulgence. An *askesis* of self and speech in conversation desires a similar vigor of spirit that studiously avoids flabby, loquacious self-indulgence.

St. Benedict intentionally began his rule for monastic life with "Listen . . . ," beckoning the monk to "incline the ear of your heart." Attentive listening has always been at the heart of the monastic and the pastoral calling. In *The Way of Spiritual Direction*, a recent but near-classic text, Francis Kelly Nemeck and Marie Theresa Coombs describe listening as "the attentiveness of our being to another's becoming in all of his or her beauty and sinfulness, struggle and mystery."[26] When we listen to others, we honor and dignify their self-revealing, reality-naming words. Thoughts, emotions, vision, anger, hope, and despair usher forth in rough draft, open to eventual revision and clarification.

LISTENING TO THE STORY

Confessing Our Personal Story

When mentors listen to mentees they offer them the rare opportunity to discover the Spirit-authored narrative coherence of their personal stories. Mentors can literally listen their mentees' stories into existence by creating space for them to pull together disparate and inchoate memories, images, and experiences into previously unseen organization. As Kenneth Pohly describes, mentors can be like theological and spiritual autobiographers when they help mentees to "become autobiographical once again about their lived experience." Together, the mentor and mentee look theologically at the mentee's emerging story in order to discern dominant images and expectations that give shape to and find expression in the mentee's life and ministry. By drawing out these dominant images and experiences the mentee can discover the Spirit's long work of directing him or her to faith and vocation, as well as the long work of the Spirit that still needs to be done. Often the mentee's calling is clarified, or at least made less muddy, through this process of "writing" his or her story verbally and tracing out the various plots and significant characters that have brought him or her to this place in the life of faith. Though this story is "written" over the course of the mentor's and mentee's time together, it may be important for the mentee to start "writing" this verbal theological autobiography in the first or second conversation.

There is an amusing cartoon that depicts Augustine stepping out of a confessional booth when the priest, who has just heard him, leans out and says, "Hey Augustine, that was a great confession today! You should write that down." A most patient confessor indeed! His *Confessions*, written in 397–8, shortly after his ordination to the priesthood, represent his deliberate attempt to record in words the Spirit-led trajectory of his life. He recalls and reflects theologically upon those crucial episodes and events in which he could see and celebrate the mysterious actions of God's prevenient and provident grace. It was a record of his journey toward true knowledge of self and true knowledge of God.

The "truth" which Augustine sought to articulate was the very truth of his person. He sought in words to faithfully represent who he was in light of the incarnation of Christ and the gradual work of being recreated in Christ's image. This is what we attempt whenever we "confess" our personhood to someone else—to become truthful by seeking the truth of who we are *coram Deo*, in the presence of God.

"Confession," for Augustine, has a double meaning. On the one hand, it refers to the free acknowledgment, before God, of the truth one knows about oneself—and this obviously meant, for Augustine, the confession of sins. But, at the same time, and more importantly, *confiteri* means to acknowledge to God the truth one knows about God. To confess is to praise and glorify God; it is an exercise in self-knowledge and true humility in the atmosphere of grace and reconciliation. Augustine explains, in a letter of 429, that his *Confessions* are to excite his readers' mind and affections toward God, that they might "praise the righteous and good God as they speak either of my evil or good." Referring to Psalm 100, verse 3, he writes to his young correspondent, "'For he hath made us, and not we ourselves;' indeed, we had destroyed ourselves, but he who made us has made us anew. When, however, you find me in these books, pray for me that I may not fail, but be perfected. Pray, my son; pray."[27]

We learn another lesson from Augustine's example, a lesson readily apparent but easily overlooked. Augustine acknowledges that human beings are opaque to themselves no less than to others. We are not who we think we are. One of the things Augustine had to confess was that he was and had been sharply different from the person he thought he was. Not only was this true of his errant youth, but it remained true even at the time of writing—he hardly knew to what temptation or self-deception he might next succumb. He admits repeatedly that his version of his own past had to be validated and verified by God. "To hear you speaking about oneself is to know oneself."[28] He could only know himself, or anyone else, through knowing God. This is the *duplex cognitio*, the double knowledge, of which so many pastors and theologians speak. Knowing God is bound up with knowing self, and knowing self is impossible apart from knowing God and the work of God in one's life.

Narrative theology, narratival identity, and the importance of "story" are common themes these days inside and outside of the academy. Many of these developments have made a significant contribution to our understanding of God's revelation and the Hebrew, if not simply human, way of communicating. They remind us that we are storied beings caught up in the larger story of God's economy, his interaction with the world as Creator and Redeemer. Stories do shape our lives and the ways we think, in much the same way they shaped Israel's identity. The stories of Abraham, Isaac, and Jacob determined Israel's identity as God's chosen people. When an Israelite child asked who she was or who they were as a people, or why things were as they were, they received a storied answer—a storied answer of covenants and promises, an elderly first-time mother, a nearly-sacrificed son, deceptive and impulsive twin brothers, a multi-colored coat, slavery, frogs, exodus, pillars of cloud and fire, golden calves, manna, walled cities, stone tablets, and on and on the story went.[29] These symbols and stories, along with the Law given in the midst of the story, served to mediate the personal identity of the Israelite people.

Recognizing Our Communal Story

This kind of communal mediation of personal identity is manifest in every people or country that celebrates holidays, commemorates events, or erects statues and sings songs in order to reinforce nationally esteemed values considered worthy of emulation. For better or worse, these stories become woven into our stories and our personal consciousness. They mediate to us who we are expected to be as citizens or members of this body of people. We become the people we are as our identities are shaped through these patterns of communication and response. These people and events become the "common objects of love," which Augustine suggests determine the character and quality of a people. Because love is a moral orientation, what is loved collectively, whether just and righteous or idolatrous and vicious, determines how we think and act. Our own age of mass media and technology holds up the lifestyles of pop culture heroes and stock market giants as the defining canons of full corporate engagement. We are immersed in these communities and can hardly avoid their influence—as the root of this word makes clear, they literally "flow" into us, flooding our self-understanding. The same is true for our traditions. When we identify ourselves as Anglican, Roman Catholic, Anabaptist, or Pentecostal, we take on the stories bound up with those traditions and adopt their distinctive ethos. The church has consciously responded to this truth by venerating certain believers as official "saints," whose piety and devotion are worthy of common estimation and imitation.

Our struggle is to learn how to proceed once our primary community and primary identity-conferring narrative has been shifted from the secular nation and culture to the eschatological community founded on Christ and the apostles, identifiable by the presence of the Spirit. In Philippians 3 Paul exhorted the church at Philippi to live as advance outposts and ambassadors of this eschatological kingdom to which their citizenship had already been transferred. Former allegiances and obligations had been broken. They were now to have the mind of Christ, to imitate Paul, and to keep their eyes on others who walked according to his example. Thus the persons and emblems commonly loved by this new community were to determine thoughts and action. In this way, stories of patriarchs, exodus and covenant, and stable, cross, and celestial city become our own. Likewise, we inherit new common symbols and practices—such as baptism, Eucharist, preaching, prayer, community—as identifying communal markers and signs. These, however, carry with them the authority of the Creator, not simply the commendation of a particular human collective at a given time.

If it is the case that our personal identities are molded through relationships and images, then there must be some connection between the truth and quality of those relationships and images and our personhood. Part of the theological retelling of our stories includes this renunciation of one set of common objects of love and the acceptance of another, and the overlapping tension between them.

Each person's theological narrative is unique. Though we all become citizens of this new kingdom through Christ and the Spirit, we are led along paths utterly our own. Some take in church and sacrament with the bottle, drawn up under the faithful eyes of parents who apprentice them in the faith. With Timothy, John Chrysostom, Augustine, Basil of Caesarea, Gregory of Nyssa, Charles Wesley, and others, they honor their parents—or, as in each of these cases, their mothers, who nurtured seeds of faith within them. Others are "surprised" into faith and calling like C. S. Lewis, burned into faith like Pascal during his "night of fire," or broken into faith like Dostoevsky, who declared, "It was not as a child that I learned to believe in Christ and confess his faith. My hosanna has burst forth from a huge furnace of doubt."[30] We each carry our own stories with us as we journey, though some stories may have been more adventurous or disastrous or pain-filled than ours.

Listening to the New Pastor

The theological autobiography of the mentee, however, does not obviously cease upon entering the internship. Usually the drama quickens and the tension heightens. Because ministry takes place in the warp and woof of people's daily lives, it shares life's characteristic high points and low points. Laughter is followed by sorrow and disappointment, frustration by joy, elation by weariness, failure by growth, birth by death, wedding by divorce, and cursing by worship—and any of these may come at any time and all may come at once. In *Spiritual Care,* a book about pastoral ministry, Bonhoeffer responds to this reality, insisting that the ministry of every church should include the provision of pastoral care for pastors. In the impassioned chapter, "Spiritual Care for Pastors," he writes:

> Everyone who cares for the soul needs a person who will care for his or her soul. Only one who has been under spiritual care is able to exercise spiritual care. Those who renounce that law will have to face the consequences in their work . . . Whoever takes the office seriously must cry out under the burden . . . Where can a pastor find rest and recollection for their work? We have to recognize that there are mortal dangers for the office and for those who exercise it. Even the responsible, serious, and faithful pastor may be driven to external or internal perplexity . . . In the end, perplexity leads to insensitivity. The load is too heavy to bear alone. *We need someone who will help us use our powers in ministry correctly, someone who will defend us against our own lack of faith. If the pastor has no one to offer him spiritual care, then he will have to seek someone out.*[31]

The apostle Paul knew the burden of ministry. He was assured that Christ's grace and power was sufficient to carry him through his ministry, and that his burden need not be lifted nor his thorn removed. However, we must also recognize that Paul was commanded neither to steel himself in a titanic act of willed, passionless endurance, nor to endure weakness and hardship alone. He was not informed that Christ's grace would be mediated exclusively through the Spirit. It seems, instead, that Christ graced Paul through the gift of companions along the way, who, as Paul testifies, "refreshed my spirit" and "have proved a comfort to me," whom Paul longed to see "with the affection of Christ," who prayed for his struggle and ministry, and in whose company he was "filled with joy."[32] "God, who comforts the downcast," he explicitly tells the Corinthians, "comforted us by the coming of Titus."[33]

Paul's letters are inundated with the personal names of his faithful companions and fellow servants who mediated grace to him. Some are familiar characters, while others are unknown but for their names: Barnabas, Priscilla, Aquila, Timothy, Luke, Silas, Gaius, Aristarchus, Sopater, Lucius, Sosipater, Jason, Stephanus, Fortunatus, Achaicus, Secundus, Tychicus, Mark, Justus, Trophimus, Ananias, Phoebe—not to mention the litany of names in Romans 16 and elsewhere.

As these persons graced Paul's ministry in particular ways and in particular moments, so mentors, and with them a "lay committee" of designated parishioners, mediate Christ's grace to mentees. Together they offer mentees space to acknowledge and examine the doubts, fears, and frustrations that they experience, along with space to celebrate all the turns to redemption and resurrection that they witness, both in themselves and in others. Bonhoeffer, as usual, aptly summarizes the reason for pastors' dependence: "The Christ in their own hearts is weaker than the Christ in the word of other Christians. Their own hearts are uncertain; those of their brothers and sisters are sure."[34]

The Offer of Mouth and Voice

In the mentoring friendship, after the offer of ears and eyes comes the offer of mouth and voice. Questions, observations, suggestions, and exhortation must *follow* listening and seeing, but they *must* follow. They follow as parts of a dialectical conversation that has its beginning in a previous act of ministry, takes its course through Scripture, theology, and tradition, spends time in the experience and history of the mentee, and reaches its destination in a new vision for future acts of pastoral ministry.

Dialectic, a favorite tool of philosophers (think Plato or Kant) and theologians (think Augustine or Kierkegaard), refers to the art of using conversation to examine the foundations underlying an argument or action to see if bedrock or sand underlies them. In Plato's dialogues, his various interlocutors, who usually embodied popular opinions and attitudes, were led by Socrates' deceptively innocent questions to recognize the fallacy of their uncritically held presuppositions. Thus they were educated, literally "led out" (*e-ducare*), from the chains of the shadowy cave of opinion to freedom under the blazing sun of understanding. His textual dialogue partners usually proved too benighted to bring their arguments to a satisfactory conclusion, or to follow Socrates' arguments out of the cave. Plato did expect, however, that his living readers would follow the argument of the dialogue toward a subjective apprehension of objective truth, and so be educated, or led out, toward understanding. Socrates referred to his dialogical practice as "intellectual midwifery," assisting at the birth of gestating ideas inherent within the person.

Mentoring practices a form of dialectic, as do all true friendships and all good graduate seminars. The aim is similar: to examine those latent images, unexamined intuitions, or implicit theologies that, though unidentified, nevertheless inform, and sometimes malform, our practice of ministry. When those Jesus called his friends and his family practice dialectical conversations, however, the adversarial and subtly patronizing edge, which often accompanies it, is replaced by humble love and respect for the other. In his letters, Paul often draws his readers' attention to the incongruity between how they are living or thinking and who they are in Christ, or, like Nathan to David, draws their thoughts around in such a way that their ready criticism of others recoils upon themselves. But his exhortations stem from his passionate desire that they live in the freedom of truth. In mentoring for pastoral formation, we are not dependent so much on the artful rhetoric of a wise, sagacious mentor—which would be to ascribe too much—but rather by the Spirit, who speaks through mentor and mentee, giving each ears to hear and eyes to see.

Dialectic or dialogue differs from thesis-driven or descriptive essays—that standard academic exercise we become so practiced at writing. The essay, while an important aid for developing our ability to organize and present our thoughts, allows the author to retain control and determine what voices or evidence are allowed to inform the argument or challenge the conclusion. Actual dialogue, however, between two or more people, wrests control from any particular speaker or author and creates space for assent, dissent, or further questions. No one gets to deliver a monologue in a dialogue, or if they do, they compromise the integrity of the dialogue and preclude it from serving its purpose. In a "dialogue," the decisive element is the immediacy of the *dia-*, the movement "across," of *logoi*, "words," immediately addressed and immediately redressed. Likewise, in "conversation," we are "together with others" *(con)*, "turning back" or "turning over" *(versare,* as in "versus" or "conversion")—and this process is grounded in the intimacy of regular association. As with most words, the definition of "conversation" has roamed a bit. It has referred to any simple association, to life together in a household, to a dwelling place—the Authorized Version of Philippians 3:20 declares that "our conversation is in heaven"—and it has referred, by extension, to sexual intercourse—in late eighteenth-century Britain, someone convicted of adultery was charged with "criminal conversation." Behind that development lies the base root, from which we receive the literary term, "verse"—a line from a poem or song, which is derived from the plowman's practice of moving from one line of turned-up dirt to another. Line after line is plowed up, turned over, turned back—and thus a poem is made.

Conversations, therefore, turn words over, back and forth between two or more persons, delivering them along with gestures, tones, body language, and facial expressions. We turn words over to others and ask them to turn faithfully responsive words back to us. But the immediacy of the turning back and forth involves a risk, because we cannot control what is turned back to us. What is turned up is not perhaps what we had expected—our plow may blunt against a rock. But that very risk of indeterminacy secures us from the temptation to let some ground lie uncultivated, and uncultivated land rarely—if ever—resembles the garden that Adam was given to keep. When sin fertilizes the ground, thorns and thistles grow unchecked, and the land must be worked by the sweat of our brow. Working alone, it is tempting to neglect the untilled ground in our souls, minds, habits, and dispositions, which has gone to seed and threatens to choke other areas of land that we are vigorously cultivating and nurturing. In conversation, however, particularly with another plowman who has offered to assist us, together we can turn over line after line of thoughts and words and so begin to cultivate the land toward the purposes for which it was set aside: to bring glory to its creator and fruitful nourishment to his creatures.

In dialogue we try to put ourselves in the place of others in order to understand them, imaginatively thinking from their perspective, and helping them to imagine and understand our perspective. This means trying to communicate our self-understanding as clearly as possible, aiding others in their attempt to understand, and listening to make sure that they have understood us. Theologically it means allowing the Word to be the ground on which we stand to converse with others, rather than our own words.

Theology itself has always been a dialogical enterprise, in that it represents the church's endeavor to talk with itself and the world about God and the things of God. The church's conversation is named theology and draws the whole of life into its purview. When this conversation is neglected, or entered uncritically or haphazardly, we risk losing our integrity and identity as the people of God and risk tossing the direction of our mission to the winds of the age. When we theologize we facilitate a dialogue between the theology implicit in our acts of ministry, the theology we think, the theology of Scripture, and the theology of the church extended through space and time. Discussions among seminary students over coffee, or between mentor and mentee, or between believer and unbeliever about the things of God represent the dialogical enterprise of the church—or, the church theologizing. Every Christian gets in on this conversation whenever we speak Christ-determined words with another person, and none of us are experts, for we are all amateurs in the things of God. But new pastors need the opportunity to develop the skill of theologizing and the discipline of living theologically, and this requires a place to practice, space to speak, and a brother or sister to listen and encourage.

Mentor as Midwife

Augustine, in a dialogue with his inordinately clever sixteen-year-old son, Adeodatus, draws out a key principle for any mentoring friendship, namely that the mentor does not serve the mentee simply by handing over answers or making decisions on behalf of the mentee. Only when knowledge and experience have been won by the mentee does it in-form the heart and mind. Second-hand convictions and borrowed insights never fit very well, for they are always too threadbare to endure much scrutiny. Augustine appropriately calls his dialogue, *De Magistro*—that is, *Concerning the Teacher*—because he intends its dialogical form to instruct the reader in the way of Christian education and formation. Near the end of the dialogue, father and son begin to draw some conclusions:

> **Augustine:** "We listen to Truth which presides over our minds, though of course we may be bidden to listen by someone else's words. Our real Teacher is he who is so listened to, who is said to dwell in the inner man, namely Christ . . . Who is so foolishly curious as to send his son to school to learn what the teacher thinks? When the teachers have expounded by means of

134

words then their pupils take thought within themselves whether what they have been told is true."

Adeodatus: "I have learned by your warning words, that *by means of words a man is simply put on the alert that he may learn* . . . I have also learned that in order to know the truth of what is spoken, I must be taught by him who dwells within and gives me counsel about words spoken externally in the ear. By his favour I shall love him the more ardently the more I advance in learning."[35]

Words, even words uttered by a professor or pastor, are thus necessary but not sufficient in themselves. They simply "put one on the alert" that personal learning is a possibility. If the student or mentee simply mimics the answers and conclusions of another, he or she is ill prepared to lead someone else to those same insights. The mentee knows the destination, but not the way. This role of the mentor is the *maieutic* role we mentioned earlier, the role of the midwife who assists at the birth of new insights and spiritual maturity. Literature written to inform the practice of spiritual care or spiritual direction often takes up this image from the world of birth. It was Socrates' first, though. His intention was to give birth to reasonable ideas latent in the soul that, like the truths of mathematics, could be apprehended with the subtle assistance of a cunning teacher. While Christian practitioners of the art of spiritual midwifery have adopted Socrates' metaphor, they have been too aware of the epistemic and relational consequences of sin to follow his methodical search for truth through unaided and immanent reason. They recognized that his injunction to "know thyself" is only ultimately realizable when it means "know thyself" before God, in Christ, through the Holy Spirit.

Margaret Guenther, in her book, *Holy Listening: The Art of Spiritual Direction*, uses the midwife image as a dominant metaphor for describing spiritual care. The parallels between the two practices are readily apparent. The midwife is present to another in a time of vulnerability. The midwife's assistance requires a relationship of mutual trust and respect. The midwife helps the birth-giver toward greater self-knowledge, inviting and asking questions. The midwife assists at a natural event and intervenes to help only when necessary. The midwife sees what the birth-giver cannot, and reassures when the birth-giver feels helpless. The midwife knows how and when to confront, how and when to encourage. Finally, the midwife rejoices at the new birth. "As midwives of the spirit, we will do a great deal of waiting and encourage others to wait, not always in comfort and sometimes in great pain."[36]

Our goal in education or mentoring is not simply to lead someone to become more adept at speaking about love or faith or Christ, but to arouse the student or mentee to love, to exercise faith, to know Christ. This is the *maieutic* role, the communication not only of the *what* of knowledge and datum, but the *how* of being and existence. The distinctive characteristic of communication oriented to this subjective appropriation of understanding by the hearer is its *evocative* nature. New insights are literally evoked, called out or drawn forth from the individual rather than handed to him or her to be mimicked later like a theological Mynah bird.

A number of verbs that branch from the root stem, *vocare*, "to call," can assist us. One of our foci in this relationship is the determination of our "calling," literally, our "vocation." We believe God has been calling us to Christ first and to a particular service for Christ second. To assist us in hearing our call we *invoke*, or "call upon," the Spirit, who calls us—this is prayer language. In turn, we are led to *revoke*, to "call back" or reject, false images of God, church, or ourselves that we construct or inherit—this is first commandment language. We regularly *convoke*, "call together," the community. We are warned against *provocation*, provoking God's anger, or provoking children to discouragement—this is the language of challenge and jealousy. The words *advocation*, to "call" upon someone to advise or stand beside us, and *evocation,* to "call forth," reflect the language of mentoring and spiritual care, or of hospitality and invitation. The mentor evokes what is below the surface and invites it out in to the open for consideration, advocating for the mentee's welfare in all its dimensions.

Paracletic Ministry

In this essential part of the mentoring friendship, the mentor participates in the express work of the Spirit, whose Johannine name, *parakletos,* is often translated *advocatio,* the counselor called to stand with and speak to the church. In the New Testament, the prominent idea behind *parakletos* and *advocatio* is turning to another person with substantial speech. Jacob Firet, the Dutch Reformed pastoral theologian, refers to this "paracletic ministry" as the third ministry of the church, alongside its *kerygmatic* and *didactic* ministries: 1) we step into pulpits to preach that the Kingdom has come and displaced all other kingdoms (*kerygmatic*); 2) we stand behind a lectern or sit with a small group to teach about life as citizens of the Kingdom (*didactic*); and 3) we walk alongside others as they begin to live new lives and speak a new language on the basis of their new identity (*paracletic*).[37] The Word is not merely content to be proclaimed and taught. Though these are primary and necessary, they are not sufficient. The Word must be experienced and lived through ongoing moments of conversion, transformation, and reformation. Jesus, who came alongside Zaccheus, the woman at the well, and the demon-possessed, was the first paraclete, the first advocate who promised that when he departed, another advocate would be sent to the church (Jn 14:16). This advocate continues the role Jesus began, and whoever receives the paraclete is called to participate in his ongoing paracletic ministry to others.

The English New Testament is full of words that translate forms of *parakalein*: to exhort, to encourage, to ask, to entreat, to urge, to comfort. It is among the *charismata* given to the church for its mutual upbuilding (Rom 12:8). Timothy was to give special attention to it along with the public reading of Scripture and teaching (1 Tim 4:13). Paul enjoins Timothy to "reprove, rebuke, and exhort, with complete patience" (2 Tim 4:2). The elders of Crete appointed by Titus were to be able to give *parakalein* on the basis of sound doctrine (Tit 1:9). Paul warns Philemon that he is "bold enough in Christ" to command him, but "for love's sake" prefers "to appeal," *parakaleo*, to him. *Parakalein* contains the idea of the Word addressed to someone's concrete and personal situation.[38] The new state of affairs that have been announced in the *kerygma* are particularized in the call to the individual. In the Septuagint this word regularly translates Hebrew words associated with consolation and conversion, words that appeal to a change in heart, mind, and will. The reality of our human situation is that we often give our full mental assent to the truth of the Word preached and taught, but fail to change those patterns of behavior and thought which contradict that truth.

This essential part of any ministry in the church bears on the mentoring friendship as well, which obviously occurs in the company of believers. In the unity of our faith in and baptism into Christ we have become responsible for one another. As Paul wrote to the Romans, we have been summoned to admonish, comfort, and exhort one another "that we may be mutually encouraged [*symparaklethenai*] by each other's faith" (1:12).[39] In the Schmalkald Articles, Luther calls this the *mutua consolatio fratrum*, the mutual consolation and exhortation that we owe to one another in the Body. As Firet puts it, "Paraklesis is liberating; it draws a person into the light. Paraklesis is never a matter of stringing together words which people have often heard before, or as Job puts it, 'strengthening with the mouth' (Job 16:2–5); paraklesis is helping, redeeming deed."[40]

Call it what you will—*maieutic,* paracletic, evocative, dialectical, conversational—this aspect of ministry or mentoring, as with most others, requires conscientious practice. But it is often here, in the offering and receiving of personal address, that the iron of one sharpens the iron of the other.

The Offer of Hands and Feet

So mentors offers their eyes to observe and look for the spirit, their ears to listen to the unfolding of the mentee's story, their mouths to encourage and to theologize with the mentee, and finally, they offer their hands and feet actively engaged in ministry as models for the new pastor to consider. Henry Zylstra, professor of literature at Calvin College in the middle of last century, explains the value of models and examples, both literary and living:

> There is a real sense in which [literature] enables us by vicarious experience in our life to bring to bear on being Christian, myriads of lives not our own . . . by universalizing ourselves in the significant experiences of others there is more of us that is Christian, that can be Christian, than there was before . . . There is more of you, after reading Hardy, to be Christian with than there was before you read him, and there is also more conviction that you want to be it.[41]

Stories, novels, and biographies of other pastors in the history of the church offer us an opportunity to live in the immediacy of their ministries in their times and places as a way of reflecting on the immediacy of our ministry in our time and place. They give us "more to be pastors with." They ask us to test our lives against theirs. Reflecting on the immediacy of some other pastor's life is always for the sake of re-entering the immediacy of our own, but in a way that brings their experiences and insights with us.

Thus we are mentored by their stories, whether fictionalized or historical.

In literature, we have many examples of "Christ-figures," characters who in some form or fashion resemble either Christ's character or his sacrifice on behalf of others. They offer us small pictures of what it could look like to "put on Christ." From Prince Myshkin's naively unconditional and uncompromising love for unlovely people in Dostoevsky's *The Idiot,* to Gandalf's sacrificial death and "resurrection" in Tolkien's *Lord of the Rings,* to Graham Greene's "whisky priest" in *The Power and the Glory,* to John Irving's Owen Meany in *A Prayer for Owen Meany,* or Faulkner's scapegoat Joe Christmas in *Light in August,* these are characters who in some way or other enflesh Christ in a particular time and place. The question that comes to us is how we, through the Spirit, may give body to Christ and become Christ-figures for others.

Paul encouraged the Philippians to put into practice whatever they learned, received, heard from him or saw in him and exhorted them to "take note of those who live according to the pattern we gave you."[42] Overhearing his counsel, we may reasonably ask how we might follow the examples of other Christ-following pastors from the history of the church and its literature. Paul's exhortation has been oft repeated by teachers from the tradition of moral theology, who "discover" that we are helped toward becoming persons of character by being in the presence of persons of character—both the living and the dead. If this is true, Stanley Hauerwas suggests, then "our seminaries have no more important function than to direct those preparing and in the ministry to reflect on those lives that have honored their calling as ministers." Not only does he emphasize the formative power of biographies and autobiographies, but he also challenges theological educators to pay more attention to the kind of people under whom younger student-pastors serve, for, he argues, character is largely shaped by example.[43]

Mentees, of course, do not work alongside Paul or Timothy, George Herbert or St. Claire, but they do work alongside equally complex pastors such as Ruth Lee, Randy Wilkins, or Heather Robinson. These pastors, with whom mentees serve, are, by the immediacy of their relationship, uniquely placed as models of pastoral ministry. They are able to offer stories of death and resurrection from their own experiences that inform the pastoral imagination of younger pastors, and assist in the shaping of their pastoral identities. What might it look like to follow a mentor as he or she follows Christ and attempts to embody Christ in his or her time and place? In this way, the mentoring pastor offers his or her hands and feet in the service of modeling one embodied way of being a pastor and doing pastoral ministry. Younger pastors can learn from where older pastors have failed and where, by God's grace, they have thrived.

Though modeling does not carry with it the assumption of perfection or expertise, it does assume at least a degree of proficiency and experience on the part of the modeler. Time, opportunity, education, and the demands of ecclesial responsibility have likely developed certain practices or habits in the mentoring pastor's ministry. Some of these may serve the new pastor as well, who by learning them from the mentor may avoid the difficulties of discovery by trial and error.

Because the pastoral ministry carries certain indigenous pressures that may crush and exhaust new ministers, it is imperative that they develop an appropriate balance between the many areas of their personal and vocational life. Even the apostle Paul comments that apart from all else he endured, he was burdened by "the daily pressure on me of my anxiety for all the churches" (2 Cor 11:28), a confession from which Calvin infers that anyone "who is seriously concerned for the Church of God harasses himself and bears a heavy burden on his shoulders," for "nobody can have a heartfelt concern for the churches without being burdened by many difficulties."[44] Therefore, the new pastor needs to establish sane patterns that include time for prayer, study, worship, pastoral care, preaching, teaching, as well as time for play, family, friends, and spiritual direction or spiritual friendship. Thus, the mentor may offer their hands and feet to model for the mentee both their *prayer (ora)* and their *work (labora)*:

Prayer

Maintaining the health of our own souls before God while attending to the souls of others is not ever easy, but it is absolutely essential. We know the faith and know the "gospel" and talk about it so regularly that we, with a little inattention, awake one morning to the threatening realization that we no longer live in faith ourselves, but simply think and speak about it. In discipling others we may abandon our own discipleship, and for the sake of our emotional and vocational security, avoid facing our abandonment. So the mentee may reasonably ask: How do your prayer and reading create shape for the rest of your pastoral ministry? How have you avoided the temptation to reduce prayer and reading to professional tasks and preaching and teaching to professional skills? We find ourselves teaching and preaching truths we neither fully understand nor know how to live ourselves, but how can we avoid the disillusionment that induces so many to abandon their faith and vocation? When the mentor offers their hands and feet as models, they may decide to share their own struggles of moral and personal formation, their own theological questions and doubts. Martin Luther, never one to conceal his own struggles, described the theologian's work as *oratio, meditatio, tentatio*—prayer to God, meditation upon Scripture, and the fiery struggle with temptation and trial that tries and proves our faith. Dietrich Bonhoeffer picked up Luther's line and suggested that when our lives are led by Scripture into prayer for the church and the world, "temptation is the sign that our hearing, prayer, and faith have touched down in reality. There is no escape from temptation except by giving ourselves to renewed reading and meditation" in the company of others.[45] Love compels us to assist one another to recognize and adopt the truths that these two pastors knew.

Work

The mentor may intentionally offer his or her practice of ministry as a model for the mentee to consider by inviting the mentee into the daily and weekly routines of pastoring. God not only reveals himself through the Spirit-assisted reading of creation and Scripture, but also through our acts of ministry. Therefore it is important that our ministries be theologically determined at their core so as not to misrepresent God and saddle children and adults with idolatrous, disabling visions. "Practical theology"—that is, theological deliberation oriented to action—is an essential discipline to learn, for it challenges and informs both the structure and content of our ministries. In modeling these various acts of ministry for the mentee, the mentor attempts to articulate in word and speech the theology of ministry which animates and shapes the various aspects of his or her vocation.

Pastoral care: The mentor may invite the mentee to accompany her on pastoral visits and to watch, listen, and speak when appropriate.

Communication: The mentor may invite the mentee into his weekly sermon or lesson preparation and explain how he studies towards a sermon, and what he is concerned to accomplish through it. Afterwards, the mentor and mentee may discuss the sermon, with the mentor inviting questions and comments. Likewise, the mentor may in some way model for the mentee personal evangelism or outreach.

Planning: Mentees may be invited to sit in on meetings of the board or elders, or planning sessions of the pastoral staff. This may include short-term events or long-term visions for the growth and maturity of the church.

Leadership care and training: The pastor may share how she cares for and encourages her fellow pastors in the church, and how she recruits and provides training and support for laypersons in leadership, including how to draw all the people of God toward ministry, regardless of gender, age, education, or race. In particular settings, one or another of these groups may find it more difficult to initiate ministry and may require additional space and support to feel prepared to serve.

Conflict resolution: Any time a group of sinners comes together to attempt anything, conflict is sure to follow. Reconciliation and restoration to fellowship can be a difficult but not infrequent task of the pastor. When appropriate, the mentor may invite the mentee to participate in some work of reconciliation or to reflect with him about a particular conflict in the church, small or large.

Care for those in need: This may include anything from seeking a just wage for someone, finding someone adequate shelter, standing with someone in court, delivering food and blankets, helping a battered woman or child, or caring for an addict. When the mentor models this "pure religion," she offers the mentee a vision for ministry that extends beyond the church.

Eyes, Ears, Mouth, Hands, and Feet Offered Gladly

For the practice of mentoring to have integrity as a distinctly Christian activity, it ought to reflect and reveal the shape of reality given in Scripture, that is, it must be theologically informed and determined from the beginning. This is simply the way of all good practical theology.

Though the natural spontaneity of love and friendship is to be welcomed, mentoring, as we have been describing it, should also be guided by careful reflection upon several related truths, which help to coordinate our efforts. Included among those truths are: 1) the church's need for competent and convicted pastoral leaders,

2) the slow and protracted process required for our formation as persons and pastors, 3) the priority of grace in calling and equipping us, and 4) the disordering effects of sin in our culture, our churches, and ourselves. These truthful coordinates have directed our thoughts thus far in this book. Alongside these, and encompassing them, however, remains a final set of truthful coordinates that orient us in this journey. These final coordinates compel us to suggest that the mentoring friendship can and should be characterized by the disposition of "mutual gladness."

To review, in the previous sections we suggested that the mentor offers, in partnership with the Holy Spirit, eyes to observe the mentee's ministry and to look for the gifts of the Spirit, ears to listen to the mentee's story of faith and vocation, voice and mouth to evoke and encourage, and hands and feet to model. We now qualify these acts by saying that the mentor offers these *gladly* and the mentee receives them *gladly*—that is, both have the Spirit-wrought dispositions of joy in the sheer presence of the other and delight in their mutual formation in ministry.

In this section, we shift from the practice of mentoring to consider the explicit and implicit biblical theology upon which this practice is grounded, and which leads us to declare this a free, joyful, and glad activity of the church. We are led to recognize this by a set of theological coordinates that place us in dynamic relation to both the "future" and the "past." First, there is an orientation from our "future" eschatological calling, and second, there is an orientation from the "past" of our created natures. These orient us, third, to the present personal and ecclesial task of loving and serving our neighbors, including the present task of mentoring for pastoral formation.

The primary event that directs us in this mapping endeavor is Christ's resurrection and ascension to the Father as the representative new creature, and our subsequent call to participate in him through the descending Holy Spirit, and so to become new creatures. Does this seem too grandiose a context for the casual conversation of a young pastor or Master of Divinity student with a middle-aged pastor over a cup of Tim Horton's coffee? Is this level of analysis superfluous, the result of a theologian's penchant for archaic jargon? To some, it may seem so initially, but remember, as we have asked our churches to think theologically about the church, and our mentees to think theologically about ministry, so here we try to think theologically about the mentoring friendship itself. We are attempting to sketch the contours of the moral-theological "space" in which we act as Christian mentors and mentees, in the hope that doing so may confirm and encourage us to boldly pursue this worthy endeavor.

Two caveats for the reader: first, like any drawing, the whole may not be fully recognizable until the end, but as we continue to draw and then shade what we have drawn, the picture should gradually become clear. Second, we recognize that simply clarifying the theological concepts that underlie mentoring will not necessarily lead to a flourishing mentoring friendship—that can only happen as both mentor and mentee faithfully commit to it in the context of mutual ministry.

MUTUAL GLADNESS AS CREATIONAL AND ESCHATOLOGICAL CALLING[46]

We begin our sketch by considering how Christ not only redeemed humanity from sin, but restored it to the primary relationship for which it was created—that is to say, how Christ as our representative before the Father forged for us a renewed way of being human in relation to the Father, a way he invites and enables us to follow. Though all of his life, including his death and resurrection, was oriented to this end, his final act, which completed his earthly mission and opened this way to us, and to which we now turn, was his ascension to the Father.

This takes us to where Jesus' earthly ministry, but not his human ministry, ended. The New Testament writers assert that when the Son ascended to the Father's right hand, he did so as Jesus from

Nazareth and that when he returns to the church he will do so as the same Jesus from Nazareth.[47] By this, they imply that just as Christ became man without ceasing to be the transcendent God, so he ascended without ceasing to be physical and historical man.[48] In other words, in the ascension he did not slough off his human skin, as some disembodied gnostic savior fleeing corrupt, fleshly confines, who could not be both fully God and fully man. Rather, in spite of the ascension, he remains the "second Adam," the *eschatos adam*, as Paul calls him.[49] Because of this, we are able to say that our reconciliation with the Father, which begins the new creation, was made possible when this man ascended to the Father as the vicarious representative of all humanity—the "first fruit of a new creation" and the "first born among many brothers" of a new humanity. Can we say then that the ascension split human history into two parallel lines, the history of the new creation begun in Christ that will endure, and the history of the fallen creation that will end and be transformed?

Though we often collapse the moment of Christ's ascension into the moment of his resurrection, the early church seemed to keep them distinct, celebrating each of the four moments of Christ's life individually: Ascension Day held equal place with Christmas, Good Friday and Easter. Augustine, in fact, considered Ascension Day the "festival that confirms the grace of all the festivals together, without which the profitableness of every festival would have perished."[50] But what, you may legitimately ask, does Christ's ascension have to do with the Spirit-induced "gladness" to which we referred earlier, or to the mentoring friendship, which is the object of our concern?

We continue sketching and begin with the relationship between the ascension and "gladness." We could legitimately argue, it seems, that the ascension alone warrants a response of gladness, for with the resurrection and ascension of the Son to the Father, sin was broken, the Son was restored, and God was proven victorious. Thus after the ascension, if we assume that all is well with the

Creator, then the creation may legitimately rejoice. But to end with the well-being of God alone, apart from creation, would be to relegate creation to its sin-drawn patterns of dissolution and self-contradiction. Instead—and at this all of creation may truly rejoice—all is not actually well with God until all is well with God's creation, for God has chosen not to isolate himself, but only to be God with his creation, and to bind his well-being to that of his creation.

Because of this, and in light of the incarnation and resurrection-ascension, Karl Barth proposed that it was not entirely accurate to call the church's speech "theology." Instead, he suggested the amalgam, "the-anthropology," since, whenever we have to do with God, we have to do with humankind as well. "An abstract doctrine of God has no place in the Christian realm, only a 'doctrine of God and of man,' a doctrine of the commerce and communion between God and man,"[51] a doctrine of God's free grace "in which He wills to be and is nothing other than the God of man."[52]

So where are we in our sketch? Christ has ascended and God the Father has received him as the representative human. What then does this have to do with particular persons or with the mentoring relationship?

PARTICIPATION THROUGH
THE ESCHATOLOGICAL SPIRIT

This question moves us to consider the first of the three orientations, or dynamic relations, previously mentioned—that is, the "future orientation" of the mentoring friendship. We begin at the climax of the apostle Peter's explanatory sermon on Pentecost, summarized by Luke in Acts 2. Since Christ has ascended to Israel's throne and God's right hand, the promised Spirit has been poured out upon the church as the decisive eschatological act. Why does that matter? It matters for us because in Jesus the covenant history between God and humankind, begun with Israel for the sake of the world, was reduced to the history of one single man, whose history culminated in the restoration of humankind to God. God established the covenant and provided the human fulfilment of the covenant in Christ. "While the old humanity consists of countless isolated units—each one an Adam . . . the new humanity is entirely concentrated in the one single historical point, Jesus Christ."[53] In Adam, humanity fell; in Christ, humanity was picked up and restored to God.[54]

Through the eschatological Spirit, therefore, particular persons—Peter, Paul, you, and me—are enabled to participate in Christ's history of restoration and to identify it as their own. This is because when the Spirit descends and indwells, he does not act independently, but draws us *en Christo* into relational solidarity with Christ as co-heirs in his sonship, co-participants in his death and resurrection. Thus, as Christ is the new creation, so we are freed to live as new creatures, though we are still under the conditions of the old creation: "if anyone is in Christ, he is a new creation" (2 Cor 5:17). This is our part in what Luther described as the *glorifica commutatio,* the "glorious exchange" that occurs between Christ and us.[55]

The presence of the Spirit in us, however, implies not only that Christ is with us and in us, but also that we are with Christ— that we are present before the Father. For though Christ is the representative human, the great High Priest and *eschatos adam* who stands in our place, he does not replace us before the Father. Rather, as Paul describes it in Ephesians 2:1–10, we have been restored to God's presence, made alive *with* Christ, raised up *with* Christ, and given a *present* seat *with* Christ in the "heavenly places." Might we be justified in saying, therefore, that there is a co-presence before the Father, that Christ is both alone and accompanied? In a wonderful theological mouthful, Douglas Farrow describes this relation: "descending, [Christ] accustoms the Spirit to dwell in an unreceptive environment, making room for him in the fallen creature; ascending, he reconstitutes that environment by means of the same Spirit, and in so doing makes room for the creature in the Father's presence."[56]

The great "participation language" of John, Paul, and Peter testifies to this co-presencing:

"But God . . . made us alive together with Christ . . . and raised us up with him and seated us with him in the heavenly places in Christ Jesus . . . For through him we both have access in one Spirit to the Father." (Eph 2:6,18)

"And because you are sons, God has sent the Spirit of his Son into our hearts, crying, 'Abba! Father!'" (Gal 4:6)

"By this we know that we abide in him and he in us, because he has given us of his Spirit . . . Whoever confesses that Jesus is the Son of God, God abides in him, and he in God." (1 Jn 4:12-13; 5:20)

" . . . your life is hidden with Christ in God. When Christ, who is your life, appears, then you also will appear with him in glory." (Col 3:3–4)

"You know [the Spirit], for he dwells with you and will be in you . . . In that day you will know that I am in my Father, and you in me, and I in you." (Jn 14:17–23)

" . . . he has granted to us his precious and very great promises, so that through them you may become partakers of the divine nature." (2 Pet 1:4)

The ascent of Christ and the subsequent descent of the Spirit are, therefore, the final, eschatological acts of God reconciling the world to himself in Christ.

Creaturely Gladness through Communion

The only appropriate creaturely response to this promise of restoration and relationship is joy and gladness—gladness that the Creator has made and is making things right with his creation, and gladness that he is drawing us into that cosmic operation of renewal, gladness in communion with God, and gladness in communion with our neighbor. The propriety of this creaturely response to the Creator's salvific acts is manifested throughout Scripture:

> The Lord says through Isaiah: "But I will create a new heavens and a new earth . . . be glad and rejoice forever in what I will create, for I will create Jerusalem to be a delight and its people a joy." (Is 65:17–18)

> "Your father Abraham rejoiced that he would see my day. He saw it and was glad." (Jn 8:56)

> John the Baptist declared, "The friend of the bridegroom, who stands and hears him, rejoices greatly at the bridegroom's voice. Therefore this joy of mine is now complete." (Jn 3:29)

> "As the Father has loved me, so have I loved you . . . These things I have spoken to you, that my joy may be in you, and that your joy may be complete." (Jn 15:11)

> "'I have made you a light for the Gentiles, that you may bring salvation to the ends of the earth.' And when the Gentiles heard this, they began rejoicing and glorifying the word of the Lord." (Acts 13:48; cf. 11:12; 15:3)

> Peter cites David's response to the resurrection: "I saw the Lord always before me, for he is at my right hand that I may not be shaken; therefore my heart was glad and my tongue rejoiced; my flesh also will dwell in hope." (Acts 2:25–7; Ps 16:8–11)

"While he blessed them, he parted from them and was carried up into heaven. And they worshiped him and returned to Jerusalem with great joy, and were continually in the temple blessing God." (Lk 24:52)

The great multitude of heaven cries out, "Let us rejoice and exult and give him the glory, for the marriage of the Lamb has come, and his Bride has made herself ready." (Rev 19:7)

Considering Scripture's witness to the creaturely and ecclesial response to God's acts of salvation, the theologian Oliver O'Donovan concludes,

In response to Christ's exaltation the church is a *glad community* . . . When we say that the church is glad in the resurrection of Christ, we point to the meaning of that event as the recovery of creation order. Gladness belongs essentially to the creature, as glory belongs to the creator.[57]

"Gladness" in the New Testament is an eschatological word, a fruit of the Spirit who mediates the overlap between this age, the "time" of Jesus' earthly life, and the age of the world to come, the "time" of the ascended Jesus. From the "time" of the new creation, when all will finally be made well, we live in this time "filled with an inexpressible and glorious joy."[58]

Returning to our previous discussion, we can say that when all is well with God, all in fact is well with humankind, or potentially so, for in the Spirit-mediated *glorifica commutatio,* we share, in a derivative and appropriately human way, in the incarnate Son's love for the Father, and in his love for other people. Thus are we turned, in another of Luther's well-known phrases, from being *incurvatus in se,* "inturned upon oneself" in sinful autonomy and self-contradiction, to being *excurvatus ex se,* "turned out from oneself" into personal communion with God and into personal communion with others. The significance for the mentoring friendship of this staggering truth should become clear: restoration of the vertical relationship with God through Christ and the Spirit carries a promise for horizontal relationships with others. Adam's sin against God and Cain's sin against his brother are both overcome through Christ, and we are now drawn "gladly" into relationship with God and other persons, given permission to risk knowing and being known.[59]

Søren Kierkegaard's simple formulation of this may be helpful. He suggests that we should not think of our relationship with other people in the form "person–person," but rather "person–God–person." God, the Spirit, he says, must be the "middle term"; otherwise, we fall back into our usual patterns of defensive self-preservation or self-aggrandizement, either fearing or commandeering the other. Instead, when even our relationships with other people are mediated through the Holy Spirit, we no longer have to coerce or dominate them, but are made free to delight in their present otherness. Expanding on Kierkegaard's formula, Bonhoeffer explains, "Human love seeks direct contact with the other person; it loves him not as a free person but as one whom it binds to itself. [Spiritual love], however, knows that it has no immediate access to other persons. Jesus Christ stands between the lover and the others he loves."[60] This is one eschatological effect of the ascension of Christ to the Father and the descension of the Spirit to the church.

We may say that in the church, created sociality becomes redeemed sociality. From this comes the forgiveness of enemies, love for the unknown neighbor in our midst, speech that upbuilds, correction that graciously restores, and a mission taken up in common. It is the place where authentic humanity, in the image and likeness of the triune God of grace, is already emerging. It is, to use Irenaeus's word, the "recapitulation" of humankind.

Mutual Gladness as Created Nature

In our theological sketch of the free and glad meeting of mentor with mentee, we now move from the eschatological "future" to draw in the background—the past, if you will—of our "created sociality." Looking "back," we discover that as we are re-created and transformed personally and ecclesially into Christ's image, we come to fulfil our original creation in the image of the triune God.[61] If, in truth, the image of God in which humans were created was fully realized only in Christ, then in Christ we are not made *ex nihilo* into something other than human. Rather, putting on "the new self, created after the likeness of God,"[62] being "conformed to the image of his Son,"[63] and coming to "bear the image of the man of heaven" as we have previously "borne the image of the man of dust,"[64] we are made to be human in a new and truer way than we were before. As John Calvin reminds us, "The end of regeneration is that Christ should conform us to God's image . . . Now we see how Christ is the most perfect image of God; if we are conformed to it, we are so restored . . . that we bear God's image."[65] Reflecting on the redemption of our original creation in God's image, and our original and restored relationship with God, we are led to wonder whether our relational openness to others may be a kind of "social refraction" of our openness to God, and, in turn, of God's fundamental self-relatedness as a triunity of persons.

We are led to move in this direction because we recognize that the categories we have been using—"person," "relation," and "formation"—are theological categories before they are psychological or sociological categories. As soon as we speak these words, we find ourselves using theological language formed and filled by centuries of Christian dialogue, which insists that "persons in relation"—the foundation of the mentoring friendship—finds its meaning in the persons of the triune God first, prior to any enfleshing of this between human persons.

Before we can turn to the persons in the mentoring friendship directly, this conversation returns us to the tumultuous

Christological and Trinitarian debates of Nicea, Constantinople, and Chalcedon concerning the "persons" of God. In order to safeguard the common divinity and distinct particularity of each person—Father, Son, and Spirit—the pastor-theologians at these councils attempted to develop a "grammar" or "rule" of faith that was faithful to the explicit and implicit theology of the New Testament concerning the mutual indwelling and common work of the persons of the Trinity—a grammar that could warrant and safeguard future theological developments.

However, to achieve the classic Nicene formulation, which the church since then has confessed, required no small semantic innovation on the part of Athanasius and the Cappadocian Fathers in the East—Gregory of Nazianzus, Basil of Caesarea, and Gregory of Nyssa—and of Tertullian and others in the West. How to describe that which we might apprehend, but could never comprehend? Struggling to force language to take account of their new experience and understanding of God, they wrested words out of their semantic fields, reshaped them, and then resubmitted them for theological use by the church. This "semantic metanoia" is a commonplace of revelation. Words we think we know are commandeered and transformed through divine redefinition— father, king, kingdom, community, love, husband, bride, servant, authority, Israel, and Messiah. Each of these are "converted" and filled out with new meaning. Part of the process of our conversion is learning to think these "converted" words with their new definitions. This happened at Nicea with the concepts of "person," "being," and "relation."

Without rehearsing the heady and impetuous debates of the councils, suffice it to say that the hard, and barely won, orthodox confession of God as both three and one—both one *ousia* and three *hypostaseis* in the East, and one *substantia* and three *personae* in the West—introduced the subsequent difficulty of describing the distinction between Father, Son, and Holy Spirit. How could one be three? At Nicea, Athanasius's answer to his Arian detractors was that the three were distinguished in their inter-Trinitarian life by their "relations": the Father is Father in that he begets the Son, the Son is Son in that he alone is begotten, and the Spirit alone proceeds from the Father and the Son.[66]

Athanasius's point is that God has not revealed himself as a relation of three divine persons who contingently gather for moments of communication or relation, only to withdraw without loss of identity. In Gregory of Nazianzus's well-known phrase, much beloved by Calvin: "I cannot think of the One without immediately being surrounded by the radiance of the Three; nor can I discern the Three without at once being carried back to the One."[67] Theologians have long argued that the God who reveals himself to the world as Father, Son, and Holy Spirit must first be triune in himself. "The God who makes communion must already be communion."[68] As Eberhard Jungel writes, God's revelation as Father, Son, and Holy Spirit is an act of "self-interpretation" to the world, in that his internal self-relatedness makes possible his external relatedness to the world in the Son and the Spirit. His being is bound up with his coming to the world and the coming of each person to the other.[69] Likewise Calvin insists that because God has revealed himself as three persons, "unless we grasp these, only the bare and empty name of God flits about in our brains, to the exclusion of the true God," for what he is toward us in his self-revelation he is inherently and eternally in himself.[70]

Therefore, from the fourth century on, as expressed in baptismal formulas, apostolic benedictions, and biblical doxologies, the Trinity has been defined as a communion of three persons who have always existed in union with another and in dependence upon one another.[71] Without prior independent existence, each participates in the others and confers identity upon the others through the movement of self-giving love.[72] Thus, while the first thing to be said about God is that "He exists as a They"—in the mutual love of personal communion—the second is that the particularity of each person—Father, Son, and Holy Spirit—is conferred through being in relation with the other persons.

What does it mean to say that each person "participates" in the other, and "confers identity upon the others"? It means, and there is no stronger way to say it, that the relation is constitutive of the particularity of each of the persons. Augustine suggested, "the names, Father and Son, do not refer to the substance but to the relation, and the relation is no accident," that is, the relation cannot be extracted without changing the substance of the person.[73] They are who they are, we may say, in the "between" of the relation.[74]

The Greek word, *perichoresis*, literally "a dance around," and the Latin, *circumincessio*, were coined as short-hand word pictures to signify what has variously, and somewhat obliquely, been referred to as "mutual interanimation," "dynamic interpenetration," or the "coinherence" of the Trinity. Now, if "coinherence" and the like generate incoherence in the reader, it is enough to maintain the substance of the words: Father, Son, and Spirit cannot be known apart from their relation, and are distinct not in spite of their relation, but ultimately because of their mutual relation. With this, we come closer to sketching the mentor and mentee relationship in our drawing of the theological space that they indwell.

A related semantic innovation, and one with direct implications for our understanding of the created and redeemed person, came when the Greek and Latin words for "person"—*prosopon* and *persona*—were attached to the definition of "being," *hypostasis*. Why is that significant? It is significant because *prosopon* and *persona* had most likely referred to the stage-mask through which an actor spoke their lines to an audience. The same actor could play many "persons" simply by changing the masks through which he spoke (*per-sonare*).[75] "Personalness" was thus a passing phenomenon, detached from "being." We have retained this concept in our word "persona," which refers to a charlatan or the phony character someone plays in a social setting. But when Tertullian used *persona* to refer to Father, Son, and Holy Spirit, the word shifted meaning to "person-in-relation" or "person-in-participation." The "person" was fundamental and substantial and existed only as it was in relation with other persons.

The logic went something like this: If God is inherently relational because Father, Son, and Spirit are eternal, and cannot be unrelated to one another, and if Father, Son, and Spirit receive their particularity from the definition given in their relations, and if the word "person" adequately identified their eternal particular identities, then "person" necessarily referred to someone only as they were distinguished from and known in relation to other persons.

Therefore, you could never go behind the "person-in-relation" to find some "person-in-isolation."[76] In God there are not "individuals," but "persons," who dwell together so completely that we cannot consider one without immediately considering the others. This definition of "person" as irreducibly relational was inevitably applied to human "persons," created in the image of the relational God to be in relationship with him, recreated through participation in Christ by the Holy Spirit, and set into the *koinonial* communion of a *body* of believers. To be made in the image of God is to be endowed with a particular kind of personal reality, one that finds its "being" in relation with the triune God and other persons.[77] Thus we can say that our sociality is, contra many modern and postmodern descriptions, not a result of human will, but of our created "nature." J. B. Torrance, with many others, has consistently argued this point, and summarizes what we have been saying thus far:

> What we need today is a better understanding of the person not just as an individual but as someone who finds his or her true being-in-communion with God and with others, the counterpart of a Trinitarian doctrine of God. The God of the New Testament is the God who has his true being as the Father of the Son, and as the Son of the Father in the Spirit. God is love, and has his true being in communion, in the mutual indwelling

of Father, Son and Holy Spirit—*perichoresis*, the patristic word. This is the God who has created us male and female to find our true humanity in "perichoretic unity" with him and one another, and who renews us in his image in Christ.[78]

Torrance makes an important distinction between an *individual* and a *person*. The "individual" is defined as a self-conscious autonomous unit endowed with intellectual, psychological, or moral qualities who intends, wills, thinks, decides, and acts—in decidedly "ungodlike isolation."[79] A "person," as we have argued, receives particularity as, in communion with others, he or she moves across the individualized boundary of the self into the "between" of personhood. As the Orthodox theologian John Zizioulas describes, it is in the communion of freedom and love that a "particular being becomes itself"—"and that should not surprise any Christian who believes that the world exists only because of God's free love and that even God himself is love."[80]

Relational Gladness as Ecclesial Task

With these brush strokes laid, we move from the future of our eschatological calling and from the past of our created being to sketch in the present task of the church, and ultimately, the friendship between mentor and mentee. In saying this we are obviously not suggesting that we can reduplicate the inter-Trinitarian life of mutual participation, even if we fully understood it, which we do not. We are not called to reduplicate it, but through the Spirit, we are called to live, as far as it is humanly possible, lives of mutual participation, in which our relations with others are not just something we "have," but something we are—relations that constitute us as persons.[81] Through the Spirit we are drawn into one another's life and into the communion of love between the Son and the Father, from which issues our love for one another.[82] We might say we love because we are created to love, commanded to love, and enabled to love through the Spirit of the God who is

Love in himself. With the apostle John we can confess this to be the defining moment and mark of the ecclesial community.

Those who are called out from the world are bound together through the Spirit in such a way that their particularity is not obscured but rather enhanced. As Paul's extended analogy of 1 Corinthians and Romans makes clear, they are like members of a body, together forming an organic whole. Any member of the body that is separated from the whole ceases to be what it truly is. Each serves the other and understands himself or herself in relation to the others.

Returning to our earlier discussion of creaturely response, we become aware that gladness and joy in relation with God and other persons comes to us also as a task for the present, for we recognize that the fruits of the Spirit are in fact virtues of life in community. One of Karl Barth's constant themes was that our new identity as persons in Christ demands an ethical response. Christians, he suggests, are "non-conformists," who offer to the world the image of a "strangely human person."[83] Oliver O'Donovan, likewise, considers creaturely gladness and eschatological delight to include a moral task:

> . . . Gladness is a moral attitude, a disposition of the affec-
> tions appropriate to the recognition of God's creative goodness
> . . . The church's active life is based on delight at what God
> has done. Delight is not a matter of contemplation and reflec-
> tion only, but of active celebration; yet the activity is founded
> on something *there*, the handiwork of God, and is not simply
> self-generated. When we care for our neighbour's welfare, it is
> because we are delighted by our neighbour.[84]

It is a given of moral discourse and practical theology that an accurate description of a situation is imperative for determining an appropriate response. God is one God, therefore idolatry is ruled out. Humans are created in God's image, therefore murder is prohibited. The dividing wall of hostility between Jew and Gentile has been broken, therefore they may eat together. We participate in

Christ's death and life, therefore we receive the Lord's Supper and baptism. The "old man" has been killed, therefore we no longer live its life. We have been forgiven, therefore we forgive. This is part of Scripture's normative discourse. Therefore, what humans ought to do is determined by what kind of beings they are and by the condition of their existence.

As we draw the mentor and mentee into our sketch, we are concerned with the principles of mentoring that flow from the truthful coordinates of our created and redeemed humanity and our pneumatological and ecclesial identity. Mentoring "works," we might say, because we are relationally determined creatures created and re-created through Christ in the image of the triune God, who is an internal and eternal relation of persons. Mentoring is counted among those things that are true, noble, right, pure, lovely, admirable, and praiseworthy when its principles and practices are oriented to these *fundamentums* of theology. Therefore, while our relationality is given to us in the structure of our creation, and as part of our calling through the eschatological Spirit, we can also affirm that it is part of our rich task and calling as the church to develop ways of being and loving that respect and contribute to the flourishing of other persons. Mentoring for pastoral formation or Christian maturity certainly takes its place as one of these ways.

Mentoring thus can be seen as a glad meeting of persons created to be in communion with one another and created to be formed in that communion. As persons, as Christians, and as pastors, we are created and enabled to love and to receive love in numerous ways from our brothers and sisters. If we consider the mentoring relationship a genre of friendship, and recall that Christ called the disciples his friends and enjoined them to love each other as he loved them, what can we say by way of implication? We can say very little, really, that has not already been said elsewhere. We have described many of the implications for mentoring already, but here take note of them, to use David S. Cunningham's phrase, as "Trinitarian virtues," dispositions "God has by nature and in which we participate by grace and practice." As gifts, these virtues "are not forced upon us; but we can allow them to form us, and thus allow God to take us up into the divine life."[85] Following are a few "Trinitarian virtues," the final details of our theological sketch, whose practice may assist the mentoring friendship to be a distinctly Christian activity that does indeed indwell and reveal the shape of reality given us in Scripture:

- Mentor and mentee create "space" for the other to be, respecting the distinct personhood of the other. On the other hand, both recognize that to be distinct persons means crossing through that space to meet the other in the "between" of personal relating.

- Withdrawing from personal communion for the sake of claiming space to be "myself" actually collapses space because my self fills the space, and no room is left for the relation that particularizes me. I am thus left with only myself as an "individual" and fail to one degree or another to become a "person."

- Truthful communication—listening and speaking thoughtfully—are primary ways to receive the person of the other "gladly."

- Mentor and mentee find their ultimate identity as persons and pastors in Christ, and neither in their work nor in the other person's approval or disapproval. We are thus freed from self-promotion and self-assertion, and freed to hear criticism and praise.

- We recognize that the Spirit bestows a plurality of gifts in his work of particularizing persons.

- Both mentor and mentee recognize that one of the first works of sin is to break relationship, and so both resist that temptation in themselves and in the other.

- Self-giving love is the essence of being a person in Christ. This call to love takes precedence over any individual gift we may have (1 Cor 13:2).

- Love is fulfilled in helping the other to flourish as a person in Christ and a pastor for Christ, helping both to live into their eschatological and present calling.

CHAPTER 6

FOUR AREAS OF PASTORAL FORMATION RECONSIDERED

To assist in the glad offer and reception of the mentor's eyes, ears, mouth, hands and feet, the following quotes, images, and questions return us to a shared exploration of Gregory of Nazianzus's four areas of pastoral formation and preparation.

I. MORAL, SPIRITUAL, PERSONAL FORMATION

The moral and spiritual formation of the pastor and priest was of utmost importance to many of the church fathers and mothers. Indeed, at times they appear to esteem an impossible ideal, demanding a level of personal holiness and purity that seems unattainable and therefore prohibitive to those of us who know our failings and faults so well. However, what they desire are preachers and pastors who indwell that to which they call others, who are able to validate and embody in their lives the gospel they share in their words.

> Who seeks a spring in the mud? Who wants to drink from muddy water? Who will think a man to be useful to another's cause whom he sees to be useless in his own life?
>
> —Ambrose of Milan, fourth-century bishop[1]

In spiritual formation seminarians learn to care for the parish of their own soul, while preparing to care for the souls entrusted to them in a parish.

—St. Charles Borremeo, SJ
sixteenth-century Counter Reformation educator

How could you acquire a tenderness and skill in speaking to them that are weary, without a taste of such trials as they also meet with? You could only be a hearsay witness to the truth, power, and sweetness of the precious promises, unless you have been in such a situation as to need them, and to find their suitableness and sufficiency. The Lord has given you a good desire to serve him in the Gospel, and he is now training you for that service.

—Reverend John Newton,
eighteenth-century pastor and hymn writer

[Gospel] things are never well known till they are felt, nor well felt till they are possessed; and he that feeleth them not himself, is not likely to speak feelingly of them to others, nor to help others to the feeling of them. How can you follow sinners, with compassion in your hearts and tears in your eyes, and beseech them, in the name of the Lord, to stop their course, and return and live, and never had so much compassion on your own soul, as to do this much for yourselves? . . . *I confess that a man shall never have my consent to have the charge of other men's souls and to oversee them in order to their salvation that takes not heed to himself but is careless of his own.*

—Richard Baxter,
seventeenth-century evangelical Puritan pastor[2]

These pastors challenge us to live coherent and consistent lives of grace and integrity. The following questions ask us to consider the health of our souls and the shape and practice of our ministries.[3]

QUESTIONS FOR CONSIDERATION

Personal:

1. From what or from whom do I seek affirmation and confirmation of who I am?

2. How do I respond to the indigenous pressures and stresses of pastoral ministry? Likewise, how do I respond to criticism and praise—can I humbly accept both?

3. Where and when have I been hurt and how does that affect the way I do ministry or relate to people? How might God use my past to prepare me for ministry in the future?

4. What might God be wanting to teach me during this season in my life? Am I willing to hear his voice?

Spiritual:

5. How is my ministry affecting my relationship with God, or how is my relationship with God affecting my ministry?

6. Is there a difference for me between the "God and Father of our Lord Jesus Christ" and the "God of my fathers"?

7. How will I carve out time for "holy leisure" with the Lord? Do I have time for sabbath prayer and sabbath play?

8. How might a "spiritual director" or "spiritual friend" assist me at this stage in my life? Should I seek one?

9. Am I intentional about my own spiritual care?

Moral:

10. How are my character and integrity being tested in life and ministry?

11. In what area do I need to be held accountable? From whom should the exhortation come?

12. Given my personality and history, what patterns of disorder or sin am I particularly prone to fall into? How will this affect my ministry? How might I begin to cultivate discipline in this area? Am I able to confess my failures or successes to someone else?

13. Do I tend to separate my faith, or lack thereof, from my work? Do I believe and live what I call others to believe and live? Where do I struggle with this?

II. PASTORAL CALLING, IMAGES, AND IMAGINATION

As we shall read in chapter 8, the Swiss Karl Barth was both pastor and theologian. For his eightieth birthday celebration, accolades poured in from around the world. He was hailed as the greatest theologian of the twentieth century, one comparable to the church fathers. No less a luminary than Pope Pius XII described him as "the greatest theologian since St. Thomas Aquinas" (bypassing the entire Reformation, of course!). The aging Barth, however, was not quite as impressed with the guest of honor as were others. When he was finally allowed to speak at the celebrations, with his usual wit he read an inscription he had made to himself on the flyleaf of his own copy of his first book, the famous 1922 *Romans* commentary: "From Karl Barth to his dear friend Karl Barth." The words which followed were originally from Martin Luther to young theologians:

> If you think and are of the opinion that you really stand secure and you please yourself with your own books, your teaching and your writings, [if you think] that you have done very splendidly and have preached magnificently, and if it then pleases you to be praised before others, yes, if you perhaps want to be praised lest you mourn and give up, then, my friend, if you are man enough, put your hands to your ears, and if you do so rightly, you will find a lovely pair of big, long, rough donkey's ears. Do not spare the cost of decorating them with golden bells so that you can be heard wherever you go and the people can

point to you and say: "Behold, behold! There goes that splendid creature that writes such wonderful books and preaches such wonderful sermons."[4]

Luther and Barth both knew very well that pastors and theologian are not called to draw others to themselves. Barth often commented how glad he was not to be a "Barthian," and exhorted his students to emphasize "the one, interesting Name."[5] What Barth knew, so many of us have seen and known in ourselves, that too often as pastors and theologians, we are seduced to hook an earring, or a bell, or maybe some ribbon in our big donkey ears. We receive some compliments on the new look and add a bow or perhaps a purple streamer. Then we trot out our newly adorned ears for others to esteem, and somewhere along the way we become caught up in our own parade and forget to carry the burden Christ asked us to carry.

Near the end of his speech on that day, Barth compared his life and his monumental work to that of another donkey, and in doing so offered us a wonderful image for pastoral ministry:

> A real donkey is mentioned in the Bible . . . It was permitted to carry Jesus to Jerusalem. If I have done anything in this life of mine, I have done it as a relative of the donkey that went its way carrying an important burden. The disciples had said to its owner: "The Lord has need of it." And so it seems to have pleased God to have used me at this time, just as I was, in spite of all the things, the disagreeable things, that quite rightly are and will be said about me. Thus I was used. I was on the spot . . . A theology somewhat different from the current theology was apparently needed in our time, and I was permitted to be the donkey that carried this better theology for part of the way, or tried to carry it as best I could.[6]

As Barth grew older, it began to appear that he might not finish his multi-volume *Church Dogmatics*. A joke was making the rounds, however, that God would not let him die until he completed it, because God was too interested to find out about himself. Barth, mildly amused, remarked,

> the angels must laugh at old Karl. They laugh at him because he tries to grasp the truth about God in a book of Dogmatics. They laugh at the fact that volume follows volume and each is thicker than the previous one. As they laugh, they say to one another, "Look! Here he comes now with his little pushcart full of volumes of the *Dogmatics*!" And they laugh about the men who write so much about Karl Barth instead of writing about the things he is trying to write about. Truly, the angels laugh.[7]

The point is that the pastor is to be about the work of the Father, Son, and Spirit, emphasizing the one interesting Name in the church, and carrying the Messiah through the streets to the world. The question that is put to us, and that we must consider together with our mentor or mentee, is how in our place and time, like Barth in his, "the Lord has need of us" to carry this burden.

Questions for Consideration

What dominant images of pastoral ministry shape the expectations imposed upon us by ourselves, by the church, and by culture? Pastor as hireling expected to meet the felt needs of those paying the salary? Pastor as resident holy person who lives righteously and prays so others do not have to? Pastor as crisis counsellor? Pastor as infallible authority?

1. How broad is my image of pastoral ministry? From where or whom have I received my image of pastor and ministry?

2. What dominant images do I want to indwell in my ministry, and how do I ensure its congruence with biblical concepts?

3. Who do I esteem as models for my faith journey and pastoral ministry? What specifically would I like to incorporate into my own character and ministry?

4. What do I hope to learn or develop or think about in the next few months during my internship?

5. How can I cultivate my pastoral imagination?

6. How do I understand ordination: as a sacramental commissioning of the church or as professional certification?

7. What are my hopes and dreams for future ministry? How can my mentor or church help me grow and develop toward these?

Classical pastoral wisdom has not only believed that one's call can be examined, but that it is dangerous if left unexamined. This call has both an external and an internal moment. The "internal call" is a result of the continued drawing power of the Holy Spirit. The "external call" is an act of the Christian community that by due process confirms the inward call by calling us into active service. This does not imply, of course, that the Spirit's call comes only to pastors. Indeed, the Spirit may call believers into many unique vocations. Among the many "calls," however, the church has always confessed that one is the call to enter pastoral ministry.

H. Richard Niebuhr, Charles Spurgeon, and John Newton offer us the following classic formulae for examining the call to ministry. Common to all three is an internal, Spirit-generated desire, a certain aptness or competence for ministry, and the recognition and confirmation by the church—all three of which ought to be present and discernible.

In his book, *The Purpose of the Church and Its Ministry*, Niebuhr suggests that the call to ministry actually includes four calls[8]. We can summarize them as follows:

1. The call to be a Christian;

2. The secret call, namely, that inner persuasion or experience whereby a person feels directly summoned or invited by God to take up the work of ministry;

3. The providential call or invitation that comes through our natural gifts conjoined with the divine guidance of one's life in all its circumstances;

4. The ecclesiastical call, that is, the summons and invitation extended to an individual by some community or institution of the church to engage in the work of ministry.

Likewise, when Charles Spurgeon discussed with his students the nature of the call to ministry, he suggested the following:[9]

1. The call must be an "intense, all-absorbing desire" for the work of ministry. The desire must be thoughtful and continual rather than anxious and impulsive. The desire must not be motivated by self-interest, but by the glory of God and the service of souls.

2. There must be some aptness to teach, preach, minister, and administer in love and grace.

3. There ought to be some response to the gospel as a result of his or her ministry.

4. His or her ministry and desire to do ministry should be confirmed by the prayerful judgment of the church and other spiritually mature persons.

Likewise, John Newton, who was "long distressed" about his own call, counselled a young friend that a call to ministry should include the following:[10]

1. An enduring warm and affectionate desire to serve in ministry even though one may be "intimidated by a sense of its importance and difficulty," and fearful of one's own "great insufficiency" to meet its demands.

2. In due season, the appearance of some competency "as to gifts, knowledge, and utterance," since "if the Lord sends a person to teach others, He will furnish him with the means."

3. These, finally, must be followed by a "correspondent opening in providence" that leads one to "the means, the time, the place, of actually entering upon the work." In other words, if God calls and equips, he also provides the opportunity.

Questions for reflecting upon one's calling:[11]

1. Am I being called to pastoral ministry of some sort? How do I know? To whom should I listen?

2. How am I being called to carry Christ as best I can? For what task does "the Lord have need" of me? As a chaplain, counselor, youth worker, social worker, teacher?

3. What is my passion? What do I think my time and culture needs to hear from the gospel?

4. How is my sense of God's call being clarified through my current ministry?

5. Where do others see the presence and power of God in my ministry? When do people seem to hear the gospel through me?

6. Am I open to the possibility that I am not being called into ministry at this time? Is it possible for me to conceive that God might be calling me elsewhere?

7. Is my internal sense of call confirmed with an external call by my church? Do professors, pastors, and parishioners confirm my ministry, my gifts, and my desire? Have they encouraged me to pursue either ordination or ministry in some capacity?

III. THEOLOGICAL REFLECTION AND DELIBERATION

Practical theologizing is near the centre of pastoral ministry and the centre of the mentoring relationship. Many of the men and women God has raised up as theologians and teachers in the church have been deeply immersed in the practice of ministry, people whose thinking and writing were the product of supple minds and hearts moving back and forth between Scripture and ministry. Likewise, pastors of the church whose lives and ministries are worthy to be esteemed are theologians to one degree or another. A pragmatic and haphazard ministry is the result of a theologically undisciplined mind. Pastors ought to be the "resident theologians" for their churches and ought to cultivate and practice theologically determined ministry. This is only possible by thinking critically about what we do when we pray and plan what to do and how to do it, and when we reflect on and evaluate what we have done.[12]

Made up of four related movements, practical theology serves both a critical and a prescriptive function. In the critical mode, we labor to avoid words, actions, and decisions that misrepresent the triune God of grace and lead people's minds and hearts astray. We scrutinize what we say, what we do, and the explicit or implicit messages that our ministry policies and programs might communicate. In its positive mode we labor to construct the ministry of our churches around a biblical and theological core, which shapes and animates them. It does not guarantee that we shall always make the right decision or take the right course of action. We will not. It does ensure, however, that our action in ministry will at least be informed and considered, and therefore potentially more accurate more often.

Following are the four moments of practical theologising.

1. *Theological Description*

This begins with reflection upon the givenness of reality—that is, reflection on what has been revealed to us about God, the world, church, and humanity in and through the Word. Scripture

174

is our primary source for this—our norming normative—though tradition, reasoning, and experience each contribute to our understanding. So our first step forward is to stand and look back at what is there. Based on what we "see" and know, how do we understand and describe our context or situation theologically rather than psychologically or sociologically? Creation, Covenant, Christ, and the Kingdom form our primary interpretive grid.

This stage is unavoidable, for without a description of the situation and space into which we are supposed to act, our actions and decisions will often be either conservative or innovative for their own sakes, rather than genuinely serviceable to the gospel and other people. Faulty descriptions of reality, of ultimate ends and immediate needs, can carry serious consequences for church and society, as is rather easily verified.

2. Theological Deliberation or Practical Reason

This attempts to move from the theological description of our situation before God in the midst of our ecclesial and social communities to some act of ministry that appropriately reflects what we know to be true about the situation. It requires the formation of guiding concepts authorized by the narratives and teaching of Scripture. This second step turns our attention forward, to where we are going to put our foot, and causes us to ask what a particular act or decision, sermon or speech, commission or omission, will communicate about God. Our action, therefore, is determined both by the backward glance at the given, and the forward glance at the anticipated effect. What do we desire to accomplish? This is a moment of action-directed thought—not yet action itself—but reasoning that justifies doing one thing in particular and not another thing.

The act of ministry occurs here, in the middle, as the falling of the foot, an act chosen before other possibilities to most faithfully mediate the Word in all its fullness to others. Though the act of ministry, whatever it may be, stands apart from the four-fold process of practical theologizing, it is a theological act, decisive for our understanding and comprehension. It reveals and confirms truths and errors unforeseeable apart from it. Thus this intentional practice and embodiment of theology in turn leads to a greater understanding of theology and future practice.

3. Theological Reflection

In this step, we reflect upon either our deliberative act of ministry, or upon a particular spontaneous conversation, or some moment in the life of the church or ministry setting. This is the moment in which we ask, after both the explicit and the implicit theology that animated the situation, Did we step where we had hoped, or did something unforeseen distract us or get in the way? Did we fall or stand? Did we accomplish what we wanted? Were we true to what we believe? Did our words or actions faithfully represent truth, or did they falsify and violate it? This leads to the fourth moment in the chain.

4. Ministerial-Theological Repentance and Confirmation:

This occurs between our reflection and our return to description and deliberation. It is the moment for renewed obedience and change, when we acknowledge patterns of sin and error, epistemic blindness, and unforeseeable consequences. We must be watchful not to pass by this moment, when we decide not to step again where we just have, or when we consider how to repair the damage done by our previous step. This step, finally, leads us back to theological description. With the knowledge gained from our action, our reflection upon it, and our repentance in the face of its shortcomings, how now ought we describe the situation anew?

Theological Reflection in Conversation

The following model for theological reflection in a supervised ministry setting is adapted from Kenneth Pohly's book, *Transforming the Rough Places: The Ministry of Supervision.*[13] We offer it as a suggestive model for thinking through the kinds of questions that mentor and mentee are likely to consider. It most naturally finds its place in the last two stages mentioned above: theological reflection and ministerial-theological repentance and confirmation. The following questions should only serve to lead our thoughts and open the door to more extensive conversations. They should not replace thought and genuine conversation by woodenly adhering to their form or order.

Information

The intention in the opening stage is simply to obtain an accurate picture of the act or situation of ministry under discussion. A variety of means may be used to communicate this. You might consider:

    a. What took place? What was the situation?
    b. What was your role? How did you expect to participate?
    c. How did you respond to the situation?
    d. How did the other participant(s) respond to you?
    e. How did the situation end?

Evaluation

The intention in the second stage is to sort out potentially core issues that may indicate larger areas for reflection and discussion.

    a. What emotions did you experience? fear? failure? delight? peace?
    b. How do you feel about the other people involved? How can you attempt to love them well?
    c. What might you have done differently?
    d. How does this affect your ability to minister?
    e. What are the key issues involved? What seems most important?

Analysis

The intention in the third stage is to remove the obstacles and find among all the possible alternatives one that seems most viable for continued ministry in the situation.

177

a. What would you like to discuss with the mentor?

b. What would you like to see happen in the situation or with the persons involved?

c. What are possible alternatives?

d. How can future encounters best be confronted or handled?

e. Are there attitudes or responses to repent?

Theologizing

The intention in the fourth stage is to discuss the theological interpretation of the experience and the relationship between Scripture, theology, and experience.

a. What theological insights have emerged about yourself, human nature, the church, God, the world?

b. What theological truths could be brought to bear on this situation? How might it be interpreted theologically in light of Scripture, theology, and tradition?

c. What implications might this have for your identity as a minister? Are there weaknesses or strengths that have been revealed?

d. What questions remain?

Commitment Stage

The intention in the fifth and final stage is to come to a theologically determined and informed decision regarding future ministry.

a. Is a similar situation likely to present itself in the future? Do you expect to find yourself in a similar position?

b. How do you anticipate responding to it in the future?

c. What resources do you need to inform and shape your future response?

d. What do you need to pray in light of this?

e. What specific steps can you take that will help? Meditating on particular passages of Scripture? Reading a relevant book? Praying with others? Journaling? Thinking through the theological argument or implications? Seeking counsel or direction from someone?

IV. PRACTICAL PASTORAL SKILLS

To preach a sermon, I think, is not the hardest part; and yet what skill is necessary to make the truth plain; to convince the hearers, to let irresistible light in to their consciences, and to keep it there, and drive all home; to screw the truth into their minds, and work Christ into their affections; to meet every objection, and clearly to resolve it; to drive sinners to a stand, and make them see that there is no hope, but that they must unavoidably either be converted or condemned—and to do all this, as regards language and manner, as beseems our work, and yet as is most suitable to the capacities of our hearers. This, and a great deal more that should be done in every sermon, must surely require a great deal of holy skill. So great a God, whose message we deliver, should be honored by our delivery of it.

—Richard Baxter, *Reformed Pastor*[14]

In his sermons too he should prefer to please with the substance of what he says more than with the words he says it in; nor should he imagine that a thing is said better unless it is said more truly; and as a teacher his words should be serving him, not he his words.

—Augustine, *On Teaching Christianity*[15]

Questions for Consideration[16]

1. What areas of my ministry will I be able to cultivate in this church at this time: preaching, teaching, recruiting, leading worship and liturgy, teaching children, pastoral care, social and community care?

2. Are there new areas of ministry that I need to attempt or areas where I need to gain experience? Church administration?

Pastoral counseling? Evangelism? Event planning? Biblical study and exposition? Grief care?

3. How do I work with others on a team? Am I willing to release others to do ministry, even if I might be more able or better equipped to do it?

4. Where are my skills being tested? Where do they need to be stretched? Do I fear them being challenged?

5. How do I respond to failure or success in ministry? Can I hear criticism and praise?

6. Baxter challenges us to "screw the truth" into people's minds and "work Christ into their affections," and both "as is most suitable" to our hearers. In which of these am I stronger, and in which weaker? Do I maintain a balance between the cognitive and the affective?

CHAPTER 7

MENTORING FOR PASTORAL FORMATION IN SCRIPTURE

When we turn into the pages of Scripture, that sanctified human work of wisdom and witness to God, what do we find? Among the stories of creation, exodus, conquest, exile, the coming of Christ, the descending of the Spirit, and the birth of the church, do we find anything that reinforces or illuminates mentoring for pastoral formation? Though "mentoring" carries particularly modern connotations, both negative and positive, Scripture does in fact offer us a number of relationships that we may legitimately describe as types of mentoring. These pictures, however brief, primarily reinforce the necessity of preparation for ministry and the importance of doing so in a very personal way.

In the following few pages, we will glance at the relationships of Moses and Joshua, Elijah and Elisha, Jesus with the apostles, and Paul with Timothy and Titus in order to consider them from the perspective of mentoring for leadership and ministry. Though the details are characteristically sparse and we should be cautious about arguing for a "biblical" mandate for mentoring, these stories unmistakably emphasize the immediacy of the personal relationships between individuals in the midst of joint service to God and his people.

What follows is by no means "exegesis," but rather a series of brief pictures of persons prepared for ministry by a "mentor" of some sort that have been given to us in the pages of Scripture. References to the biblical citations are included for your own reading and further reflection.

MOSES AND JOSHUA

Exodus 24:13, 33:11; Numbers 11:28; Joshua 1:1, 5:24, 24:29

Central to the spiritual formation and religious education of any Hebrew child was the family. Central to Hebrew faith is the *Torah*. Rather than a set of rules legislated by a cosmic lawgiver, this covenant-law is a way of life to follow that, as Joseph Grassi affirms, "had to be learned through the close association with a teacher . . . The first and most important place this came about was in the heart of the Jewish family. Any further instruction was considered an extension and continuation of what was begun at home."[1] The home was the initial arena in which theological instruction would take place, and this would have been the primary source of Joshua's spiritual, moral, and theological formation in the years prior to his service to and alongside Moses.

Exodus 33:7–11 refers to Joshua as Moses's ever-present aide who, as we see from Numbers 11:28, had been with Moses from his youth. Joshua not only accompanied Moses during the execution of his legislative and judicial tasks, but was also with him in the Tent of Meeting, when Moses spoke with the LORD face to face. When Joshua became the spiritual and political leader of Israel upon Moses's death, Deuteronomy 34 indicates that he was "full of the spirit of wisdom, for Moses had laid his hands on him." However, it is clear that Joshua's preparation for leadership did not occur only at that moment of the Spirit's quickening, but was the result of years of close personal companionship with and the exercise of leadership under Moses.

ELIJAH AND ELISHA

1 Kings 19:19ff; 2 Kings 2–6.

The role of the prophet in Israel was largely to call the people back to the covenant faithfulness that they had abandoned when they went whoring after other more attractive gods and goddesses. The prophet was often that unwelcome gadfly who proclaimed the LORD's holiness and his displeasure with rulers, priests, and people who had long despised and neglected him. Their activity included not only the sharp use of their tongue, but also the sharp end of the sword to preserve the LORD's holiness. Likewise, the prophet often represented the lament of the people to the LORD in the midst of their suffering, giving verbal and physical expression to their plight. Consider Moses, Samuel, Elijah, Isaiah, Jeremiah, Amos, Hosea—to speak for the Holy One of Israel to an unholy people was a weighty vocation. For this vocation it seems that some were prepared not only by the immediate presence of the Spirit, but often through their extended companionship with another prophet or a school of prophets.

This is obviously the case of Elijah and Elisha—from the enigmatic call of Elisha by Elijah in 1 Kings 19 to the dramatic departure of Elijah in 2 Kings 2 and his authorizing of Elisha to take his place, symbolized in both instances by the giving of Elijah's cloak. This cloak or "mantle" was a physical sign of the office of Prophet, a vocation that required a singular focus. The LORD had directed Elijah to anoint Elisha, and when he threw his cloak over Elisha's shoulders, Elisha immediately left his previous labors and his family to travel at Elijah's side, assisting in the last years of Elijah's life and ministry. We can imagine that Elisha was often on the run with his master and teacher, watching, listening, and learning from him. He was a faithful pupil and servant who

183

eventually was to receive from God a double portion of his master's spirit, and to become God's new mouthpiece to the kings and people of Israel. Likewise it seems that both Elijah and Elisha were involved in the teaching and training of other men, called the "sons of the prophets," mentioned in 2 Kings 2–6, whose role is unknown. What is clear is that Elisha was not called to take up the prophet's mantle without having been trained and mentored for that role by his zealous and tempestuous predecessor.

JESUS AND HIS DISCIPLES

Matthew 4:18ff; 8:19–22; 16; 28:18–20; Mk 1:16ff; 14:18–42; 16:14–20; Luke 5:10; 6:12ff; 9:22ff; 24:49; John 1:37ff; 12:25—26; 13:3–20; 14–16; 17:18.

It would be an impossible and rather foolhardy task to attempt to describe and define the totality of Christ's relation as teacher, mentor, friend, and saviour to those twelve men who were to become the foundation of the New Israel around him, the teachers and leaders of the church. However, we would also be remiss to neglect what we do know about their time together and about Christ's diligent attention to their formation and preparation for ministry during the three years that they travelled with him, ministered alongside him, learned from him, and were instructed and at times rebuked by him. Though obviously their relationship was unique in that the Spirit of Christ descended upon them at Pentecost, we should not fail to consider his ways of being with them as their rabbi.

As was his custom, Jesus spent all night in prayer before he chose from among all his disciples the twelve who would accompany him. Jesus lived his life in utter dependence upon the Spirit and in continual communion with God. If the Son of God so depended on the Spirit for his ministry, so also ought we in our roles as mentor and mentee, trusting the Spirit to sustain us and to grant us words and wisdom.

Jesus called and invited and, largely without hesitation, the disciples followed. They were instructed to forsake their old ways of living in order to embark on a radical new way of life.

Though Jesus taught great multitudes at times, he invested the majority of his time in but a few people rather than a host. He drew to him a small cluster of rather motley and indistinguishable individuals and taught them in close proximity. Through the direct experience of seeing Christ at work through words and actions, the disciples were being prepared for the ministry that they would have once their teacher had departed.

Jesus' role as teacher and mentor was marked by humble service—that divine humility that is as characteristic of God as his thundering power. This humility determined the character of his apostles and the church, which emerged from the disciples' witness. If the pastoral mentor learns this ready willingness to wash feet from the character of the Lord, the mentee will learn it from both of them and in turn wash the feet of those to whom he or she ministers in the future.

PAUL, TIMOTHY, AND TITUS

2 Corinthians 7 & 8; 1 & 2 Timothy; Titus

Paul was immensely concerned with equipping people practically, morally, and spiritually to serve Christ, and involved in supporting, encouraging, and challenging those already involved in ministry. He exhorted them, offered them wise counsel, and entrusted them to carry on ministry apart from his direct supervision. As we previously mentioned, Paul also often called upon scores of individuals and churches to encourage and to care for those set aside for service in the church. Though he was the primary teacher and mentor to many, he, of all pastors, knew the importance of the myriad gifts given to particular members of Christ's body, and was not hesitant to call upon them. These various traits and practices are readily discernible in Paul's relationship with two particular young men, Timothy and Titus.

Timothy was Paul's long-serving assistant, who received training for his ministry by accompanying his teacher in evangelism and church planting. He was also Paul's "beloved son," whom Paul was nurturing and encouraging toward maturity in faith and ministry. As we saw earlier, Paul rather strongly exhorted Timothy to diligently fan into flame the *charismata* that he had received as a gift from God through the laying on of Paul's hands, lest it cool and die out. The importance of Timothy's close friendship with Paul for his own preparation and formation cannot be overstated.

Paul commends Timothy to other churches, lists Timothy as a co-author of some of his letters, and implores Timothy to carry on the mission of establishing the church in his absence. In 2 Timothy 4, we read of Paul's charge to Timothy to preach the word. Paul's ministry was coming to an end and Timothy was entrusted, as a son, to "fight the good fight and finish the race."

Titus, like Timothy, was commended as being a "co-worker" (2 Cor 8:23), Paul's "true child in a common faith."

The letter written to Titus is immensely practical and encouraging. It does appear that Titus is experiencing problems within his church community and it is through the authority of Paul that he is better equipped to maintain order and discipline.

Paul, while affording Titus the room to minister as he saw fit, gently directed and guided Titus through the difficulties he was experiencing. This suggests that despite commissioning his 'co-workers' for works of service, his teaching, direction, or mentoring in their lives continued. In many ways, 1 and 2 Timothy and Titus are mentor letters: words of experience, wise counsel, sound direction, and godly exhortation from an older pastor to younger pastors.

SUMMARY

In summary then, what lessons can we learn from each of these examples that can be practically applied in mentoring for pastoral formation?

First, in spite of the sketched nature of these relationships between mentor/teacher and mentee/student, the depth and immediacy of the relationships are obvious. Attending to the spiritual, emotional, moral, and theological life of the pastor is fundamental in preparing and being prepared for ministry, whatever it may be. Second, both mentor and mentee were immersed in practical ministry together. Rather than simply observing the mentor at work, each mentee ministered and worked alongside his or her teacher. Third, each relationship began with an invitation. Only when they humbly chose to forsake their old ways of life in favor of a radically different and uncertain life were the mentees in a place where they could be prepared, shaped, and molded for their impending ministry. This required a commitment of their whole person to their vocation. Finally, each person recognized the divine calling of the other and saw the other as a servant called to minister to God's people, responding and ultimately responsible to God alone.

CHAPTER 8

MENTORING FOR PASTORAL FORMATION IN THE CHURCH

Even our brief reflection on these biblical examples reveals that the people of God have always engaged in some form of mentoring for the formation and preparation of godly servant-leaders for the community. Thus those who continue this practice in the church take their place in a very long and old tradition. From Israel and the early church, we now turn to consider a cross-section of pastoral mentors from the history of the later church: Augustine in fourth- and fifth-century Africa, Catherine of Siena in twelfth-century Italy, John Newton in eighteenth-century England, Dietrich Bonhoeffer in twentieth-century Germany, and Karl Barth and Eduard Thurneysen in twentieth-century Switzerland and Germany. Our hope is that the experiences and reflections of these fellow pastors may open up space into which today's mentors and mentees may step, joining in the ongoing conversation about acts of ministry and how to prepare to serve God's church.

We shall see that this tradition of education and preparation was perpetuated in various ways through diverse times. Though each individual maintained a unique emphasis and perspective, they share a remarkable congruence in both their thought and practice concerning what is required for pastoral ministry. And would we expect otherwise from a people shaped by a personal God who calls them into love and fellowship—a people who in their corporate and their intimate relations are a foreshadowing of the heavenly community toward which we hasten? We, too, are part of this community and listen to those who have gone this way before us.

This is the glory of the communion of the saints, the great diverse cloud of witnesses that beckons us to learn from their historically embodied attempts to live from and to the truth.

One Spirit has drawn us into their train and has given them to us so that we might listen and learn. The Spirit utterly disregards our modern nearsighted prejudice that disdains to look behind the productions of the demanding present. The confusion of the passage of time with progress, which assumes that the more modern we are the more advanced we must be, is a most flattering but arrogant mistake. It hinders us in the formation of wisdom because it casts us back upon our own limited resources. As the theologian Thomas Oden argues, when we turn to study the best practitioners of pastoral ministry and pastoral formation and education, the effectiveness of our own practice is greatly improved. "The best preparation for pastoral service," he suggests, "may be more like an apprenticeship to an excellent sculptor, or a medical internship, than academic study in a university." When we turn to try to think the thoughts and hear the stories of the following fellow pastors, we open ourselves to be apprenticed by them in the way of pastoral ministry and pastoral mentoring.

At the end of each historical vignette, we offer a few leading questions that the mentor and mentee may choose to discuss together or reflect upon alone. As you read the following pages, be alert to the overlapping concerns and common practices that mark these six pastoral mentors as a people of God who share in the one

Spirit of God, and consider how you might adopt and embody the same in your own time, place, and culture.

The Humble Service of Love: Augustine

First and foremost, I beg your wise holiness to consider that there is nothing in this life, and especially in our own day, more easy and pleasant and acceptable to men than the office of bishop or priest or deacon, if its duties be discharged in a mechanical or sycophantic way; but nothing more worthless and deplorable and meet for chastisement in the sight of God; and on the other hand, that there is nothing in this life and especially in our own day, more difficult, toilsome, and hazardous than the office of bishop, priest, or deacon; but nothing more blessed in the sight of God, if our service be in accordance with our captain's orders.[1] Augustine, to his bishop, upon his ordination, 391

The Augustine with whom we are most likely familiar is Augustine the theologian, author of the *Confessions*, *The City of God*, and *On the Trinity*—the Augustine seated at his desk with parchment and pen whose original and fertile mind produced scores of other philosophical and theological works that significantly shaped the Middle Ages and the Reformation and continue to shape theological and cultural discussions today. This is Augustine the defender of Christian orthodoxy against theological heresies and pagan calumnies. The Augustine with whom we are less familiar is Augustine the pastor and pastoral mentor.

Born in 354 in northern Africa to a Christian mother and an unbelieving father, he turned away from the Christian faith due to its high moral rigors, its low intellectual credibility, and its lack of philosophical refinement. He turned instead to sensual indulgence, ambitious careerism, and neo-Platonic philosophy in a search for certain truth. Eventually, through the prayers of his mother, the influence of Ambrose of Milan, and a "chance" reading of Romans, his defenses were broken and, as he says, God converted him to Himself in 386. Death came to him in 430, as Vandal hordes swept across North Africa and into his city during the waning days of the Roman Empire.

Our immediate interest in Augustine, however, begins in 391, when he traveled to the coastal town of Hippo Regius in Numidia, intent on persuading a friend to join the fledgling semi-monastic community he had just established in his hometown of Thagaste. Though a Christian only a scant five years, Augustine's reputation as an apologist and theologian had grown so considerably that he began avoiding towns with vacant bishoprics from fear he would be compelled into public service and forced to give up his private life of study and community. Hippo posed no perceivable threat, for its bishop was secure. However, unbeknownst to Augustine, the Greek bishop of Hippo, Valerius, was finding his ministry sorely pressed and was actively looking for someone to assist him. His halting knowledge of the local Latin dialect made communication difficult, and the Catholics of Hippo were a minority regularly harassed by Donatists and Manichees.[2] Knowing Augustine's reputation and spying him in his congregation one Sunday, Valerius spoke urgently during the sermon of his need for a worthy assistant. He concluded by asking his congregation to help him find such a person. Conveniently, the people discovered Augustine in their midst, to Valerius's delight and to Augustine's dismay. So with the usual clamor and shouting that attended one of these forced ordinations, they pushed him forward to the bishop, and Valerius conscripted Augustine into service and ordained him a priest on the spot.

Augustine, unable and unwilling to flee like many others forced into ordination, was, however, greatly alarmed. As he describes it, he felt like a novice seaman thrust to the helm of the ship before he had even learned to handle an oar. In his ordination, however, he felt a graced judgment, a divine chastisement for his hasty and arrogant derision of other priests, for criticizing "the faults of many sailors before I had learned by experience the nature of their work." The Lord, he says, laughed at his rash over-confidence and "was pleased to show me by actual experience what I am."

In preparation for the awesome responsibility of his unexpected calling, he implored Valerius to allow him time to examine the Scriptures—not, as we might imagine, to explore exegetical or theological matters of doctrine. These he knew and believed. The overwhelming concern of this great doctor of the faith was a practical one: "How am I to use this truth in ministering to the salvation of others, seeking what is profitable not for myself alone, but for many, that they may be saved?" Anticipating Valerius's skepticism at his request, he pleaded,

> what shall I answer to the Lord my Judge? Shall I say, "I was not able to acquire the things of which I stood in need, because I was engrossed wholly with the affairs of the Church"? . . . or "the aged Valerius is to blame; for, believing me to be instructed in all things necessary, he declined, with a determination proportionate to his love for me, to give me permission to learn what I had not acquired"?

And how can these things be known, he asks, "except, as the Lord Himself tells us, by asking, seeking, knocking, that is, by praying, reading, and weeping?"[3] Valerius did grant him six months leave, but his experience of being suddenly thrust into pastoral ministry sensitized Augustine to the great need of the church to adequately prepare and care for the ongoing formation of those it called into its service. He doubted that the experience of feeling overwhelmed by the daunting responsibility of ministry and administering the truth to others was his alone.

AUGUSTINE THE URBAN BISHOP

Like scores of theologians after him, Augustine was bishop and shepherd before anything else. He had been charged with the spiritual well-being of his local congregation in Hippo and with the intellectual preparation and spiritual formation of those who would come alongside him in ministry. His vocation was preacher and pastor first, theologian second; or rather, theologian because he was preacher and pastor. This is Augustine the letter writer, preacher, social activist, legal reformer, and mentoring pastor. Many of these roles are less well known because they have as much to do with the localized culture of fifth-century north Africa as they do with the "timeless truths" of Christian theology. Thus, the medieval scribes turned to copy his letters and sermons much less frequently than his other works. As bishop of a large Roman, and largely pagan, port city, however, Augustine was embroiled in the immediate social affairs and ministry of his church.

For instance, the elderly Augustine led the faithful of his city in vigorous protest against the rampant slave trade enjoying free reign on the coast of Africa. The local authorities colluded with the slave-traders to give them safe passage to transport kidnapped African peasants and Roman citizens to serve as slaves on estates in Italy and Southern Gaul. When they passed through their port city, Augustine and the congregations of Hippo worked vigorously to gain the release of many of these slaves. Some they ransomed with money, and some they freed against the wishes of their captors. On one occasion the parishioners of Hippo raided a slave ship and freed 120 slaves from captivity. In turn, the powerful protectors of the slave trade sued Augustine and his church for damages. Undaunted, Augustine not only preached against slavery as an unnatural perversion of the created order of human equity, he also sought to reform Roman law. He studied law texts, consulted lawyers, made legal appeals to governors, and was determined to make his case to the Emperor. Through his friend and fellow-bishop, Alypius, Augustine appealed to the courts in Rome on several occasions.

Likewise, Augustine lobbied against the use of the death penalty, the excessive torture of prisoners and criminals, unjust imprisonments, criminal warmaking, the exploitation of tenant farmers, and, surprising to some, against the inequitable legal treatment of women in marriage and society.[4] His church attempted to rescue children abandoned to die, taking them in as wards until married or able to support themselves. The church at Hippo also heard their bishop's constant exhortation to comfort their "fellow poor and needy" by providing food and clothing.[5] His biographer and friend, Possidius, records that Augustine would often sell church property or melt down vessels of the church in order to raise money to ransom captives or care for the needy.[6] Along with these affairs, his time was consumed with the usual ecclesial demands of preaching, traveling, providing spiritual counsel, and, albeit reluctantly, directing the financial and administrative affairs of his large urban church. Despite these many demands on his time, to which he frequently refers,[7] near the heart of his role as bishop was life in community for the sake of mutual encouragement and formation for ministry.

BISHOP AND CLERGY IN COMMUNITY

Upon his surprise ordination in 391, Augustine immediately set about drawing together a loosely organized monastic community of like-minded friends and young priests for the sake of common study and worship. He had already established two other such communities, but without the focus of public ministry. The fatherly Valerius recognized that Augustine needed learned conversation with others to develop and refine his thoughts, and needed shared prayer and devotion to strengthen and sustain his spirit. So he granted Augustine's wish to form a new community in the houses of the church's garden courtyard. Augustine thought it proper to call his community a "monastery," though the word, which comes from *monos*, would in his community no longer refer to individual solitude, but instead to a oneness of heart and mind in love and service of God.[8] As God is love in himself, so because we live in God through the Spirit, we are enabled to love one another. Eventually, Augustine's new form of "monastery" included laity and priests, educated and illiterate, freed slaves and aristocrats, elderly men and young boys.

Despite his powerful intellect and personality, this influential church father desired to direct the devotion of these individuals solely to God rather than to himself.[9] To receive that devotion is a powerful temptation to every ecclesial leader or mentor. Augustine was determined to release to God in heart and mind those entrusted to his care so that they could think and pray for themselves.

> We who preach and write books, we write in a manner altogether different from the manner in which the canon of the Scriptures has been written. We write while we make progress. We learn something new every day. We dictate at the same time as we explore. We speak as we still knock for understanding . . . If anyone criticizes me when I have said what is right, he does me an injustice. But I would be more angry with the one who praises me and takes what I have written for Gospel truth (*canonicum*) than I would be with the one who criticizes me unfairly.[10]

His biographer, Possidius, noted that Augustine's "disinterested interest" in these many persons led to no less than ten bishops and numerous priests coming from his community prepared to serve the church. After Valerius died and Augustine became sole bishop of Hippo, he invited the clergy of his diocese to live in community with him in the bishop's residence—a first in the African church. Frederic Van der Meer, in his book on Augustine as bishop, explains, "Augustine recognized that he could render no greater service to the Church in his part of the world" than to prepare new priests for service, "largely educated under his supervision, in his own house, and largely by his own efforts, for there was obviously quite a shortage of priests" with adequate intellectual education, practical training, and spiritual formation.[11] Remembering his own want of preparation and direction, he attempted through daily discourse, sermons, texts, and letters to mentor those given to him by God for their salvation and their preparation for service to the church. Augustine's model was imitated throughout northern Africa and by several of his friends and disciples—Alypius at Thagaste, Possidius at Calama, Fortunatus at Cirta, Evodius at Uzalis, and Boniface at Carthage. It provided—and we may say continues to provide, as Van der Meer concludes, "an excellent atmosphere for training candidates for the priesthood."[12]

ON CHRISTIAN FRIENDSHIP

Augustine inherited from the classical world its hallowed respect for friendship, immortalized in Cicero's *On Friendship.* The opening chapters of the *Confessions,* in fact, are filled with descriptions of his passionate, and at times idolatrous, devotion to the friends of his youth. Augustine's mature and "baptized" understanding of friendship, however, differed from that of the classical world: only after his love and desire had been reordered toward God first did love for his friends find its proper place, and did he begin to turn not to Cicero, but to the description of the common life of the early church in Acts 4.

First, Augustine declares that true friendship is authored by God. In his *Confessions,* he prays, "There is no true friendship unless You weld it between souls that cleave together through that charity which is shed in our hearts by the Holy Ghost who is given to us."[13] Commenting on this prayer, Sister Marie McNamara suggests that for Augustine, "the only true friendship is that sent by God to those who love each other in Him. He considers it a gift of God like chastity, patience, charity, and all the virtues. It is God alone who can join two persons to each other."[14]

197

Second, only through Christ can a friendship endure: "No friendship is faithful except in Christ; in Him alone can it be happy and eternal." In him alone are friends turned toward each other, able to meet each other in free and frank exchange. "Let us resolve to maintain between ourselves," Augustine wrote in one of his many letters to Jerome, "the liberty as well as the charity of friendship, so that in the letters which we exchange, neither of us shall be restrained from frankly stating to the other whatever troubles us."

Third, friendship must be based on a true knowledge of the other person's strengths and weaknesses. Otherwise, the relationship exists only between two phantom figures, and neither is truly known. "I take no pleasure in being thought by my dearest friends to be such as I am not. Obviously they do not love me, but another in my name, if they love, not what I am, but what I am not."[15] Correlative is a sane and humble assessment of one's own ignorance and need. Replying to one of his student-priests who came with numerous liturgical questions, Augustine readily admitted, "there are innumerable things of which I am ignorant, and even in the Holy Scriptures themselves, my ignorance is greater than my knowledge."[16] This latter recognition prompted him to declare to Jerome that not only was he ready and willing to receive in a brotherly spirit any contrary opinion or interpretation of Jerome's, but he asked and insisted that Jerome offer it out of love.[17] To another correspondent he argued, "No age is too advanced to learn what needs learning, because, although it is more fitting for old men to teach than to learn, it is even more fitting to learn what they teach rather than to remain ignorant."[18]

Fourth, Augustine could not see how a true and deeply mutual friendship could be maintained between a believer and an unbeliever:[19] "it necessarily follows that he who despises things divine esteems things human otherwise than as he should and that whoever does not love Him who has made men has not learned to love men rightly."[20] Instead, friendship requires that each desires the other's spiritual well being: "To love the neighbor in the right way demands that we act towards them in such a way that they come to love God with all their heart, soul, and mind."[21]

Fraternal charity, in fact, rather than prayer or study, was the first rule Augustine established to guide those living in community, co-inhabited by the same Spirit. This was the heart of the Christian life and was indispensable for attaining wisdom. In daily intercourse, charity of this sort refused the mutual self-indulgence of easy tolerance; instead it led to the gracious practice of loving correction. "Love mingled with severity is better than deceit with indulgence," Augustine wrote to an erring friend. The true good of the other must be the sole criterion. At their common meals, however, he insisted that the character of an absent cleric should never be touched. On the common table he had engraved: *Quisguis amat dictis absentum rodere vitam, Hanc mensam vetitam noverit esse sibi*—"Whoever loves to peck at the life of the absent, will himself be prohibited from becoming familiar with this table."

Fifth, one of the chief aids of friendship that Augustine commonly referred to was the mutual sharing of sorrow and struggle:

> If poverty pinches, if grief saddens, if physical pain unnerves us, if exile darkens our lives, if any other misfortune fills us with foreboding, let good people be present to us, people who know how to "rejoice with those who rejoice" as well as to "weep with those who weep" (Rom. 12:15), people who are skilled in helpful words and banter. If such people are with us then in large measure our bitter trials become less bitter, the heavy burdens become lighter, perceived obstacles are faced and overcome. But He who makes them good by His Spirit effects this in and through them.[22]

True friendships are a divine gift; therefore, the comfort and solace found through the physical presence and words of friends are no less than the effects of God's grace coming through those he has given us:

> I confess that upon the love of such friends I readily cast myself without reservation, especially when chafed and wearied by the scandals of this world; and in their love I rest without any disturbing care; for I perceive that God is there, on whom I confidingly cast myself, and in whom I confidingly rest . . . "for God is love, and he that abides in love, abides in God."[23]

AUGUSTINE'S PRACTICE OF MENTORING FOR PASTORAL FORMATION

Augustine penned hundreds of carefully composed letters, responding to nearly everyone who wrote. Some came with substantial theological questions, some wanted to impress the illustrious scholar, some brought trenchant criticism, and some a simple inquiry about religious matters mundane and eccentric. To Possidius he admitted being overwhelmed by the correspondence that came "unannounced from here, there, and everywhere." He corresponded with contemporary luminaries such as Jerome, Pope Boniface, Cyril of Alexandria, Atticus of Constantinople, and also with cantankerous country parishioners, recent converts, and with many other priests and bishops devoted to the faithful execution of their pastoral ministries. His motivation to carry on this unflagging epistolary mentoring was chiefly his love for the church and secondarily his love for the individual pastor, as his response to the priest Deogratias reveals:

> If . . . the Lord requires me to offer any manner of aid to those whom He has made brethren to me, I feel constrained not only by that love and service which is due from me to you on the terms of familiar friendship, but also by that which I owe universally to our mother the Church, by no means to refuse the task, but rather to take it up with a prompt and devoted willingness. For the more extensively I desire to see the treasure

of the Lord distributed, the more does it become my duty, if I ascertain that the stewards, who are my fellow-servants, find any difficulty in laying it out, to do all that lies in my power to the end that they may be able to accomplish easily and expeditiously what they sedulously and earnestly aim at.[24]

Chief among his correspondents were those many priests and bishops who had been called out from his community in Hippo. The letters that passed between them were extensions of the conversations and discussions that had begun when they enjoyed the immediate proximity of each other's company. By glancing into them, we are able to listen in on a conversation between pastoral mentor and mentored pastor. Each letter was the result of Augustine's theological reflection and deliberation upon the immediate pastoral and ecclesial concerns of the clergy. As a fellow priest and bishop, he shared with them the responsibilities and pressures of the pastoral office. Though his letters differ in content, style, and tone, depending on the personality, intellectual acumen, and particular need of the recipient, each is marked by the profound love and humility that characterized his ministry to the church and clerical community of Hippo.

> Love is in labor with some, becomes weak with others; strives to edify some, dreads to be a cause of offense to others; stoops to some, before others stands with head erect; is gentle to some and stern to others; an enemy to none, a mother to all.[25]

To the priest Januarius's inquiry about the variety of liturgical practices between churches, Augustine recalled the counsel he and his mother, Monica, had received from Bishop Ambrose concerning the same question: follow the custom of the local church. If a particular variance in custom or observation addressed a real spiritual need in the church, induced holiness and true devotion, and was not contrary to faith or Christian morality, it should be accepted, supported, and celebrated.[26]

201

To the deacon Deogratias of Carthage, Augustine offered lengthy counsel on teaching basic doctrinal catechesis: what to teach and how to teach it. Deogratias had confessed what every teacher has felt: he found the precise articulation of doctrine difficult and that it often became "profitless and distasteful" to himself, let alone to his hearers, during "the course of a lengthened and languid address."

To Castorius, struggling with the decision to enter ministry, Augustine and his lifelong friend Alypius, urged him to receive ordination and "devote to Christ" his "talents, prudence, eloquence, gravity, self-control, and everything else which adorns your conversation . . . To what service can they be more fittingly devoted," they continued, "than to His by whom they were bestowed, in order that they may be preserved, increased, perfected, and rewarded by Him?"[27]

To Bishop Evodius of Uzala, a former member of his community, and the friend who comforted him at his mother's death, Augustine urged restraint of his impatient and impetuous nature, which regularly caught him in trouble with his people and fellow priests. Augustine only barely hid his exasperation at Evodius's urgent and demanding requests, but while his reproaches were justifiably stern at times, they were still shaped by his concern for this "beloved friend": "While I have been dictating this letter to you, I have had a mental picture of you, though you are far away and unaware of it, and, according to my interior knowledge of you, I have imagined how you would be affected by these words." [28]

To one former member of his monastery, Bishop Paul of Cataquas, Augustine delivered a severe reprimand for his embezzlement of church funds and tax evasion, reminding him that the ministry was not a way to self-indulgent ease. The hurt he had caused could not be remedied "unless the Lord sets you free from all your worldly cares and calls you back to the true life and diet of a bishop."[29]

To Bishop Auxilius, a young and inexperienced bishop who had rashly driven from the church a local family, he wrote that though he by no means despised Auxilius's youth or inexperience and, though old, was in fact ready to learn from one so young, he did not see that Auxilius's action could be justified according to Scripture. So Augustine encouraged him to cancel his harsh sentence so that mutual love and peace might be restored. "Think not," he wrote, "that, because we are bishops, it is impossible for unjust passionate resentment to gain secretly upon us."[30]

To Bishop Honoratus's urgently practical question of whether he and the other clerics should flee the Vandal invasion of his city of Thiave in 428, Augustine replied that while an individually pursued clergy may flee, like Paul or Athanasius, "when the danger is common to all, that is, to bishops, clerics and laity, those who depend upon others are not to be forsaken by those on whom they depend"—in other words, no, they should not flee, because those who could not flee needed their ministry.[31] The small coterie of God's people needed the pastoral ministry of Word and sacrament, which was so necessary "in a time of such peril."

To his close friends—Aurelius, the influential Bishop of Carthage, and Alypius, Bishop of Thagaste—he gave counsel with the frankness that is the privilege of friendship concerning the necessary cessation of the all too common drunken revelries taking place at the tombs of martyrs on feast days.[32] At another time, Augustine and Alypius together heaped lavish praise upon Aurelius, now archbishop and the veritable leader of the African church, for his pastorally beneficial and personally humble decision to allow priests and presbyters to preach regularly to congregations in northern Africa, even if the bishop was present. Augustine saw the obvious benefits of this innovation both for the people and for the priests, "through whose tongues thus engaged your love sounds louder in the hearts than even their voice does in the ears of men." His joy and respect broke like a deluge upon Aurelius:

Thanks be unto God, who has endowed you with a heart so true to the interests of your sons, and who has brought to light what you had latent in the inner soul, beyond the reach of human eye, giving you not only the will to do good, but the means of realizing your desires. So be it, certainly so be it! Let these works shine before men, that they may see them, and rejoice and glorify your Father in heaven.[33]

Not only did it allow priests the beneficence of preaching, but Aurelius's act of trusting others with ministry thrust before the priests an example of humble service: "Let the stronger lead; let the weaker imitate their example, being followers of them, as they are of Christ."[34]

With his lifelong friend, Alypius, who was present with him at his conversion and baptized with him by Ambrose, Augustine was in constant conversation regarding the practice of ministry. The two studied, prayed, and lived together in each of Augustine's communities, until Alypius was called to serve as bishop of their home town. Whereas Alypius relied on Augustine for clearer and deeper insight into the understanding of spiritual and theological mysteries, Augustine relied on the many practical talents and devout example of Alypius: "You [Alypius] have no difficulty in following these rules of conduct. You have eagerly put them into practice with such wholeheartedness that if I am your master by my words, you have become mine by your example."[35]

To Bishop Possidius, another student from the clerical community at Hippo, whose love for the church Augustine deeply respected, Augustine offered encouragement and counsel regarding Possidius's debates with the aggressive Donatist bishop in his city, and his struggle with the pagan civil officials.[36] When Possidius was troubled by women in his own congregation, who continued to wear pagan amulets after their conversion, Augustine wisely counseled him not to respond too hastily: "It requires more consideration to decide what to do with those who refuse to obey you, than to discover how to show them that things which they do are unlawful."[37] Possidius eventually wrote the biography of Augustine, at the end of which he asked his readers to pray that he might "strive to imitate a man with whom God gave me the happiness to live in friendship for forty years."

AUGUSTINE , THE PASTORAL MENTEE

Augustine not only helped to clarify the pastoral identity of others, but we can also see how his own pastoral ministry as priest and bishop was decisively influenced by the character of the elderly bishop, Valerius, whom he worked alongside for five years. In his relationship with Augustine, Valerius modeled many essential characteristics of the pastor-mentor. He recognized Augustine's obvious abilities and unique interests. He took measures to see Augustine ordained and offered him opportunities unheard of among priests in the West, allowing him to preach even when the bishop was present in his own diocese.[38] Knowing his desire to live in community, Valerius granted him the garden enclosure of the main church for his monastery. He bent the custom of the church again and had Augustine elected co-bishop with him in 395.[39] Valerius not only drafted Augustine into the service to the church, but, as we see, freed him to flourish as pastor, theologian, and educator.

Most significantly, he modeled for Augustine the character of a humble leader and impressed upon Augustine the need for him to become the same. Any incumbent bishop or minister might justifiably feel threatened by a successor with the mind and heart of Augustine, or become jealous of the acclaim that Augustine received, for he was constantly being invited to preach and speak in cities across north Africa, and to deliver essays on theological and ecclesial matters. As Bishop Paulinus of Nola reported, there was a great celebration at Augustine's ordination, because "the Lord now had a powerful trumpet through whom he could play."[40] Bishop Valerius, however, "a man of moderation and mildness, of prudence and vigilance in the Lord," as Augustine described him, felt no envy, it seems, but rejoiced in Augustine's ministry. Possidius recalled that as Augustine's reputation and influence increased, "the blessed Valerius rejoiced more than all the others and thanked God for having accorded him such a favor." Valerius's humility, his disdain for personal acclaim, and his service borne by love of the church profoundly marked Augustine's practice of pastoral ministry.

PASTORAL HUMILITY

In Augustine's letters, his own desire for humility became a constant theme. Likewise, when he described pastoral ministry, his constant themes were humility, service, and love. How could it be otherwise, he exclaimed, when we are called to active imitation of Christ, who let go of equality with God and became man to die in service of the church? In conscious imitation of Christ, therefore, he rejected honors, status, and privilege, and constantly exhorted his fellow priests and bishops to do the same. He praised particular bishops who had stepped down from their positions when it seemed necessary to do so in order to advance the unity and peace of the church, bishops who had not regarded their rank something to be grasped at the expense of the gospel.

At the consecration of a new bishop, Augustine charged:

> He who is head and leader of the people must first of all realize that he is the servant of many. And do not disdain to be the servant of many; do not, I repeat, disdain to be the servant of many, seeing that the Lord of Lords did not disdain to make himself our servant.[41]

To the people present on that day he explained:

> Here, then, is the sum of the matter: we are your servants and your fellow-servants at once. We are your servants, but we all have one single Lord; we are your servants, but in Jesus . . . We are servants of his Church and most especially of the weakest members, whatever be our position as members of that same Body.[42]

This humility the pagan philosophers did not know and could never know, according to Augustine, because they did not know Christ. Whereas they arrogantly "wear the actor's high boots of a supposedly more sublime philosophy," bishop and priest are but ministers and servants, those who feed the flock with food drawn from a storeroom not their own. To one haughty young Ciceronian scholar who hoped to impress and receive an endorsement from the bishop, Augustine patiently responded:

> Construct no other way for yourself of grasping and holding the truth than the way constructed by Him, who as God, saw how faltering were our steps. This way is first humility, second humility, third humility. And however often you should ask me I would say the same, not because there are no other precepts to be explained, but, if humility does not precede and accompany and follow every good word we do, and if it is not set before us to look upon, and beside us to lean upon, and behind us to fence us in, pride will wrest from our hand any good we do while we are in the very act of taking pleasure in it.[43]

To numerous priests and bishops and in numerous sermons, Augustine emphasized that in order to balance the tremendous temptation to pride that came with the office of priest or bishop, and in order to follow the example of Christ, whose ministry they mediated, pastoral ministry must be marked by humility and service. What he taught and modeled to his monastic clerics he preached to his congregation: "But we, who are we? His ministers, his servants."[44]

This is one of the first lessons to be learned. The pastor, he insisted, is first, with his fellow believers, under the tutelage of Scripture and the one Master, Jesus Christ.[45] Preaching at the consecration of another bishop, this time in Carthage, Augustine testified, "We are chiefs and leaders, and we are servants, we are at your head, but only if we are at your side." To his own church, he declared, "For you I am a bishop, with you I am a Christian. The former is the name of an office received, the latter is the name of a grace received."[46] Only by being at the side of the community as a fellow disciple could one be in authority.[47] "For you we are shepherds, but under that Good Shepherd we are sheep together with you." The pastor who would care for souls must do so "by action and exhortation, not aiming to be at the head but to be by the side."[48] Unless a pastor set out to serve Christ's church, Augustine warned, he would soon be "pasturing himself and not the sheep."

QUESTIONS FOR CONSIDERATION

1. Augustine, though inundated with calls for his attention, balanced his life between ecclesial responsibilities, prayer, study, and life in intentional community. Augustine the bishop, Augustine the theologian, Augustine the theological educator and pastoral mentor—these were three interrelated strands of one vocation, woven so tightly together that each reinforced and gave shape to the other two. What kind of space does Augustine open for us to do the same?

2. With Augustine, no topic was closed for discussion. No matter the subject or question, he attempted to help his correspondent understand the interrelation between theology, practical ministry, and spirituality. Is there freedom to explore any relevant question or concern in our mentoring conversations?

3. Do we attempt to trace out the connecting threads between doctrine, practice, and devotion?

4. Despite his formidable intellect and capabilities, Augustine had no interest in furthering his own career or in overwhelming any of his fellow priests and bishops. He served alongside them, not over them. He desired their formation as pastors and theologians and rejoiced with them in their success and maturity. What place does humility have in pastoral ministry? In the mentoring relationship?

5. How can we practice learning how to release others to do ministry and rejoice in their success?

6. The service of ministry was exhausted in the pastor's humble offer of the Word in speech, in act, and in sacrament. He directed those priests in his community to direct their attention to exegesis, preaching and teaching, to caring for the most needy in their community, and to offering the sacraments to the praise of God and the nourishment of the people. None of these were to be neglected. Am I prone to neglect any of these in my ministry?

7. Which of these do I need help in developing?

8. Augustine shaped his conversation and letters according to the person's specific needs, thus modeling through his practice an important principle of pastoral ministry. How can we cultivate this same posture of attentive listening and personal counsel in relationships with either mentor or mentee, or parishioner?

9. Augustine offered life-long friendship and support to those priests who came from his community. His relationship with them was the farthest thing from being perfunctory or expedient. His life was invested in theirs and theirs in his because of their common investment in Christ through the Spirit. How might Augustine's verbal and embodied articulation of Christian friendship inform the mentoring relationship?

Pious Mentor to Pope and Priest: Catherine of Siena

Among the women who have had significant roles in the history of the church is Catherine of Siena, a young woman passionate for Christ and his bride, the church. In spite of the conventional confines of the mid-fourteenth century, Catherine became, through her letters of spiritual and ecclesiastical counsel, a powerful instrument of God's grace, love, and restoration. Women in the medieval period were particularly central to the mission of the church to the sick, elderly, and marginalised persons of society, and it was in this context that Caterina di Iacopo di Benincasa (Catherine of Siena) shared her ministry.

Catherine was born on March 25, 1347, the twenty-fourth child of parents, Lapa Piacenti and Giaciomo Benincasa. From historic records of her early life as a child, it appears that Catherine had a deep conviction regarding the road she would later travel—that is, the road of dedication to God and ministry to the church and the world through the Dominican Order. Whilst this life decision was not the first choice of her parents, confirmation of the authenticity of her calling came through a mystical communion with Christ in 1368, at the tender age of twenty-one. Though she had several such mystical experiences, these were but more intensive moments of her continual life of prayer and devotion.

Catherine was respected for her role as mediator within the church during the struggles for Papal power between France and Italy during the period of the Avignon Papacy. For the purposes of this text, however, the aspect of her life on which we will focus is the written counsel and direction she offered to noblemen, the Pope, and peasants alike. Catherine's wise counsel in her letters is far out of proportion to her youth. This seems to have come in part from her strict routine of prayer and meditation—a routine that confirms that any ministry of service must be balanced by restful communion with God.

SELF UNDERSTANDING

I pray you then, you and me and every other servant of God, that we devote ourselves to understanding ourselves perfectly, in order that we may more perfectly recognize the goodwill of God, so that enlightened we may abandon judging our neighbour, and acquire true compassion.

The freedom that marked Catherine's ministry to both church leaders and lay persons grew from the humble acknowledgment of her frailty, her sinful nature, and her pride before God. Lacking pretense she was free to serve indiscriminately and selflessly. Her desire to be a vessel of God's grace and peace to others led her to search the deep enclaves of her heart in order to discern who God had created her to be and the direction her ministry ought to take. She sought to rely on God's good nature to guide and discipline her in love and grace. Her increasing "self-knowledge," her hunger for intimacy with God, and for passion to draw others into God's presence dominates the almost 400 letters that have endured.

CATHERINE'S COUNSEL

While many of her letters were written to the Pope and clerics, she also offered extensive spiritual direction to her closest friends. The form of her letters, however, does not differ greatly according to the recipient. Whether Pope (at that time, Gregory XI in Avignon), acquaintance, or friend, Catherine was adept at communicating her love for Christ and concern for her correspondents with openness, subtlety, and humility.

One such friend, with whom she shared a close relationship, was Raimondo (Raymond) da Capua. Raymond was appointed to be Catherine's confessor and spiritual director during the last six years of her life. Though his first inclination was to humbly decline from assisting such a well-known person, Catherine's character and unique mission fascinated him. As they began to journey together through the strife of the Black Plague, the political unrest of Europe, and Catherine's deteriorating health, their friendship and trust of one another deepened. The lines between mentor (the role designated to Raymond by the Master General of the Dominican Order) and mentee (Catherine) were quickly blurred. Raymond, in fact, was the one who probably most benefited from the relationship, in many ways being mentored by Catherine. For her part, Catherine came to trust Raymond implicitly. Indeed, it is due to Raymond's intimate friendship with Catherine that we have such a comprehensive understanding of her life, spirituality, and ministry.

Raymond and Catherine exchanged numerous letters throughout their friendship, though none better capture her mission, prayerful life, and love for the church than the letter written to Raymond while he was in Avignon preparing for Catherine's arrival to speak with Pope Gregory XI. On the night of April 1, 1376, while in prayer, Catherine had a vision of the Pope's return to Rome and the unity of the church—a vision she was eager to share with her friend and mentor.

> Love, love, love one another! Be glad, be jubilant! Summertime is coming! For on the night of April first God disclosed his secrets more than usual. He showed his secrets more than usual. He showed his marvels in such a way that my soul seemed to be outside my body and was so overwhelmed with joy that I can't really describe it in words. He told and explained bit by bit the mystery of the persecution the holy Church is now enduring, and of the renewal and exaltation to come. He said that what is happening now is being permitted to restore her to her original condition.[49]

This letter marks her move from private spiritual devotion to public spiritual and ecclesial counsel. In large part, this move can be attributed to Raymond, who saw in his mentee a young woman who had remarkable gifts of wisdom, insight, love, and counsel. At a time when the Papal seat in Avignon was undergoing severe opposition from Italian factions in Florence and Rome, Raymond encouraged and enabled Catherine to speak her words of counsel, to share her love of Christ, and to mediate between the Pope and his Italian opposition. Though some have painted the picture of a genteel Catherine, her letters add vibrant color to the image—that of a strong-willed and often fiery young woman. Indeed, her passion for the church and sheer exasperation with the difficult situation which she had been appointed to mediate came across in her direct, unwavering use of language. In writing to the Pope and encouraging him to return to Rome and bring an end to the warring factions within the church, this young "positionless" woman wrote:

> I am begging you, I am *telling* you: come, and conquer our enemies with the same gentle hand. In the name of Christ crucified I am telling you. Don't choose to listen to the devil's advisors. They would like to block your holy and good resolution. Be a courageous man for me, not a coward. Respond to God, who is calling you to come and take possession of the place of the glorious shepherd, Saint Peter, whose representative you still are.[50]

CATHERINE'S CHALLENGE

In the context of the twenty-first century, such strong words spoken to one's elder or authority would not likely be considered appropriate. Many times we choose to totter around an issue in order to avoid the possibility of hurting another. Indeed, it is right and prudent that we prepare our words so they may be clearly understood by the other and avoid needless offence. As persons, and particularly as ministers and pastors, however, we need both words of encouragement and words of challenge throughout our lives. Without words of encouragement we may simply give up when we stumble on failure or trip over criticism, when we timidly hide the gifts we have been given to share. Without words of challenge we may begin to serve our own desires, gorge our own egos, and so fail to serve our neighbor and the community in which God has placed us. In many ways Catherine knew the pitfalls of remaining silent. Her example challenges us to speak words of grace and wisdom to those with whom we live and minister.

A second noteworthy theme found throughout Catherine's letters is her deeply rooted pastoral concern, which reflect her passion for the church and the mission to which Christ called her. Therefore, it is no surprise that she returned again and again to Word, Sacrament, "calling," and servanthood. In writing to a group of elders in Lucca, who had decided to place their support in an antipapal league, Catherine implored the group to recover their call to serve the church, and in particular the Pope. She wrote:

> I had been happy, jubilant about the courage you'd had up to now, to be strong and steadfastly obedient to holy Church. But now, when I heard the opposite, I was really sorry. This is why I came here in the name of Christ Crucified: to tell you and beg you not to let anything make you do this. You should know that if you were to do it to save yourselves and to have peace, you would fall into greater warfare and ruin than ever—physically as well as spiritually. Don't get involved in such stupidity! No, be true and steadfast children.[51]

Catherine's passion was evident as she pleaded with her friends to recover their calling to serve Christ and his Body: "Be true and remain faithful. Remember why you are serving God and His bride the Church!" In letters written to Raymond she referred to his need to "keep the good, holy, and true faithful will that I know God in his mercy has given you."[52] She understood that God called each person to a unique ministry of service, to share in his servant work. To be reminded of that call and to reflect upon it is central to understanding who we are as people called to wash feet, serve tables, and meet spiritual and physical hunger.

Sacrament is another recurring theme throughout her works, and in particular the image of "Christ's blood." The "blood of Christ" not only referred to the celebration of the Eucharist, but more acutely to her understanding that through Christ's blood, as one "tasted" and "drowned" oneself in it, the believer begins to know self and God more fully. In other words, Catherine understood that it was only because of Christ's sacrificial death on our behalf, and the shedding of his blood, that her mission had any purpose or significance. As one commentator writes, "The blood is for Catherine the symbol of the whole reality of cross and resurrection. It is not a gruesome obsession as some have considered it, but rather the glorious Love-gone-mad that dyes the whole cloth of God's truth in us red with life—God's life and our life."[53] Thus she left no space for an autonomous ministry carried out in one's own name or power, or for the sake of personal acclaim and affirmation. To her colleague, Stefano di Corrado Maconi, in Siena, she wrote:

> Here, I am saying, is how we gain this glorious virtue of strength and steady perseverance: since our reason is made strong in Christ's blood, we must drown ourselves in this sweet glorious ransom. How? With our mind's eye and by the light of most holy faith we see it within the vessel of our own soul, in the knowledge that our being comes from God, and that God created us anew to grace in the blood of his only-begotten Son. And in that blood we were freed from our weakness. Oh dearest son, look, and be happy! For you have been made a vessel that holds the blood of Christ crucified—if you are but willing to taste it in the affection of love![54]

WHAT CAN WE LEARN?

Having considered this brief snapshot of Catherine's ministry amongst her peers and church leaders, what principles can we draw on in our service as pastors, mentors and mentees? We suggest that Catherine's example provides us with a number of significant insights, though four are particularly pertinent in the context of the pastoral role.

First, Catherine led an incredibly busy life. Yet, in the midst of mediation, counselling, and furthering the work of her Dominican brothers and sisters in Italy and abroad, she still devoted herself wholeheartedly to setting apart hours of prayer and meditation. She knew herself intimately. It was, without doubt, through this intentional devotion that she journeyed into that close communion with God, gaining understanding of herself, her calling, and God's heart. In today's society, where we can become so consumed by expectations and the need to fulfil many roles and ministries, Catherine, through her example, encourages each of us to forego our inclination to be busy people and consciously to allow ourselves time alone with God in prayer and meditation. For it is a life lived in constant communion with God that ought to under-gird our service, rather than our busyness.

Second, we should seek out the counsel and direction of older, wiser women or men who will walk with us through our decisions, problems and joys, and who will aid us in our theological reflection when we are faced with difficult or challenging ministry issues. Prior to Raymond's involvement in Catherine's life as her spiritual director, we are told that Catherine was fervent in her prayers that God would lead her to a person who would fulfil the mentoring role in her life. So it ought to be with us. If we have not yet found a mentor, or we have not yet allowed ourselves to be mentored, or indeed to mentor, we should prayerfully seek someone with whom we can share our lives, and who will disciple us through the many challenges that life may bring. Openness, encouragement, challenge, counsel, and direction from another is very often the path that leads us into a deeper understanding of ourselves and of who we are before God.

Third, Catherine, in spite of being pushed and pulled in all the various directions of her ministry, still found time to share her life both with those who were in high positions and those who were marginalized in society. While it may be easy for us to selectively spend time with certain people, for many the very nature of the vocation we are following does not allow such a comfortable choice. Many of us will be required to be diligent in weekly pastoral visits to those who are unwell or unable to attend church regularly. We may be called upon to visit with the homeless at the soup kitchen run by the church. For many, such visits are difficult.

They make us vulnerable, unsure, even afraid. Yet the very nature of our calling is to person-centred ministry, sharing our lives and the gospel with people with whom we would not ordinarily choose to spend time. For others of us, we delight in such scenarios. They make us feel alive, while the thought of having to spend another wet evening in a cold church hall with the Presbytery committee fills us with dread. Whatever the scenario, Catherine teaches us that it is indeed a good thing to serve the vast array of people in our church or parish with the same grace, humility, and love as we would our closest friend, husband, wife, mother, or father. At the same time, it is important to remember that Catherine also knew her own limits. She could not be in Avignon counseling the Pope while also nurturing the Dominican community in Siena. Here she whispers a warning to us: *We cannot be all things to all people all the time, and we violate the diverse gifting of the Body when we attempt to be.*

Last, but by no means least, Catherine loved and served the church. We have already noted that she was given the tremendous task of mediating between those factions within the church that were vying for power whilst the Pope resided in Avignon. In the midst of what must have seemed an overwhelming task for such a young woman, there is no doubt that she would have been unable to cope with the strain without her mentor, without that person who walked with her through her struggles and pains. So often in our own lives, we try to achieve the unachievable in the hope that through some titanic act of will, we will be able to deal with difficult decisions or solve the most complex of problems. The underlying principle of Catherine's life was devotion to mentoring and being mentored. While we may certainly have the tools to deal with the challenges we face, the worth of being able to share and seek counsel or confirmation from another cannot be overvalued. We will all have experienced the pain of making a quick and rash decision without thinking of the consequences, or the sense of being lost as we go round and round in circles seeking a way out of an awkward situation. Having a mentor to walk with us through these times, as well as to share times of joy, is vital in our lives as servants of Christ.

QUESTIONS FOR CONSIDERATION

1. Do you know your weaknesses, fears, failings, strengths, joys?

2. Do you spend time with God in prayer and meditation?

3. How will you as a mentor enable your mentee to see and use his or her gifts?

A Graced Pastor and Mentor: John Newton and the Eclectic Society

The Eclectic Society was instituted early in the year 1783 by a few of the London clergy, for mutual religious intercourse and improvement, and for the investigation of religious truth. The first meeting was held at the Castle-and-Falcon Inn, Aldersgate Street, January 16, 1783, and consisted of the Rev. John Newton, the Rev. Henry Foster, the Rev. Richard Cecil and Eli Bates, Esq.[55]

—John Pratt, 1856

I am not fond either of assemblies, consistories, synods, councils, benches, or boards . . . Ministers' associations, in my judgment, should always be voluntary and free. Thus there are ten or a dozen of us in London, who frequently meet; we deliberate, ask, and give advice as occasions arise; but the sentiment of one, or even of the whole body, is not binding on any.[56]

—John Newton, 1783

Thus John Pratt and John Newton described the regular meeting of irregular evangelical pastors and lay persons who, in various configurations of membership, gathered fortnightly for over thirty-one years to discuss the pressing theological and practical concerns of its members. It was a group irregular by design, counting among its members over the years Church of England ministers, Moravians, Anglican laypersons, Dissenters, and Freechurchman, whose ages ranged, in 1798 at least, from the seventy-three-year-old John Newton to the twenty-nine-year-old John Pratt.

Pratt, who kept the notes of the group from 1798 to 1814, described the personalities of some of the eclectics who contributed to these lively and serious affairs. The Rev. H. Foster, a plain and pious man, was without any peculiar decoration of taste, style, or eloquence in his general preaching, though his soul-searching comments were much valued. The Rev. G. Pattrick was a humble and retiring man much esteemed by his church. The Rev. W. J. Abdy, a mild and affectionate man, was better known for his devout spirit than his powerful mind. The Rev. John Clayton was an Independent minister of piety and judgment. John Bacon, Esq., was a celebrated sculptor, a man of imagination, and a keen judge of character, whose genius outshone his sound judgment. And, of course, John Newton, the senior member of the group, respected for his even-tempered and independent theological mind, beloved for his penetrative insight into spiritual matters of the soul.

In 1783, Newton had invited a handful of ministers and laymen to his home to discuss matters relating to Scripture and pastoral ministry. A few months later this group gave birth to the Eclectic Society, which in turn gave birth to the influential Church Missionary Society, responsible for sending Christian missionaries to Africa, India, and Australia.

NEWTON'S JOURNEY TO THE PASTORATE

This was the age of the great evangelical revivals. This generation had seen John and Charles Wesley, Isaac Watts, George Whitefield, Charles Spurgeon, William Cowper, William Wilberforce, and John Newton, a former slaver whose hymn, "Amazing Grace," recounted his wonderment at finding a wretch like himself forgiven and called to administer the gospel to other sinners. This slaver's conversion is well known. To sea at the age of eleven with his father, Newton was pressed into service on a naval man-of-war at eighteen. He recalls in his autobiographical account, *An Authentic Narrative*, that the ruin of any latent moral principles he might have had was made complete on this ship. Led by his passion for a girl, one Mary Cattlet (who later became his wife), he impulsively deserted the Navy soon after. Once captured, he was stripped of rank, whipped, clapped in irons, and (in hindsight) providentially transferred to a merchant ship bound for Africa. An impudent and profligate midshipman, he sailed on several vessels serving the slave trade off the coast of Africa,[57] where he became, he says, "a ringleader in blasphemy and wickedness," the "sport and the pity of slaves."[58] Famously, on March 21, 1748, despairing of life and ship in the middle of a tempestuous storm in the North Atlantic that swamped his vessel, broke its mast, and stripped its sails in minutes, Newton breathed a prayer for mercy.

Probably every sailor on any ship ever in such a situation has muttered a similar prayer.[59] For Newton, however, it was the moment grace began to lay hold of his wanton heart. He recounted that his thoughts turned first to his black pile of sins—unforgivable, he thought—but then to the life of Christ, who had died on account of sins not his own. When the storm finally abated and the ship hobbled into an Irish port, its crew half-starved, he recalled, "About this time I began to know that there is a God who hears and answers prayer. I was no longer an infidel. I heartily renounced my former profaneness . . . and was touched with a sense of God's undeserved mercy. I was sorry for the past, and purposed an immediate reformation . . . yet still I was greatly deficient in many respects."[60] Every year to the end of his life, Newton observed March 21 as the day on which grace broke upon him.

He remained in the slave trade for another six years, however, and left only after suffering an epileptic seizure. In the meantime, his new faith and Christian conduct had waned. Gradually he came into contact with a godly ship captain, certain evangelical ministers, including George Whitefield and John Wesley, and numerous other Christians who nurtured his faith. During the next ten years he taught himself Greek, Hebrew, Syriac, Latin, and began a regular course of reading in theology. Identifying with St. Paul, the "chiefest of sinners" turned preacher of the gospel, Newton himself began, in 1759, a five-year journey toward ordination and ministry in the church. From 1764 until 1780, he served first the rural parish of Olney in the East Midlands, where, with the poet, William Cowper, he published the influential *Olney Hymns* in 1779 and a collection of his letters of spiritual counsel, *Cardiophonia* ("utterances of the heart"), a year later.[61] In 1780, he transferred to the London parish of St. Mary Woolnoth, where he served until his death in 1807.[62]

ON PASTORAL FORMATION AND PREPARATION

As Newton knew well, the gospel was no trifling matter. "It is a poor affair to be a stage-player in divinity," he wrote. Eternal life and death, gracious forgiveness, and divine recompense were its subject matter, the grace of Christ unbending sin-bent hearts and minds its plot. Therefore, evangelical clergyman who would honor their high calling could not afford to play at their vocation, nor could their parishioners afford for them to. Therefore, their formation for ministry by educator and mentor was of utmost concern to Newton, who spent much of his life mentoring and counselling pastors and divinity students.

He wrote to a young minister in 1750, "The Gospel is the power of God unto salvation," and the minister is charged to preach this gospel with due conviction and personal knowledge of its salutary character. "So study the Word of God, and the working of your heart . . . thus you shall come forth as a scribe, well instructed in the mysteries of the kingdom . . . thus your trumpet shall not give an uncertain sound, nor shall you appear like a cloud without water." Newton insisted that when preaching, the minister must combine a confidence of the truth with a sense of the importance of the message, a love for the souls entrusted to his care, and a perception of the presence of God. D. Bruce Hindmarsh summarizes Newton's pastoral ideals:

> He believed that a minister must aim above all to awaken sinners through the preaching of the gospel. He must also be zealous, disciplined, and humble, expert in the Scriptures and widely experienced in spiritual matters, athirst for the glory of God and the salvation of souls. He must pray often and earnestly in private and in public, must preach plainly and affectionately, must speak individually to his hearers of Christ, and must seek to spread the gospel near and far.[63]

PASTORAL AND THEOLOGICAL EDUCATION

Newton's thoughts were turned to the formation and preparation of pastors throughout his adult life, first for the sake of his own ministry, and second for the sake of the countless ministers, both young and old, who turned to Newton for wise counsel. His letters of spiritual and pastoral counsel rank among the classics of the church for their clarity and depth. Like David, he spoke from his heart directly to the heart of his correspondent, and as is commonly testified, to the hearts of many who have continued to read his writings during the past two hundred years. His deft counsel is like that of a wise surgeon, whose skillful application of healing balm restores one to health. One of his biographers, Rev.

Josiah Bull, the son of one of Newton's close friends, described him perfectly as "a moral anatomist," a student of the human heart. Newton studiously practiced the advice he had once given to a young seminarian:

> Converse much with experienced Christians, and exercised souls. You will find advantage in this respect, not only from the wise, but from the weak of the flock . . . Observe how their spirits work, what they say, and how they reason in their several cases . . . Compare these with the Word of God and your own heart. What you observe of ten persons in these different situations, may be applied to ten thousand. For though some circumstances vary, the heart of man, the aids of grace, and the artifices of Satan, in general, are universally the same.[64]

Besides sitting with his colleagues in the Eclectic Society, to whom we shall return shortly, Newton wrote several essay-length letters to young ministers and seminarians beginning their journey of pastoral formation. So well respected was Newton as a minister, and so evident was his concern to come to the aid of other pastors, that in 1782, shortly after his move to London, he was asked to draft a curricular plan for a new academy to be established "for preparing young men for the ministry in which the greatest stress might be laid upon truth, life, spirituality, and the least stress upon forms, modes, and non-essentials."[65] Despite his protest that his own studies had been conducted not at university or academy but rather in "the wilds of Africa," his plan was adopted and used by the academy at Newport Pagnel for over fifty years.[66]

The plan he submitted for the college was a distillation from the wisdom his letters had been carrying to innumerable pastors for years. His first word to both pastor and mentee was, "None but he who made the world can make a minister of the gospel"— an absolutely fundamental truth that has profound practical implications for pastoral formation and ministry in any age.

The choice of the tutor or mentor for inexperienced student-pastors was the most important question to be settled according to Newton. [67] He recognized that this person would not only exert a profound influence upon the students, but through them would be "remotely the instrument of all the blessings and benefits which the Lord is pleased to communicate by their ministry" to other people until the end of their life. Therefore, whoever will be tutor or mentor to others must remember that they are in the service of many more people than simply the individual person before them. Through their diligent, intentional relationship, they love well a whole host of unseen neighbors, sisters, and brothers.

Newton's first qualification for the tutor or mentor concerns their spirit: their mind must be "deeply penetrated with a sense of the grace, glory, and efficacy of the gospel" and their heart "attached to the person of the Redeemer as God-man." Second, the tutor must be able to teach, to be ready to adapt patiently to the individual "states, attainments, and capacities" of each student, in order to lead each one forward "step by step, in such a manner, that the sentiments he instills in them may be their own, and not taken up merely upon the authority of his spoken word."[68] Third, the tutor-mentor should exercise sound theology, a lively imagination, prudential judgment, and with a quick eye, look for teachable moments beyond the lecture room "in all places and at all times, whether sitting in the house or walking by the way."

As for the students, Newton's concern, in common with other evangelicals, was that as knowledge was acquired, it would lead to wisdom, and as understanding increased, it would lead them to experience the truth. He had warned a young divinity student against picking up bits of theological and exegetical knowledge too hastily without ensuring that they were properly "balanced by a proportionable depth of spiritual experience."[69] The chief means for attaining this pastoral wisdom, according to Newton, are Scripture, prayer, and meditation—"the wisest can do nothing without them; the weakest shall not use them in vain." And in order for these to lead one to wisdom, they must become habits. They must be cultivated by an industrious "spiritual diligence," whose source and goal is a heart acutely aware of "the love of God, the worth of souls, the shortness of time, and the importance of eternity." Without a mind quickened by these truths, "though a man should spend sixteen hours every day in his study, he may be a mere trifler."[70]

Though Newton was never one to disparage learning or education, he was determined to secure it in its proper place. Only after attending to the spiritual formation of the students did he turn to the students' orderly and comprehensive understanding of theology and Scripture. Ideally, they should acquire this knowledge through learning the original languages—as Newton himself had done. Second, they should develop a competent knowledge of ancient and modern aids to Scripture. Third, the course of study should include a general knowledge of literature, history, and philosophy, as well as the study of logic so that students might more competently distinguish and explain truth from error.

Finally, the students must have some instruction and practice in the art of preaching and writing, the normal means through which the Spirit deigns to work. They should learn to preach "in a pertinent and collected manner, with freedom and decorum, with fidelity and tenderness."[71] Echoing Gregory of Nazianzus and Gregory the Great, Newton reminds the young divinity student that grace and sin will be playing out in each person of the congregation in different ways—some are maturing, some weakening, some contending with temptation, some buried in sin, some rejoicing, some weeping. "Remember that some of all these sorts will probably be before you, and each should have something said to their own peculiar case."[72]

Are we dependent upon the Spirit for the efficacy of our words? Absolutely, according to Newton. Does that imply we might forego the hard work of careful study and preparation for sermons? "Not in the least," he answers, "the blessing [of the Holy Spirit] and the means [of the sermon] are so closely united, that they cannot be separated." Therefore, though we expect the Spirit's assistance in the preparation and delivery of sermons, we must still prepare and deliver them as articulately as we are able. Newton laments that many persons, however, despite their hard work, venture too hastily into the pulpit, believing themselves called, only to discover later "that the Lord had neither called them to it nor furnished them for it." Instead, he exhorts young preachers and pastors to habitually consult the advice and seek the approbation of ministers and preachers more experienced than they—the very practice of mentoring for pastoral formation and preparation we have been considering. "You will likewise find advantage, by attending as much as you can on those preachers, whom God has blessed with much power, life, and success in their ministry."[73]

In a letter to his wife, after hearing one eloquent young preacher in London, Newton remarked, "young men, not having had time to be duly acquainted with the depths of the heart and the depths of Satan, cannot ordinarily be expected to speak with so much feeling and experience as they who have been in many conflicts and exercises." However, even young preachers, he continued, have much to offer:

> I love young preachers, for they are sprightly, warm, and earnest. I love old preachers, for they are solid, savoury, and [experiential]. So I love them all, and am glad to hear all as occasion offers. But I own I like the old wine best. It is a mercy that the Lord not only gives us food, but such a variety that every one may in his turn have his palate pleased if he be not quite unreasonable and dainty indeed.[74]

Newton was also keenly aware that no matter how capable the tutor or how deep the curriculum, there remained a portion of pastoral knowledge and understanding that could only be acquired in the thick of ministry. In this, too, he echoed the sentiment of countless other pastors who labored before him. Comparing a new pastor to a soldier's first step on the battlefield, he warned a newly ordained minister, "a distant view of the ministry is generally very different from what it is found to be when we are actually engaged in it . . . If the Lord was to shew us the whole before hand, who that has a due sense of his own insufficiency and weakness, would venture to engage?"[75] For Newton truth and grace had to be lived and practiced, not just preached and studied. If true for the individual Christian, then this was doubly true for the pastor. Newton wisely counseled several young pastors that their formation and preparation for ministry were ongoing, and in some ways quickened upon ordination. Almost twenty years after his ordination, Newton wrote to the Rev. Cadogan concerning the ongoing formation of pastoral wisdom:

> The doctrinal parts of our message are in some degree familiar to us, but that which gives a savour, fullness, energy, and variety to our ministrations is the result of many painful conflicts and exercises which we pass through in our private walk, combined with the proofs we receive, as we go along, of the Lord's compassion and mercies under all the perverseness and folly we are conscious of in ourselves. It is only in the school of experience that we can acquire the tongue of the learned, and know how to speak a word in season to those that are weary.[76]

To the inexperienced Rev. Coffin, anxious about his own lack of spiritual maturity compared to other pastors, Newton responded:

But some of those [ministers] you deem [more mature] were planted in the Lord's garden many years before you. Why then should you complain that you are not so tall, nor your branches so wide, nor your root so deep, in two years' growth, as others who have been growing twenty or thirty years? Should a little sapling, just springing up from an acorn ask, "Why am not I as large as the stoutest oak in the wood?"[77]Newton's attentiveness to the quickening ways of the Spirit in his own heart and life allowed him to speak apt words of counsel to these other pastors. In many ways, he was quite similar to Augustine: each reflected theologically on their autobiography and offered it to others as evidence of God's grace and providential care. Neither entertained any perilous naïveté regarding sin, nor were they blind to the distinct temptations faced by leaders and servants in the church. Humility, grace, and love were the watchwords set on both their lips. Through correspondence and the immediacy of their homes, they lived in active, intentional community with other pastors and priests, offering and receiving counsel on all manner of things throughout their lives. Each relationship they had was unique and to each correspondent they responded according to his or her specific need or situation.

NEWTON AS PASTORAL MENTOR

Numerous young pastors turned to Newton for just this reason. In Newton's time, the usual course into the pastorate led from the halls of either Oxford or Cambridge to a placement with an established pastor or priest, with whom the new pastor might live for a number of years before receiving his own parish. We are not surprised, therefore, to find that many students lived with Newton and his wife as part of their preparation for ministry. Many of them, due to their dissenting views from the Church of England, had been disallowed from studying at Oxford and Cambridge.

Thomas Jones

One Oxford student, Thomas Jones, who was expelled from Oxford for his evangelical practices, had lived with Newton before attending the famous academy. An eighteen-year-old wig-maker from London, he had written to Newton in 1765 about his desire to enter the ministry. He subsequently moved in with Newton for two years, and under his tutelage apparently made considerable progress in Greek and Hebrew. In 1768, however, when a student at St. Edmund's Hall, Oxford, he was formally dismissed along with five other students. As the local paper recorded, they had been charged with "holding Methodistical tenets, and taking upon them to pray, read and expound the Scriptures, and singing hymns in private homes."[78] The charges were ludicrous, as the Principal of their college argued, defending their action from the

39 Articles of the Anglican Church.[79] Nonetheless, they proved effective. Jones was eventually ordained, however, and entered the curacy of Clifton. From here, just a few miles from where Newton was in Olney, the two began a regular correspondence.

Newton's experience of being plunged deep into sin and then deep into grace seems to have created space where others, including pastors and divinity students, felt safe to pour out to him their own moral weakness and spiritual frustration. For instance, while Jones was still at Oxford, he confessed to Newton some kind of moral failure. Aware of his friend's sincere desire for holiness, Newton, the gentle pastor and mentor, reminded him not to expect habits and tempers to die too quickly. However, "by perseverance in prayer, and observation upon the experiences of every day, much may be done in time. Now and then you will (as is usual in the course of war) lose a battle; but be not discouraged, but rally your forces, and return to the fight."[80] After responding to his confession of past failure, he turned Jones forward and commended his sincerity and integrity, encouraging him to persevere in his pursuit of humble dependence upon Christ's grace. "I do not know that I have had any thing so much at heart in my connexions with you, as to impress you with a sense of the necessity and advantages of a humble frame of spirit."

Besides his intimate acquaintance with sin and grace, Newton also possessed deep pastoral and theological wisdom. Though reticent to engage in speculative theological controversy that seemed devoid of pastoral implication, he recognized the salutary effects of truth and thus the importance of doctrine for pastoral care. His discussions with Jones and others, therefore, were not limited to matters of morality and spirituality. For instance, late in 1767, he responded to Jones's questions concerning the relationship between Calvinism and the free offer of the gospel to sinners, a live topic among evangelicals of this period. Newton counseled Jones to avoid the extremes of either Arminians or hyper-Calvinists, but to search the Scriptures and pray. Our task is to preach to all, he said, and leave the effects to the work of the Spirit: "I do not reason, expostulate, and persuade sinners because I think I can prevail with them, but because the Lord has commanded it. When I have done all, I know it is to little purpose, except the Lord speaks to their hearts." By this fine bit of theological reflection and deliberation, therefore, he was able to relieve Jones's anxiety about preaching to a "mixed" crowd.

Newton engaged in theological and pastoral questions with numerous other pastors as well. In the collections of his letters, we find him conversing with Rev. Bowman on confidence in preaching and about John Owen and Jonathan Edwards; with Rev. Symonds about the manifold gifts of the Spirit; with Rev. Powley on Richard Baxter, spiritual discernment, and Christian prudence. He wrote Rev. Howell about the peculiar difficulties of the pastoral office and the pastor's susceptibility to depression, and to Rev. Scott about the Athanasian Creed, the Trinity, and predestination. With the influential Hannah Moore, he discussed God's providence and the comfort of grace. He counseled Rev. Rose about the danger of prosperity, Rev. Barlass about the temptations of Satan, Rev. Campbell on Calvinism, Arminianism, and the distraction of politics to seminarians, and Rev. Cadogan on the value of afflictions to a minister and the strong temptations to pride. To the young Rev. James Coffin, he spoke of false humility in the minister and the need to wait upon the Lord for spiritual maturity. These people were his colleagues and friends in ministry for whom he gave counsel and from whom he received it. Like the other pastors and priests from whom we have heard, Newton was acutely aware of the high calling of the pastoral office, the weakness of he and his colleagues, and the grace and mercy of Christ that sustained them. To that end these pastors offered each other the gracious consolation and exhortation of co-laborers called to the same task.

John Ryland

Another young pastor that Newton took special care for was John Ryland, who began corresponding with Newton in 1771, when Newton, age forty-six, was at Olney, and Ryland, age eighteen, was just beginning his ministry in Northampton under his father. They became acquainted through Newton's regular visits to Ryland's father, a rather staunchly Calvinist minister who kept a school for boys. Though John was only fifteen when Newton first invited him to Olney, their subsequent friendship endured for nearly forty years. Newton fondly recalled these early years, when "we could see each other often, take sweet counsel together, and go to the House of our God in company." They corresponded until their last letter of 1803, when Newton was in London, and Ryland, an accomplished scholar, was pastor of Broadmead, Bristol, and President of Bristol College.

The elder in the relationship, Newton regularly offered his wisdom and experience to Ryland, who often turned to Newton with all manner of issues: personal, theological, pastoral, and vocational.[81] In 1776, Ryland wrote to Newton for advice on his courtship of Elizabeth Taylor, wondering whether Newton thought it wise to pursue marriage. Newton did think it wise and directed Ryland how to proceed in such an affair: pray, get the lady's consent, and approach her guardians. When Elizabeth died seven years later, Newton wrote to comfort the inconsolable Ryland. Two years hence, Newton took up pen to encourage Ryland to consider remarrying: "Everybody knows you loved your Betsy while she lived, and was a true mourner for her after she was gone," but due to his despondency and some unidentified "uneasy circumstances," Newton urged him to "pair yourself to another gracious suitable partner." Ryland also discussed questions of vocational discernment with Newton: should he move from Northampton to Bristol? Newton discouraged the move, owing to the fact that "the removal of ministers from place to place where they are acceptable and useful is often hazardous. But not always improper." Though Newton tried to dissuade him, once Ryland had in fact moved, Newton accepted it as a response to the Lord's leading, and admitted, "I am a shortsighted creature."

The elder pastor played the role of the attentive mentor for Ryland many times, staying alert to the dangerous patterns into which the younger pastor was prone to fall. Out of love for him and concern for his ministry, Newton offered at times difficult counsel. For instance, in 1771, Newton was dismayed at a collection of impetuous theological poems that Ryland had composed and published. In the preface, Ryland had belligerently declared his high Calvinist principles in defiance of Arminians and touted the fact that no one had assisted him in the composition of his poems. Newton pointed out his folly on both accounts. The poems would have benefited from external criticism, and the theology from a little sane humility: "For a young man under eighteen to pronounce *ex cathedra* upon a point in which the majority of the most learned, spiritual and humble Divines, are of another opinion, was such an offense against decency as grieved me."[82] For his part, Ryland accepted Newton's counsel, and Newton commended his teachable spirit. During at least the next ten years under Newton's influence, Ryland underwent a significant theological shift from the hyper-Calvinism of his father to the more moderate, evangelical Calvinism of Newton.[83]

In 1774, Newton confronted the now twenty-one-year-old Ryland again, this time about reports of his preaching and excessive workload: "I have occasionally heard sad tales of you that by the loudness, length, and frequency of your public discourses you are lighting the candle at both ends." Newton commended his zeal, but warned that such a blaze was a sure way to lay "a foundation for an early old age and distressing bodily complaints." From the perspective earned by patience and experience, Newton reminded him, "the Lord is seldom hasty in his operations." He concluded by encouraging Ryland and acknowledging their mutual benefit to one another: "In a word as I approve of your zeal, I shall be glad for your own sake if you will approve and adopt a little of my prudence. I wish my letters may be a bridle to you and yours a spur to me." At other times, their epistolary conversation turned to the extent of Christ's care for the church, the failure of theological professors, the hope of heaven, and the faithful service of Christ and church. Newton not only counseled this younger pastor, but also summoned his prayers for his own moral and spiritual well-being.

In his final letter, in 1803, Newton explicated what had been the foundation of their friendship from the beginning. They enjoyed communion with one another through their letters, and assisted one another through their prayers, because they both were caught up as "living members of that body of which Jesus is the living Head."[84] Chronological and geographical distance mattered little in the face of that.

The Eclectic Society: Collegial Mentors

And now, having walked through Newton's proposal for the education and formation of any minister, and through examples of his counsel to specific ministers, we finally return to the Eclectic Society of London, that regular meeting of ministers and laypersons who converged upon a London pub each fortnight for the sake of mutual edification through practical and theological discourse. Rarely, in fact, do we catch a glimpse of actual conversations between persons involved in mentoring for pastoral formation. Rarely do we get to listen in on any conversation from history. Unfortunately, this is also true for the first sixteen years of the Eclectic Society, during which no formal notes were taken. Newton kept a few notebooks of the meetings, but it is essentially to John Pratt, the junior member of the group, that we owe a debt of gratitude for keeping detailed notes of the society's conversations from 1798 to 1814. His notes are a marvelous record of what might now be referred to as "collegial mentoring"—the intentional mentoring between peers.[85]

Each time these evangelical pastors and laypersons met, after tea and prayer, a previously designated person would bring forth some question or concern for discussion. The situation or question would be explained and soon the conversation would gallop along, apparently without pause for nearly three hours. Early in its life, Newton wrote to a friend of this new found delight: "Our new institution at the Castle and Falcon promises well . . . I think they are the most interesting and instructive conversations I ever had a share in."[86] In another letter he notes that as their unanimity on essentials holds them together, their differences of sentiment "conduce to give the conversation a more agreeable variety, and tend to illustrate our subjects to greater advantage."

Given that they met for thirty-one years, their conversations ran the gamut of possibilities. So what came up for discussion among these servants of the church? Were the questions confined to eighteenth-century London or early evangelicalism? Problems quaint but outdated? Of historical interest but irrelevant? Actually, they are the same questions pastors have asked each other since the early church. These records of their meetings reinforce what we have seen throughout this text, that we are neither the first ones to be ministers, nor that we need to do ministry isolated from other ministers.

The following examples are selected from the hundreds of questions considered by the society over three decades.

On March 5, 1798, Mr. Bacon proposed to discuss the question *"What constitutes what is termed effect in preaching?"* He suggests "effect" depends on the preacher's character, the simplicity of the text, and the ability of the minister to awaken his hearers, or as he describes it, to "open the pores that they may inhale the sentimental effluvia." The Rev. Thomas Scottresponds that the greatest hindrance to preaching is the lack of apostolic spirit that aims to work miracles of grace in the conversion of sinners, a comment which leads to a discussion on the morality of preachers. Pratt, the editor, then summarizes the preaching styles of each of the members present, perhaps as a way of demonstrating that neither personality, experience, nor expertise preclude a preacher from benefiting from such a discussion: Rev. Cecil was apparently the pre-eminent preacher of the group capable of "commanding the attention of a congregation and producing upon them a corresponding effect." Newton's preaching was characterized by truth spoken in simplicity and affection; Rev. Basil Woodd's by a mild, persuasive, and affectionate statement of the gospel; Rev. John Venn's by his fidelity to Scripture and his sublime originality in "rich copious, and varied streams of piety, truth, and eloquence;" and the Rev. Thomas Scott's, though rich and original in content, was apparently kept from being too popular by his peculiar nasal accent.

What else did these ministers discuss? On March 19, 1798, the Rev. Basil Woodd proposed the topic, *"What is an external call to the ministry, and how far is it indispensable?"* On January 22, 1798, the Rev. R. Cecil asked the perennial question, *"What may be done towards the interests of the children of a congregation?"* The Rev. R. Cecil proposed on June 11, 1798, *"How far is it expedient that a minister should confine his preaching within his own experience?"* On October 15, 1798, the Rev. J. Clayton brought for discussion, *"How are we to understand doctrinal, experimental [experiential], and practical preaching?"* Later that year, on November 26, the Rev. J. Venn wished to discuss the practical question, *"What is the best way of improving the next Thanksgiving Day?"*

The question that would lead to the establishment of the well-known Church Missionary Society came from Venn on March 18, 1799, *"What methods can we use most effectually to promote the knowledge of the gospel among the heathens?"* On April 14, 1800, from the Rev. B. Woodd came the theological question, *"Is redemption general or particular?"* On June 21, 1802, the Rev. B. Woodd introduced the still pressing question, *"What is the best method of fortifying the minds of youth in schools against infidelity?"* For the meeting on June 20, 1803, the Rev. H. Foster asked the often-debated question, *"Does St. Paul, in the 7ᵗʰ chapter to the Romans, speak in the person of a regenerate or unregenerate man?"* A pastoral question came from the Rev. W. Goode on April 23, 1804: *"How far does the Word of God encourage Christians to expect consolation in the present life?"* At the meeting of March 9, 1807, they discussed another question from the Rev. W. Goode: *"What are the just bounds of typical [typological] interpretations of the Scripture?"* Related to our discussion of pastoral mentoring, the Rev. W. Fry asked on November 30, 1807, *"What are the chief duties of Christian ministers with respect to one another?"* On June 26, 1809, the Rev. H.G. Watkins proposed the hermeneutical question, *"What is the best method of studying the epistolary writings, as to their general use and application?"*

And so it goes, week after week, year after year, the members of the Eclectic Society meeting to discuss common questions of faith, practical ministry, exegesis, morality, theology, and spirituality. Nearly all of them were ministers called to the same vocation of pastoral service to the church. They believed that the pastoral ministry was not to be undertaken alone and were committed to listening to one another and learning from one another. The Eclectic Society is a picture of the kind of community—spontaneous in origin and intentional in execution—that often emerges among persons indwelt by a common Spirit. It is altogether natural that communities like this should spring up among fellow-believers and altogether wise to attend to their salutary continuation.

The concerns of these pastors and preachers are our concerns, for as Newton declared, "the heart of man, the aids of grace, and the artifices of Satan, in general, are universally the same." Not only, therefore, might we dip into their conversations to learn from them, but we ought to model their commitment to one another in the face of the indigenous pressures, demands—and joys—of pastoral ministry.

QUESTIONS FOR CONSIDERATION

1. How does your conversion experience influence your understanding of and vision for ministry?

2. How might you integrate your knowledge with your spirit? Your understanding with your devotion?

3. How feasible would it be to form a group similar to the Eclectic Society with your peers? What contribution to your life and ministry could it have?

4. Has there been a preacher or minister who has influenced your ministry? Have there been others you wish you would have consulted? Do you know a younger pastor you might exhort and encourage?

Death to Self and Life in Community: Dietrich Bonhoeffer and the Finkenwalde Seminary

We call you [pastors] to order your lives anew. We have suffered long enough from the desire of individuals to go their own way and separate themselves from their brothers. That was not the spirit of Jesus Christ, but the spirit of individualism, indolence, and defiance. To a great extent it has done serious harm to our preaching. Pastors cannot perform the duties of their office alone. They need their brothers. We call you faithfully to keep regular times for prayer and for the contemplation and study of scripture every day. We ask you to claim the help of brothers who can discuss matters of concern with you and receive your personal confession. We impose on each of you the sacred duty to be available to your brother for this ministry. We ask you to come together to pray as you prepare your sermons and to help one another find the proper words.

— Dietrich Bonhoeffer,
from an unpreached sermon, 1942[87]

Dietrich Bonhoeffer lived through what could reasonably be considered the most turbulent period of the twentieth century. A child during the First World War, he eventually witnessed the rise of Adolf Hitler, whose promise to restore glory and dignity to Germany's national identity led the country into the Second World War. During the unstable years of economic and moral decline between the Wars, Bonhoeffer became theologian, pastor, professor, musician, author—and near the end of the war, eventually martyr, losing his life because of his staunch opposition to the Third Reich's brutally dehumanizing policies. On April 9, 1945, he was hanged at the concentration camp in Flossenbürg by Gestapo prison guards, barely three weeks before Hitler took his own life and the Third Reich crumbled. Bonhoeffer had been involved with the resistance movement against Hitler and, along with several high-ranking German officials, was party to a plot to assassinate him. Though he desperately struggled with the ethical implications of his decision and the unknown fate of a post-Hitler Germany, he could foresee no other option than to remove Hitler from power by any means ready to hand—a conviction that cost him his life. Despite his early martyrdom at age thirty-nine, however, Bonhoeffer's powerful theological and pastoral voice still resonates with great promise for the church and theological education. In turning away from the demonic spirit of the times that was fracturing Europe along nationalist and ethnic fault lines, he turned to the community of faith and to the neighbor, receiving them as given by God, and serving them as he was led by God. Despite his relatively few years of service, he became a mentor to many pastors and students.

Bonhoeffer was born into a privileged home on February 4, 1906, along with a twin sister, Sabine. His father was Karl Bonhoeffer, a prominent university lecturer in psychiatry and neurology. His mother, Paula Bonhoeffer, was a university-educated teacher who home-schooled her eight children. Although Though Dietrich's decision to study theology and serve the church baffled his parents, he began his study of theology in1923 at the University of Tübingen and concluded in 1927, while only twenty-one, with a highly praised doctoral dissertation at the University of Berlin.[88] An accomplished scholar, Bonhoeffer's move into the pastorate was surprisingly uneventful. He was a curate in Barcelona, Spain, until 1930, assisted at the Abyssinian Baptist Church in Harlem, New York, until 1931,[89] and served two churches in London from 1933 until he returned to Germany in 1935.[90]

Bonhoeffer always seemed to move from one of his loves to the other—from theological studies to the church, and from the church back into theology, drawing the two into passionate conversation with one another. His first doctoral dissertation, called *Sanctorum Communio,* "the communion of the saints," was a theological exploration of the church as it is called to represent Christ to the world as a redeemed community of sinners; his second, *Act and Being,* was a description of how Christ becomes present in and through individual Christians and Christian communities. In April, 1935, he was finally given the opportunity to wed these two passions together when he became principal to twenty-three students at the underground Preachers' Seminary in Zingst, Germany.

After a few months, the school found its permanent home in the now well-known town of Finkenwalde, in Pomerania. A "practical theologian" from the beginning, Bonhoeffer's ministry, his ethics, and his theological pedagogy moved along lines set by theology. He shaped life at Finkenwalde, therefore, according to the understanding of Christology, discipleship, and Christian community he had formulated in his dissertations and experienced in his pastoral ministries. He knew the most solid foundation possible was necessary for the young men who would soon pastor the small coterie of "Confessing Churches." To find that foundational cornerstone, they had to dig beneath the shifting sands on which sat the German National Church, sands that rolled whenever the tides of nationalistic theology and state policy washed over them. These "Confessing Churches" dissociated themselves from the German National Church in protest against its collusion with National Socialism. The first spade broke through the sand and struck rock when the leaders of these churches signed the well-known Barmen Declaration penned by Karl Barth in 1934. They immediately established several illegal Confessing Church seminaries, including Finkenwalde, with its then twenty-nine year old principal. Like their teacher, many of these Confessing Church seminarians would eventually give their lives in martyrdom when the Gestapo closed the Finkenwalde seminary in 1937 and arrested twenty-seven students; others were drafted against their will into the German army and were killed in battle; others did survive, however, and assisted the rebuilding of the devastated post-war German church.

FINKENWALDE

Though Bonhoeffer is rightfully remembered for his courageous stance against the Third Reich, and for his theological acumen, his greatest contribution to the fledgling Confessing Church was his role in the education and formation of its emerging clergy. Finkenwalde's primary task was pastoral formation in the midst of a community that thought, worshipped, played, and prayed together. The spiritual aridity and isolating competition of the universities received little nourishment at Finkenwalde. Here, students were given space to question their chosen vocation, to think through the meaning of the faith, and to form the devotional habits of prayer, solitude, confession, and worship that would prepare them and sustain them while they served their churches as leaders through dark times. Here these young pastors explored the complex intersection between the fracturing world, the God who entered that world, and the kind of faithful ministry and witness that world desperately needed.

We argued earlier in this text that mentoring for pastoral formation moves against the stream of popular culture. Finkenwalde is a case in point. Bonhoeffer's vision for the seminary was formed in reaction to the spiritually vapid education students received in state-controlled universities that left them, as Bonhoeffer wrote to Barth, "burned out . . . and empty not only as regards theological insights and still more as regards knowledge of the Bible, but also as regards their personal life."[91] He wanted to resist the faithless religiosity and custom that drained the soul of the church. He wanted to resist the Romantic individualism and nationalistic triumphalism that were at their height both in Germany and the rest of Europe at this time. He wanted to resist the blatant commandeering and complicit adulteration of the German Lutheran Church, which, in 1933, agreed to force potential ordinands to prove their purely Aryan descent. The Third Reich had been steadily increasing its attempt to suffocate any and all political, social, and ecclesial opposition to its policies. As it had seduced the German people, so it successfully seduced the German church. Because the German Evangelical Church "was not accustomed to opposing state legislation," it began to do so rather hesitantly and haphazardly.[92] Moving against the culture of its time, Finkenwalde was heavily scrutinised by the German church and had to be careful not to expose itself to the German authorities, who vehemently opposed the Confessing Church seminaries.[93] To prepare ministers to step into such a hostile culture, Bonhoeffer would not tolerate a sentimental, self-indulgent approach to education and formation. A resistance movement had to begin with discipleship and education that was led by the Spirit from Scripture to personal holiness and worldly action. Jay Rochelle captures the essence of the seminary when he comments:

> The seminary involved the training of pastors as theologians, preachers, pastors, teachers and administrators under the Word of God, [as] persons who lived as committed disciples . . . Unlike the traditional preachers' seminaries, in which only the practical aspects of ministry were taught in a technical-school setting, Bonhoeffer wrestled theologically with his students in order that they might confront the impact of the theology of the Word on pastoral work.[94]

Anticipating his return to Germany in 1935, Bonhoeffer began visiting monasteries and seminaries throughout Britain in order to witness firsthand how they combined communal life with theological education. As he understood it, because Christians were unavoidably given to each other as brothers and sisters through the Spirit, life together in a community of believers reflected the essence of faith as a true picture of the church. For several years he had been attempting to give a practical shape to this truth with his students.

Though it was not customary for German professors to foster warm relations with their students, while Bonhoeffer was a professor in Berlin, he met regularly with students during the week and on weekend retreats in order to worship, pray, and theologize with them. However difficult or uncomfortable it was for some, and he himself was hardly an extrovert, he refused to leave "Christian community" a pious sentiment. Many of these students later followed him to Finkenwalde as its first seminarians. Together with Bonhoeffer, they sought to form an intentional community dependent on Spirit-engendered spontaneity and authenticity.

> Bonhoeffer wanted a genuine, natural community in the Preacher's Seminary, and this community was practised in play, in walks through the richly wooded and beautiful district of Pomerania, during evenings spent in listening to someone

reading, in making music and singing, and last but not least in worship together and holy communion. He kept entreating us to live together naturally and not to make worship an exception. He rejected all false and hollow sentiment.[95]

The seminary at Finkenwalde, therefore, was actually something of an experiment in communal living and theological education. It was certainly, at least, an innovation for German education, where, as a rule, students did not live together in common houses or dormitories. Here, however, we find a small seminary dedicated to the training of young clergy in the often disorderly context of community, formed around companionship and solitude, study and worship, speech and silence, intercessory prayer and service.

It was an experiment, however, from which Bonhoeffer expected not only his students, but the whole church to benefit—one individual contribution whose lessons were to be studied and incorporated into other future "experiments" for the general increase of Christian fellowship through the Spirit. Commenting on Finkenwalde after its closure, he insisted, "We are not dealing with a concern of some private circles but with a mission entrusted to the church. Because of this, we are not searching for more or less haphazard individual solutions to a problem. This is, rather, a responsibility to be undertaken by the church as a whole."[96]

Recognising that the pastorate often left the minister isolated, stumbling over hurdles alone, he desired his seminarians to cultivate habits and patterns of mutual dependence and care that would be taken with them into ministry. In a letter explaining life at Finkenwalde to the mentor of ministry candidates in another German province, Bonhoeffer wrote that along with biblical, theological, and practical studies, for which he was responsible, they needed to learn

> how to lead a community life in daily and strict obedience to the will of Jesus Christ, in the practice of the humblest and the noblest service one Christian brother can perform for another. They must learn to recognize the strength and liberation to be

found in their brotherly service and their life in a Christian community. For this is something they are going to need.[97]

Though theologically grounded and feasible in design, it proved far more difficult to achieve in practice. Not all those who lived at Finkenwalde were of one mind from the beginning. The students were rather unaccustomed to Bonhoeffer's emphasis upon disciplined community. Yet slowly, the seminarians began to understand and embrace the necessity of community. Wolf-Dieter Zimmerman, a former student at Finkenwalde, later commented,

> The spiritual order was what was new to us, a burden difficult to bear, a discipline to which we did not like to submit. We made jokes about it, mocked at this cult and behaved like stubborn Asses. Pietism and enthusiasm were for almost all of us a form of Christianity which we rejected. Prayers in the mornings and evenings, meditations, periods of silence—it was too much. We were not accustomed to keep quiet if we had words that could be spoken. Yet, apart from being a salutary exercise, this "method" was a way of making the common life of people bearable. Bonhoeffer later told us that this second point of view had been very important for him.[98]

Life in community extended beyond Finkenwalde as well. After the closure of the seminary in 1937, Bonhoeffer spent two years sending circular letters and traveling secretly from village to village in order to encourage and supervise his former students, most of whom were working illegally in small east German churches. The experience of life in community, however, prepared not only the seminarians, but their teacher as well, who was to spend many days isolated in a Nazi prison. In his letters he testifies that this experience of community provided him with the hope and the determination to remain emotionally and spiritually stable through the horrors of solitary confinement and separation from family, fiancé, and friends. He knew he was not alone, but was borne up by the prayers and the ministries of those who had gone out from Finkenwalde.

It was in the context of community at Finkenwalde that Bonhoeffer wrote his well-known work, *The Cost of Discipleship.* His other much beloved book, *Life Together,* hastily written down a year after the seminary was closed, is a record of the "experiment" of Finkenwalde. Bonhoeffer did not want to fail to preserve for the church what had gone on there, so he compressed his thoughts and the experience of the seminarians into five short, profound (and unusually quotable) chapters: *Community, The Day Together, The Day Alone, Service,* and *Confession and the Lord's Supper.* Though written in only four short weeks, while the Nazis were threatening to invade Czechoslovakia and crush the Confessing Church in Germany, it has become a classic text on the meaning of true companionship and fellowship with others in and through God the Father, God the Son, and God the Holy Spirit.

As is clear, Finkenwalde's main purpose was to establish a community for the sake of pastoral formation, not because it was expedient or efficient—it was hardly that—but because pastoral formation had to be done in community. Bonhoeffer was clear that the way in which someone is prepared for ministry directly informs and shapes the way they do ministry. "The goal," he contended, "is not cloistered isolation, but the most intense concentration for ministry outside the seminary."[99] What were some of those theological guiding lines that shaped and directed this community that we would do well to consider? What did Bonhoeffer expect other such "experiments" in pastoral formation to learn?

First in order was Bonhoeffer's view of personhood. In everyone he met, he looked for Christ. His relation with them was never immediate, but was only mediated through Christ. Authentic relations could not be predicated on the instability of natural desire or common affection that sometimes drove people together and sometimes apart. It could only be predicated on mutual participation in Christ through the Holy Spirit, which identified the other as brother or sister before anything else. Community meant learning, growing, worshipping, living, grieving, and serving together in and through Christ, and not apart from Christ. In *Life Together,* he reflected on this Christocentric companionship:

> Christian community means community through Jesus Christ and in Jesus Christ. There is no Christian community that is more than this, and none that is less than this. We belong to one another only through and in Jesus Christ. The fact that we are brothers or sisters only through Jesus Christ is of immeasurable significance . . . What persons are in themselves as Christians, in their inwardness and piety, cannot constitute the basis of our community, which is determined by what those persons are in terms of Christ.[100]

This decisively shaped his relations with students. He was dedicated to them and invested in them. The community spent many evenings in theological discussion, prayer, worship, or, as mentioned above, taking walks and playing music together. Through this investment of time and energy he was not only able to contribute to the formation of those present at Finkenwalde, but also to the formation of all those to whom these seminarians would minister and teach after dispersing. Bonhoeffer recognised that by investing in the formation of these students even beyond the classroom setting, he could raise in them an awareness of the necessity of sharing their lives with others.

In the context of community every person, including the principal of the seminary, was both teacher and student. Humility, therefore, was an essential virtue and listening an essential practice. He considered each of his students to be a gift of grace from whom he expected to learn much, and a member of Christ's Body through whom he expected to hear Christ's Word. In his original work on the community of the church, he argued that, as Christ's Body, it lives Christ's life and manifests his being. Therefore, he concluded, "It is not only Christ who is both *donum* [gift] and *exemplum* [example] for us human beings, but in the same way also one human being is so for another . . . God has made it possible for human beings to seek counsel from others; it would be presumptuous folly if one were not to accept this offer."[101]

Bonhoeffer knew that the active life of the community had to be balanced with intentional solitude by the individual. It was not a luxury; it would be indispensable to restoration and recreation in the midst of busy pastoral life. So solitude and meditation were woven into the daily routine of the seminary. Bonhoeffer cautioned, "Whoever cannot be alone should beware of community. Whoever cannot stand being in community should beware of being alone. The day together will be unfruitful without the day alone, both for the community and for the individual."[102] Bonhoeffer knew that life at Finkenwalde and life in ministry depended on the cultivated practice of this difficult discipline of holy seclusion with God. If only alone, Christians pitch into the pit of vanity, self-infatuation, and despair, but if only together, then into the void of chattering words and sentimentality.

Bonhoeffer's fatherly approach to the spiritual care of his own students stemmed in part from his great desire to see pastors in general cared for spiritually through the encouragement and challenge of peers and pastoral mentor. Though the terms "discipleship" and "mentoring" were not in vogue in 1930s Finkenwalde, as they are now, they accurately describe Bonhoeffer's way of theological, spiritual, and pastoral formation. As is obvious, however, his was a form of mentoring that transcended the confines of weekly appointments. Rather, it was an immensely holistic form of mentoring, an invited invasion into the other's life. As one former student writes, "It was not a naïve but a highly conscious love that drove Dietrich Bonhoeffer to become the father, pastor and neighbor of his seminarists, . . . serving his brother became the centre of Bonhoeffer's life."[103] In his book, *Spiritual Care,* Bonhoeffer insists that in the church we are bound to offer one another the kind of support and encouragement each one needs, which includes taking into consideration the unique needs of the pastor.

> Whoever takes the office seriously must cry out under the burden . . . Where can a pastor find rest and recollection for their work? . . . The load is too heavy to bear alone. We need someone who will help us use our powers in ministry correctly, someone who will defend us against our own lack of faith. If the pastor has no one to offer him spiritual care, then he will have to seek someone out.[104]

Bonhoeffer was careful, however, to avoid the potentially destructive converse of care—caring too much. He cautiously reminds us of the spiritual atrophy that results when we rely too heavily upon the care afforded us from others, and we fail to mature. Like the warp and woof of community and solitude, spiritual care from others must be balanced with learning to tend to our own faith and devotion. He writes, "The goal of spiritual care is rather to lead people along in their own struggle to the point where they can break through it on their own. Excessive dependence on spiritual care can result in lack of resistance and inner laxity. One's own experience thus never matures, and we abandon the attempts too soon."[105]

Finally, Bonhoeffer recognized that he was but a tool in the hands of God, who alone determines the unique gifts and vocation of each person, who alone determines how each person in his seminary and church would show forth Christ to the world. That implied that Bonhoeffer, and pastoral mentors who would learn from him, must look for the work and unique equipping of the Spirit.

> God does not want me to mold others into the image that seems good to me, that is, into my own image. Instead, in their freedom from me God made other people in God's image. I can never know in advance how God's image should appear

in others. That image always takes on a completely new and unique form.[106]

Despite his short life, Bonhoeffer's many theological works have been exceedingly influential in the lives of individual Christians and the theologizing of the church in general. The students at Finkenwalde, however, had a fuller comprehension of the man behind the books. In Bonhoeffer they initially met an intelligent man with an acute theological mind, yet they soon experienced relationship with a humble man, ever willing it seemed to explore the complexity of calling or discuss the meaning of Sacrament, a man prepared to journey with them in faith at a time when maintaining faithful witness was a difficult and dangerous cross to bear.

At the beginning of this text we described what mentoring for pastoral formation is and what it is not. We proposed that mentoring is not self-mastery for the sake of self-sufficiency, that it does not provide us with rational techniques for the sake of speedy progress, and that it does not lead us toward a fashionable lifestyle promising self-fulfilment. Instead, we described mentoring for pastoral formation as a) grounded in deepening friendship, b) turned toward the work of Christ and the Spirit, and c) taken up with dying to self, putting on Christ, and preparing to serve the church and the world. Without question, Bonhoeffer's ministry at Finkenwalde embodies these characteristics.

a) Though Bonhoeffer was conscious of maintaining a teacher-student relationship, there is little doubt that students counted him a friend in whom they could confide and a pastor to whom they could confess.

b) Bonhoeffer was immensely concerned with the work of Christ and the Spirit within the church and within the individual seminarians.

c) Finally, he attempted to prepare both himself and future pastors for death to self. For Bonhoeffer, this led to physical death in the most literal sense. Before his final days in Germany,

Bonhoeffer taught in New York and London, and could have easily stayed in either place. He returned to Germany, however, to stand in solidarity at whatever cost with his fellow Germans and fellow Christians, who were enduring the crush of National Socialism. Bonhoeffer captured the essence of putting on Christ in service of the known and unknown neighbor. At the seminary he died to self by making himself available to his students, pouring out his time and energy for them. Outside of the relative safety of Finkenwalde, he died to self through his involvement with the resistance movement. Both of his deaths, we might say, were freely offered for the sake of others—a quality at the heart of pastoral ministry and mentoring. Bonhoeffer provides us with a remarkable example of the depth and commitment required to participate in the formation and preparation of ministers of the gospel of the crucified God.

QUESTIONS FOR CONSIDERATION

1. "Freedom is a relationship between two persons. Being free means 'being-free-for-the-other', because I am bound to the other. Only by being in relationship with the other am I free."[107] What has been your experience of being in an intentional relationship with someone? Was it positive or negative? How might your experience shape your approach to mentoring?

2. Has your life been touched through the investment of time and energy from another?

3. What did you learn? In what ways has that shaped you and made you the person and pastor you are today? How have they helped you "find the proper words" as Bonhoeffer describes?

4. What has been your experience of investing in another? Did you find this difficult or easy?

5. Bonhoeffer claims that formation for ministry must be done in community, and that pastors should reconsider it their "sacred

duty" to be available to one another in this. Is there room in your ministry to accept this "sacred duty"?

6. How does the way we are prepared for ministry affect the way we do ministry?

7. Bonhoeffer expected the church to benefit from his "experiment" at Finkenwalde. What can we learn and adopt from it? How can we move "Christian community" out of being merely a pious sentiment and into a lived reality?

Liturgical Conversations and Substantial Words: Eduard Thurneysen and Karl Barth

New Pastors and Colleagues

In 1911 and 1913, two former seminary acquaintances inaugurated their pastoral ministries in obscure agricultural and industrial areas in the Aargau canton of northern Switzerland, between Basel and Zurich—one in Safenwil, the other in Leutwil. Though separated by a three-hour walk over valleys and high ridges, they struck up an ardent friendship which not only deepened their ministries as local pastors, but which also strengthened their faith and shaped their theology.

The one pastor was twenty-six-year-old Karl Barth, installed in Safenwil—a town we read of "247 houses, 1625 inhabitants, 1487 Protestants, and 318 Protestant children."[108] Barth's days were spent like any new pastor in a country town—teaching catechism classes to rowdy children, preaching to empty pews, and forcing out sermons "with terrible birth-pangs." Like many such pastors, he later recalled with some amusement both the protracted length of the sermons he foisted upon his bewildered congregation and the late hours during which most of them were composed.

The other pastor was twenty-five-year-old Eduard Thurneysen, installed in Leutwil in 1913. Thurneysen was the lifelong pastor, but a consummate theological pastor and pastoral theologian, whose thought always moved from, to, and for the sake of the church. Barth was a pastor who became a theologian, but one whose theology grew from the roots of his twelve years in Safenwil. Their friendship was significant for their formation as both pastors and theologians.

Both of these young pastors were educated in the Romantic theology of Friedrich Schleiermacher, the Kantian theology of Albrecht Ritschl, and personally under the liberal theologian Adolf von Harnack. Yet together, now away from the academy in parish ministry, they began to discover—or, more accurately, to be discovered by—the blazing "holy otherness" of God, who resists being commandeered by human projects, and who shatters the human pretensions to religious, moral, and epistemic autonomy that had nourished the theology of their forbears. Scandalized by their dawning awareness of the immediacy of the God of Abraham, Isaac, and Jacob, they met to try to comprehend the implications for both their ministries and their theology. It was time, they decided, to dig up and examine the foundations of the theology they had inherited. Barth, for his part, began fervently studying Kant, the foundation for both Ritschl and Harnack, but quickly moved to Paul's epistle to the Romans, filling up notebook after notebook with paraphrases and explanations for he and Thurneysen to discuss. With great zeal and anticipation, they undertook biblical and theological study in parallel with each other in order to compare notes on their discoveries.

So taken were they by their newfound camaraderie, and so in need of concrete discourse were they, that they met at least weekly, one or the other making the early morning trek. Their meetings were apparently the stuff of lore. Always accompanied by pipe and cigar, they became so engrossed in conversation week by week that Barth surmised that the local villagers must have taken them for "two strange wanderers between two worlds." Once Barth procured the first bicycle in the area, the journey became his to make:

> Thus the old parsonage in Leutwil, which has now vanished off the face of the earth, became the scene of innumerable conversations about how to carry on our ministry: especially about our sermons and about the church in general and its task in the world. We did not know what great changes were in store at that very time. We only knew that we had to look for decisive, compelling words, more substantial than those which we heard around us. And we knew that we could no longer do theology in the traditional style of the discipline.[109]

Thurneysen likewise recalled:

> we walked untiringly backwards and forwards to meet each other, but that was not enough. We had the most urgent need to be real brothers, to share our thoughts about everything that was going on, as we used to say at the time, in the church, the world and the kingdom of God. And because we had no telephones in our parsonages . . . we began a lively correspondence which was carried on almost week by week.[110]

Their correspondence in fact grew to over a thousand letters between 1914 and Barth's death in 1968.[111]

BARTH THE PASTORAL THEOLOGIAN— THURNEYSEN THE THEOLOGICAL PASTOR

One defining mark of both men was their unabashed love of and service to the church. All ministry and theology had to be done in and for the church, Barth often reminded his students. Theology is simply the church reflecting critically upon what it teaches, in conversation with itself. In a letter that was intended to serve as the preface to a collection of Thurneysen's essays, Barth recalled his friend's desire to re-ground theology in the life of the church and the work of the pastor:

253

To understand these addresses of Eduard Thurneysen and to understand that the Church is the basis, starting point, and subject of theology are one and the same thing . . . It should be known, however, on the one hand that Eduard Thurneysen saw the need for a church theology of this kind before anyone else; *at any rate, he stimulated me to work in this direction.* On the other hand, it should be noted that of all those who have made a reputation and a name within this new theology, there is hardly anyone who embodies it as a movement from the church for the church as characteristically as does Eduard Thurneysen.[112]

After eight years in pastoral ministry, Barth published his celebrated *Romans* in 1919, which he had begun as running commentary for he and Thurneysen. The Roman Catholic theologian, Karl Adam, famously described it as having "dropped like a bomb on the playground of the theologians." It was the first volley, and a powerful one at that, of a soon to be unleashed theological barrage against the entrenched anthropocentric liberalism of his forbears, and its impact led to Barth's move from pastor to professor. In the preface to his substantially revised second edition, Barth warmly acknowledged the silent part played by his faithful friend and interlocutor. Thurneysen, he writes,

> has read the whole manuscript with approval, and has suggested many additions. Some of these penetrated deeper than my original comment, others were explanatory and added greater precision of expression. I have adopted these additions for the most part without alteration, and they remain a silent testimony to his self-effacement. So close has been our cooperation that I doubt whether even the specialist could detect where the one leaves off and the other begins.[113]

So close was the cadence into which their life and thought had fallen that when the two Aargau pastors published collections of their sermons in 1917 and 1924, they chose not to delineate which sermons came from which author's pen.[114]

These mentoring fellows convened not only as new preachers passing each other sermons and articles for comment and critique, and not only as weathered theologians in the twilight of their lives still searching for substantial words, but also as friends who cared pastorally for one another. Thurneysen, in particular, it seems, cared for Barth. Thurneysen offered intimate counsel to Barth and his wife, Nelly, concerning their painfully strained marriage; he shared Barth's frustration and dismay over deteriorating relations with former theological allies like Emil Brunner and Rudolph Bultmann; and he upheld Barth's spirits during many times of critical self-doubt in his life. And Barth, in turn, upheld his friend at times when, like after Easter, 1922, Thurneysen had preached to countless people who would not be seen again for another year, and he confessed,

> now the preachers take a long breath—but really *for what?* I am no longer at ease in the pulpit; even in my dreams it has become for me a place that is full of ambiguity and distress, and the long, long road and the many, many Sundays until the day of retirement take on a questionable enough aspect for me. I sit by the brook Kerith after each Sunday and can only wait for the marvelous ravens which will somehow bring the food—or perhaps they will not?[115]

In short, these two friends brought to each other all that it means to be persons, pastors, and theologians in relation, and they brought it all expecting to hear the Word of God in and through the other.

In an introduction to a 1958 Festschrift for Thurneysen, Barth recalled Thurneysen's "Johannine nature," so different from his own, and the way it shaped his six decades of pastoral mentoring in ministry:

> All my personal impressions of him can be summed up in the word *openness* . . . He gets on with people in an astonishing way. He can put himself in their place, walk with them,

and help them by understanding them (though from a more
lofty vantage point and in a transfiguring light). He shares
their sorrow or their joy. The very evident criticism, which he
brings to bear on them, is almost always a radical, immanent
criticism which is constructive by being comforting, helpful
and friendly . . . I would be omitting the chief thing of all were
I not to say that his openness toward all things human has a
secret correspondence to the openness with which, apart from
all human voices, he seeks to hearken to the Holy Scriptures.
. . . He devoted special pastoral care to me.[116]

A clearer description of the spiritual friend or pastoral mentor is
hard to find: open, understanding, graciously critical for the sake
of being genuinely transformative, attentive to Scripture.

In his book, *A Theology of Pastoral Care*, Thurneysen
demonstrates the deep theological foundations of the practice
of pastoral care that so evidently informed his friendship with
Barth. Published in 1946, it is a far-reaching, splendid work of
systematic, biblical, and historical theology in the service of the
practical ministry of the pastor. From the history of pastoral care,
Thurneysen demonstrates that the practice of pastoral counselling
is unavoidably predicated upon theological assumptions. Proving
a wise guide in these matters, his text not only illuminates his
own practice of pastoral ministry, but also offers us a vision for
mentoring and being mentored, pastoring and being pastored.[117]

Pastoral care . . . intends to be a conversation that proceeds
from the Word of God and leads to the Word of God. The
conversation is integrated by the fact that the two partners in
conversation are already engaged or at least about to be engaged
in a confrontation with the Word of God. They are already or
soon will be addressed by the Word of God. For this reason
and purpose they now talk to each other. *Being initially and
continually addressed by the Word of God is the one great assumption each of the two partners makes for the other.* It permeates and
determines their whole conversation. At first, they perhaps do

not mention this Word of God and its content at all; instead they speak of certain very concrete problems and concerns of their lives. Even so they proceed on the assumption that the Word of God whereby they are addressed or are to be addressed is important for these very problems and concerns . . . Our speech must be measured by the question of whether it can exist before the Word of God or not.[118]

BARTH THE GOTTINGEN PROFESSOR

In 1921, Barth left Safenwil to teach at the university in Gottingen, Germany. Thurneysen, however, remained a pastor, moving from Leutwil to Brugge, and finally to the Reformed Cathedral in Basel. Although the move created distances well beyond the capacities of biking or walking, their correspondence allowed them to continue their habit of thinking with and through the other. In Gottingen, Barth relied on Thurneysen's support more than ever. Not only was the volatile political climate and rampant nationalism of post-war Germany inhospitable to the Swiss Barth, he also felt entirely unprepared for his new academic post. Any fledgling professor, budding author, or newly installed pastor can knowingly smile—or cringe—at the picture Barth paints for Thurneysen of his early days in the university.

The university had assigned Barth to teach, with only three weeks to prepare, a course on the Reformed confessional writings—the only problem was that Barth neither owned a copy of them nor had ever even read them. His own need being as great as his students, he lectured for the next five semesters on the history of the Reformed tradition. Not content to preserve the "sweet illusion that indeed I know something" simply because he kept talking, Barth writes that he was studying day and night, "going to and fro with books old and new." "Thus 'teaching office' = groaning . . . More than once, the lecture which I gave at 7 A.M. was not ready until 3–5 A.M."[119] He lamented to Thurneysen, who was both concerned and amused by his friend's new plight, "I have to find my way through the fog like a poor mule, still hampered above all by a lack of academic agility, an inadequate knowledge of Latin and the most appalling memory!" His "dreadful theological ignorance" and "quite miserable memory" were his "thorn in the flesh."[120] He asks, "Shall I always be this wandering gypsy among all the honourable scholars by whom I am surrounded, one who has only a couple of leaky kettles to call his own and, to compensate, occasionally sets a house on fire?" He confesses that the inside of his head felt like "a cage full of hyenas *before* being fed." Which of us has not kept a similar cage at times? Who has not shared Barth's anxious sense of inadequacy and ill preparation for ministry? And what pastor does not know the need for an encouraging or understanding word of grace from a friend?

Barth needed Thurneysen to listen more than anything else at this time, for he was still in the process of his own theological reformation. Though, in some ways, this theological reforming never ceased for Barth, at this time in particular, his thinking was being radically quickened by his intensive study of the New Testament and the Reformed theological tradition. In a moment of remarkable transparency, Barth acknowledged that to understand himself he needed to be understood by Thurneysen.

> During my time in Gottingen, too, the correspondence and exchange of thought with him was more necessary to me than daily bread . . . because there was in me constantly the deepest need to hear his judgment concerning what I had done, and while I followed my star as he followed his, to take my bearing ever afresh in relation to him, since I had to understand him and to be understood by him in order to understand myself aright. Which one then preceded the other? Which one followed the other? We were closely united—in a unity that could never become tiresome because we continually approached both things and men quite differently and saw them differently.[121]

Their theological understanding to this point was remarkably convergent, but not because either the theological pastor or the pastoral theologian overwhelmed the other. Over time, their vastly different experiences and influences did, in fact, lead to occasional disagreements in theological, political, and pastoral matters, but they held a high regard for the other's particularity, and their friendship endured in spite of, and perhaps because of, their particularized perspectives and calling.

LITURGICAL CONVERSATIONS

In his *A Theology of Pastoral Care*, Thurneysen explains: "God's 'I' says 'thou' to us and gives us the neighbor as a brother as he addresses him together with us and redeems us from that loneliness which we cannot pierce by our own power."[122] God's Word comes to us, he writes, in the Scriptures and through preaching, and our response to his Word is shaped by our liturgy of hymns, prayers, confessions, and equally in our pastoral conversations. "One now tells the Word of God to another . . . and he answers not with prayer or hymns but responds conversationally. What now occurs is properly human conversation placed under the proviso of the Word and Spirit of God . . . As they speak with one another, both men endeavor to hear and utter God's word." Thurneysen designated these "*liturgical conversations*" one legitimate human response to God.[123]

We offer up in worship many ordinary things—bread, wine, water, space, words, time—all set aside and offered in responsive praise to God. Their ordinariness belies the fact that in worship they become visible signs and emblems of grace. So, Thurneysen suggests, we should also think of pastoral conversations as eucharistic liturgy, thankful responses to God for the gift of the other person, or the other pastor. In fact, conversation is already present in the liturgy of many of our traditions. Many services begin with the reading of Scripture as God's communication to his people, which is followed by a response of the people to God in the form of prayers, confession, and song, but also with conversation. The priest initiates the conversation by saying to the people, "The

259

Lord be with you," and the congregation responds, "And with thy spirit." The priest prompts with, "It is right to give thanks . . . ," and the people answer, "it is very meet, right, and our bounden duty to give thanks . . . "[124] This form of liturgical conversation is carried on as a response to the Word that was read, the Word that was preached, and the Word of forgiveness that was promised. It is modeled on all the extemporaneous conversations that occur in and through the Spirit. Thus the Spirit is the qualifier of "liturgical conversations," and the Spirit beckons us to worship in truth wherever such conversations take place.

LIFELONG FRIENDS AND MENTORS

Barth's need for Thurneysen's friendship went well beyond Gottingen. His path carried him into the heart of the political, theological, and cultural crisis of pre- and post-war Germany, and into the ensuing Cold War between East and West. [125] When Barth delivered his trumpet blast of the Confessing Church, "The First Commandment as Political Axiom" in 1933, when he drafted the Barmen Declaration in 1934, when he was expelled from Germany by the Gestapo in 1935, when he joined the army in 1939, when he was banned from speaking publicly in Switzerland and put under surveillance in 1941 for his stringent criticism of National Socialism and Swiss complicity,[126] when he began covertly assisting refugees and smuggling messages to former students within Germany and occupied France, when he returned to Germany after the war to lecture in the semi-ruins of Bonn University, when he appealed for friendship to the Germans after the war, when he protested loudly against German re-militarization and nuclear proliferation, all the while bringing out volume after volume of his *Church Dogmatics,* and delivering an endless stream of occasional pieces—in the midst of all this, Thurneysen continued unflaggingly to offer pastoral and personal counsel.

Unlike many of their professional and personal friendships, theirs endured for nearly sixty years. Thurneysen was, in fact, the last person with whom Barth spoke before he died. Thurneysen called on the evening of Monday, December 9, 1968, interrupting Barth's revision of a lecture for an ecumenical week of prayer at the Paulus Academy in Zurich on the character of the church. Eberhard Busch, Barth's theological assistant at the time, tells us that Barth left his address mid-sentence—a sentence to which he never returned—in a paragraph on the church's need to return again and again to the Fathers and listen to those who have gone before in the faith. He was writing, "'God is not a God of the dead but of the living.' In Him they all live—from the Apostles down to the Fathers of the day before yesterday and of yesterday."[127] That these were Barth's final words and that his final conversation was with his lifelong friend, though an accident of circumstance, form an appropriate close to his searching friendship with Thurneysen. They had each been for the other mentor, confidant, and colleague. Together, they had consistently followed Barth's final word of counsel by returning again and again to be mentored by fathers and pastors who had labored before them, in order that they might discern how to carry on the faithful ministry of Christ today, which others had carried on yesterday and the day before yesterday.

THOUGHTS FOR REFLECTION

Are our situations distinctly different from Barth's and Thurneysen's? Yes and No. Will our mentoring friendships influence the course of theology, or bear us up in the midst of a world war, or be sustained through six decades? Probably not, though the differences are relatively trivial. The distinctions only mean that the hand of providence has not given us to such tasks or such times—and for that we may be grateful. But we have been given the task of theologizing in and for the church. "For such a time as this," we have been given to people in our churches, and they have been given to us. While we may not be forced to confront the ecclesial commandeering by a totalitarian state, we do confront the totalitarian demands of a hegemonic culture impatient with Christianity's declaration that freedom comes through service, life through death, and victory through surrender. Therefore we, too, seek out substantial words. When Barth protested against the nationalisms of Germany, the U.S., and Soviet Russia, he did so on the basis of the first commandment: "I am the Lord your God who brought you out of the land of Egypt; Thou shalt have no other gods before me." When he protested against the anthropocentric theology of Schleiermacher, Ritschl, or Bultmann, he did so on the basis of Christ's claim: "I am the way the truth and the life, no one comes to the Father but through me." His protests *against* were always rooted in a concern *for* something more substantial: *for* the honor of God, *for* the freedom of the church, *for* true human freedom in Christ, *for* humanizing socio-political righteousness, and his protests were always made *with* others, like Thurneysen, so that together they might search for substantial and compelling words through which God might mediate his one Word, Jesus Christ.

QUESTIONS FOR CONSIDERATION

1. How might we foster "liturgical conversations" with our mentor or mentee? Do we speak and listen expecting to hear the Spirit in and through him or her?

2. How are we called to speak and to help our congregations speak decisive, substantial words that resist being absorbed into the ephemeral din of cultural chatter?

3. Barth and Thurneysen revealed their personal and vocational unrest to each other in their mentoring friendship. Are we able to do the same? Do we create the space necessary for others to do so?

4. What unique interests or experiences does the other person bring to the mentoring friendship, and how can we create opportunities for those to flourish?

5. What difference does it make to consider that we have been given our mentor or mentee by God, as a neighbor who has become a brother or sister?

6. How important is it for us to have support in times of transition, doubt, or unfaithfulness?

7. What kind of support do we need and can we offer?

8. How important is it to be known by someone else in order to know ourselves or to gain clarity about what we actually think and believe?

9. Barth and Thurneysen made a weekly five-hour round-trip walk when they were pastors so they could talk about things that mattered—God, the kingdom and their churches—what efforts are required of us to do the same with our mentor or mentee?

CHAPTER 9

TOOLS FOR PASTORAL MENTORING

Here we are, you and I, and I hope a third, Christ, is in our midst. There is no one now to disturb us; there is no one to break in upon our friendly chat, no man's prattle or noise of any kind will creep into this pleasant solitude. Come now, beloved, open your heart, and pour into these friendly ears whatsoever you will, and let us accept gracefully the boon of this place, time, and leisure.[1]

Aelred of Rievaulx

Our journeys of faith and vocation are not ones that we travel alone. We have been born into relationship with God the Father, God the Son, and God the Holy Spirit, and called into the body of believers, Christ's bride, the church—that great myriad of persons, past and present, with whom we share faith in the resurrected Christ Jesus. We acquire knowledge of ourselves, and thus our identity, through the lenses that these two primary relationships offer us. Aelred of Rievaulx, though his invitation quoted above sounds rather romanticized to our ears, was acutely aware of this, and demonstrated his love for Christ through the mutual friendships and spiritual direction he shared with companions and strangers alike. Before and after Aelred, many others, some of whom we have already walked alongside in this book and some of whom you will walk alongside in your ministry, made the decision, sometimes at no little cost to themselves, to open their lives, thoughts, and ministries to others for the sake of service to Christ and the church. In this final section of the book we offer a few structural and practical examples that others have found useful in their practice of this form of service.

However, a small *caveat* first: the following are indeed suggestions, none of which represent the definitive way to shape such a relationship. As we have tried to emphasize, and as most people's experiences will verify, mentoring friendships are pluriform in kind. We are created and redeemed in all our particularity as individuals, and we find ourselves in unique situations in life and ministry, and in various ecclesiastical communities. As such, a given example may or may not be appropriate for you, though they all have proven helpful to someone at some times. Therefore, we encourage you to carefully consider which of these might be useful in your unique vocational or ministerial situation.

MENTEE & MENTOR

Prayer

> Directors and directees alike should prepare for their sessions together by listening to God: that is, by contemplative prayer.[2]

We begin with prayer, the one "suggestion" exempt from the above *caveat*. This one is not optional. Without question, prayer is fundamental to our growth and maturity as Christians. Indeed prayer is an expression of our need for God and a reflection of our desire to know him. It is a discipline that needs to be taught, learned, and practiced, even though, as many have reminded us, it is actually our "first language" as humans. Prayer—invocation of the triune God—for all its complexity and simplicity is not a heavy burden laid upon us for the sake of shaming and guilting us if we neglect it. Kierkegaard described it rather well as being "like breathing—if you don't breathe you die. If you don't pray you spiritually die."[3] New creatures in Christ breathe the air of prayer as rhythmically and—potentially—as naturally as physical creatures breathe air. Catherine of Siena, along with most Christian "mystics," seemed to understand this. She spent days in solitude, sustained by praying and meditation. Prayer became her daily bread, to change the metaphor, that nourished and sustained her life and ministry and that gave substance to her words and actions.

Both mentor and mentee should also feed upon prayer. Prepare for your time together in this way. Afford ample time to "feast" upon prayer while you are together. On the final page of his book, *A Theology of Pastoral Care,* Eduard Thurneysen reflected on the necessity of prayer in pastoral conversations.

> To pray means here that our listening to the neighbor, like our priestly speaking to him, is embedded in our listening and speaking to God. This prayerful hearing and speaking brings about the powerful protection, the great help, the liberating, purifying clarity which must surround, penetrate, and sustain the whole conversation . . . then the atmosphere is created for a mutual encounter without any false dependency, but in true unity before him who is the Lord of this conversation and wills our conversation to become the place where we may hear and transmit his gracious and saving call and word.[4]

Covenant

> Spiritual mentoring is a relationship. Whether that relationship is formal and structured, informal and casual, consistent or sporadic, the heart of spiritual mentoring is relational.[5]

Many have found that a written commitment and semi-formal structure are helpful, if not essential, for maintaining the regularity and depth of the relationship. This written "covenant" is like staking out boundaries for a garden. In the midst of the legitimate, but often encroaching, demands of school, church, family, and friends, the covenant dedicates particular temporal space to the cultivation and growth of this relationship. While occasionally a particular pairing of mentee and mentor may need to be ended due to some sort of conflict or ill-fit, both parties should take care that neither a lack of attention nor the clamoring demands of other pressures are the reason. In a society where many people—including each of us—suffer from broken relationships, isolating autonomy, and the careless inattention of others, we are called to tend to other persons and afford them the respect and care that is their due as our "neighbors." Therefore, the mentoring relationship should not be entered into lightly, but with due diligence, commitment, and willingness to offer your own spiritual, personal, and vocational landscape for shared exploration. The covenant, which usually includes both formal and substantive issues, is one way of assisting you in this.

The formal commitment to meet at the same predetermined time each week can reduce anxiety for both persons. It frees the mentee from wondering if the mentor has made time to meet, or whether she will be imposing upon the mentor, or from feeling that she must conjure up some burning question for the mentor when in fact there may be none. Likewise, it frees the mentor from wondering when the mentee will want to meet, or whether she will have to track her down to schedule a suitable time. In many ways, establishing a norm of this sort is an act of love in that it keeps the relationship from becoming haphazard and less formative than it otherwise could be.

Writing general expectations into the covenant also gives both parties concrete norms to refer back to if a particular meeting drifts into routine planning or casual conversation and away from reflection upon the mentee and his participation in ministry. This includes articulating particular areas that the mentee would like to explore during his time in ministry alongside the mentor. These areas should emerge from the mentee's own questions, weaknesses, needs, or desires in any of the four areas we have been considering: a) moral, spiritual, and personal formation, b) pastoral identity and calling, c) theological reflection and deliberation, or d) practical pastoral skills.

For instance, under a) spiritual and moral formation, a mentee may express their perceived need to combine truth-telling with love, or their need to learn how to learn from failure, or how to respond to members of the opposite or the same gender; under b) pastoral identity and calling, she may desire to reflect upon her call or gifts, or reconsider her pastoral vision or values; under c) theological reflection and deliberation, she may include a particular biblical, theological, moral, or practical issue that needs clarification; under d) practical pastoral skills, she may articulate her desire to learn how to listen attentively, or to teach more creatively, or to moderate a discussion, or to comfort the homeless, or to confront the comfortable.

Articulating these at the beginning of the relationship provides some orientation and direction for the extended discussion between mentor and mentee over the following months. One practice many have found useful is to draft together at least a tentative plan for addressing the mentee's particular concerns. In conversation with the mentor, the mentee may be able to determine how she anticipates making progress in these areas to improve her ministry. Some have found it helpful to consider addressing each of these needs or concerns through the four categories of *knowing, being, doing,* and *relating*:

> *Knowing*: consider relevant practical, theological, or biblical study. This may involve reading, memorizing, researching, or observing.

Being: consider reflecting or journaling about the implications both for attending to or neglecting the area of concern, and about past experiences that alerted you to the need, or possible fears you may have relating to it.

Doing: consider what you might do to help you develop in the area, such as teaching, counseling, serving, etc.

Relating: consider meeting with someone who might be able to directly speak into the area or offer direct feedback.

The mentee may offer occasional progress reports along with a final assessment or reflection on her development in these particular areas.

The covenant should not hamper the relationship, however. Inviting the Holy Spirit to be a third discussion partner means that your discussions may take unanticipated turns. The Spirit has a way of doing that. In order to avoid merely executing the meeting in a rather clinical or perfunctory manner, both mentor and mentee need to be sensitive to this third member of their dialogue.

See **Appendix 1** for an example of a covenant.

The Lay Committee

In addition to the mentoring relationship that students may have with pastors or staff members in the church, some kind of "lay committee" of church members may also be formed to provide periodic feedback to mentees. Usually comprised of three to five people agreed upon by the mentee and mentor, this committee represents the congregation with whom the student is ministering and provides a unique but significant contribution to the mentee's growth and development. The purpose of the lay committee, like the mentor, is to assist the student in his self-knowledge as a pastor and in the refinement of his skills and abilities. They should make conscious efforts to encourage and challenge the mentee as he works alongside the congregation or organization. The committee's role is to provide honest and sensitive feedback regarding their experience and perceptions of the student in certain situations. Though the primary mentor should assist and counsel the committee, he or she would not have to attend the mentee-lay committee meetings.

We have listed a few suggestions below that may be helpful for the formation of the lay committee. As with the primary mentor, formalizing the commitment, meeting times, and learning goals with the student may prove helpful.

1. The mentee and mentor should each suggest a few names of people who they feel might be helpful and insightful members of the committee. These should be people who are involved in the church and who may have opportunity to work alongside the mentee or to witness him at work.

2. The mentee should draw up a list of learning goals, as explained earlier in this section, toward which he can work over the course of his time with the mentor and the lay committee.

3. The committee, however, may have its own objectives as it looks to the ongoing formation of the student. If this is the case, these should be tentatively agreed upon by the committee prior to meeting with the mentee.

4. Each party should commit to regular meetings throughout the entire term of the student internship.

5. When discussing the mentee's ministry, the lay committee should draw upon concrete examples from his ministry experience in order to help him understand and learn from his experiences. For many this is a new and perhaps intimidating experience, so concerns and questions should be offered gently and wisely, and encouragement and prayer often and lavishly.

6. Appoint a facilitator/chairperson to ensure that the meeting focuses on the agreed areas or some other significant aspect of his ministry.

7. Appoint someone to take notes during the meeting. This will help enormously in charting the progression and development of the student and will provide him with a helpful tool as he reflects upon his ministry experience.

8. Leave ample time for prayer during your time together.

9. Consider how to end the formal relationship well—a shared meal, a service of some kind, a blessing from the committee, etc. Both the lay committee and the mentee should be given time to express their gratitude for the other and to offer final thoughts and encouragement.

Reading and Reflecting Together

Many mentoring pastors have found that one way of shifting the focus of the relationship off themselves as "ministry experts" is for both mentor and mentee to read and discuss either books on pastoral ministry or novels about pastors. What Henry Zylstra said about good literature applies equally well to good novels about the lives and ministries of pastors and priests. He said they are able to give order and form to the chaotic nature of life, "so that it is available for appraisal and evaluation . . . To read such a novel is to have entered a universe comprehensive in scope and intensive in quality. It is to have confronted the moral issues of men, not in the skeletons of theory or the bones of principle, but in the flesh and body of concrete experience."[6]

Books, whether fiction or non-fiction, could be read a chapter at a time, week by week. The following short list contains four kinds of books: classic and contemporary texts on pastoral ministry, books on spiritual direction and spiritual friendship, and novels that give flesh to the life and vocation of pastors. Each of these should be somewhat easily obtainable. Since most pastors will be able to draft their own list and may be disappointed to find a particularly formative book absent, consider this list a mere beginning and a spark for your imagination.

CLASSIC TEXTS ON PASTORAL MINISTRY

Richard Baxter, *Reformed Pastor*

John Chrysostom, *On the Priesthood*

Gregory of Nazianzus, *Flight to Pontus,* or *The Second Oration*

Gregory the Great, *Pastoral Care*

George Herbert, *Country Parson*

John R.H. Moorman, ed., *The Curate of Souls*

Reinhold Niebhur, *The Notebooks of a Tamed Cynic*

Andrew Purves, *Pastoral Theology in the Classical Tradition*

Samuel Rutherford, *The Letters of Samuel Rutherford*

Spurgeon, Charles H., *Lectures to My Students*

Jeremy Taylor, *Collected Works*

William A. Clebsch & Charles R Jaekle, eds., *Pastoral Care in Historical Perspective*

William Willimon, *Pastor: Reader in Ordained Ministry*

CONTEMPORARY BOOKS ON PASTORAL MINISTRY

Ray S. Anderson, ed., *Theological Foundations For Ministry*

Ray S. Anderson, *The Soul of Ministry*

Kenda Creasy Dean and Ken Foster, *The Godbearing Life: The Art of Soul Tending for Youth Ministry*

Kenda Creasy Dean, Chap Clark, Dave Rohm, eds. *Starting Right: Thinking Theologically about Youth Ministry*

Jacob Firet, *Dynamics in Pastoring*

Michael Jinkins, *Transformational Ministry: Church Leadership and the Way of the Cross.*

David Hansen, *The Art of Pastoring, A Little Handbook on Having a Soul*

Eugene H. Petersen, *The Contemplative Pastor, The Unnecessary Pastor* (with Marva Dawn), *Working the Angles, Under The Unpredictable Plant, Five Smooth Stones for Pastoral Work*

Kenneth Leech, *Spirituality and Pastoral Care*

Henri Nouwen *Creative Ministry, In the Name of Jesus, Wounded Healer*

Greg Ogden, *Transforming Discipleship*

Derek J. Tidball, *Skillfull Shepherds*

Eduard Thurneysen, *A Theology of Pastoral Care*

T.F. Torrance, *Royal Priesthood: A Theology of Ordained Ministry*

Joe E. Trull and James E. Carter, *Ministerial Ethics*

William Willimon, *Pastor: The Theology and Practice of Ordained Ministry*

BOOKS ON SPIRITUAL DIRECTION AND SPIRITUAL FRIENDSHIP

Aelred of Rievaulx, *Spiritual Friendship*

David G. Benner, Gary W. Moon, eds., *Spiritual Direction and the Care of Souls*

Dietrich Bonhoeffer, *Life Together, Spiritual Care*

Keith R. Anderson & Randy D. Reese, *Spiritual Mentoring: A Guide for Seeking and Giving Direction*

Peter Ball, *Journey Into Truth: Spiritual Direction in the Anglican Tradition*

Margaret Guenther, *Holy Listening: The Art of Spiritual Direction*

James Houston, *The Mentored Life*

Kenneth Leech, *Soul Friend*

Martin Luther, *Letters of Spiritual Counsel*

Thomas Merton, *Spiritual Direction and Meditation*

Francis Kelly Nemeck & Mary Theresa Coombs, *The Way of Spiritual Direction*

274

Neufelder and Coelho, eds., *Writings on Spiritual Direction by Great Christian Masters*

John Newton, *Letters of John Newton*

Eugene H. Petersen, *The Wisdom of Each Other*

Martin Thornton, *Spiritual Direction*

Frederick von Hugel, *Letters from Baron von Hugel to a Niece*

NOVELS ABOUT PASTORS

Wendell Berry, *Jayber Crow*

Frederick Buechner, *The Final Beast*

Georges Bernanos, *Diary of a Country Priest*

George Eliot, *Scenes of Clerical Life*, or *Romola*

Shusaku Endo, *Silence*

Graham Greene, *The Power and the Glory*

Susan Howatch, *Glittering Images*

Aldous Huxley, *Grey Eminence*

THE MENTOR AND MENTEE: ROLES AND TOOLS

The following suggestions and tools will pertain to either the mentor or the mentee specifically.

Mutual Responsibility

> The director never assumes personal responsibility for the directee's life. We advise, instruct, correct; confirm, encourage, affirm; even give specific directives at times. However, the directee always retains full responsibility for his/her decisions and choices.[7]

As we have seen, both persons in the mentoring relationship face unique challenges and temptations. We need to think ethically about these as well as so many other pastoral situations. The potential for subtle or overt abuse of power does indeed accompany this relationship. Therefore, the mentor should be aware of his or her influence and avoid subtly manipulating the mentee, or forcing him or her towards making a decision of one kind or another. We referred to this earlier as the temptation to become a "demonstrative mentor." On the contrary, the mentor is a prayerful servant who offers prudent, humble, and sober words of counsel and direction. Student mentees will usually be doing pastoral ministry, and so will regularly confront situations that challenge their sense of calling, test their theological minds, and question their emotional maturity. As a mentor, your role will be to create the space for these deep and trying concerns to be raised in a place of security and trust. Your role is to prayerfully listen to them and hopefully point their thinking minds and their praying souls in the right direction. Remember that in many ways, as you mentor them, so will they pastor and mentor others.

For mentees, your role is not that of the passive pupil seeking answers and direction from a life- or ministry-guru. Though Augustine's correspondents regarded him highly, they still had to determine whether and how to follow his counsel in their own situations in life and ministry.

Questions for Consideration

1. Have you suffered pain from being domineered by someone you trusted? If so, are you cautious about entering into a mentoring relationship?

2. What is your motivation for mentoring/being mentored?

3. Do you find it difficult to trust your own decision-making? Are you seeking someone to make difficult decisions on your behalf? Or are you looking to make decisions for someone else in an attempt to rectify poor decisions in your own life?

4. Do you feel an excessive need to challenge or to please someone who is older or in a place of authority, such as your mentor?

MENTOR

Offer of Space

Space should be offered to the mentee, both physically and spiritually. First, the physical space you create may greatly affect the mentee's sense of safety and comfort, and therefore his or her ability and willingness to share life and thoughts. Therefore, neither the cold, bare storage room nor the bustling staff lounge will likely be conducive to open and frank discussions.

The second space you should offer is spiritual space. We live in a world full of upheaval and worry, busyness and fatigue, selfishness and isolation, where the space given for spiritual reflection is often minimal or non-existent. For many, the kind of mentoring relationship we have been discussing will be rather foreign. We can, however, allow the Holy Spirit to begin the work of deconstructing fatigue, busyness, and feelings of isolation by providing sacred, holy created space for the sake of reconstruction and renewal. This space is a place of safety and refuge, encouragement and challenge.

Questions for Consideration

1. How do we allow ourselves the space to commune with God? When or where do you find it difficult? What causes you to be distracted?

2. Reflecting back over your life, when were you truly listened to? What was it that distinguished that occasion from others?

3. If you are extremely busy, how will you afford your complete and undivided attention to the mentee? Will you be a clock-watcher, longing for the session to end so that you can get on with some other important task? How might this affect the meeting?

4. How easy is it for you to be vulnerable as a mentor?

Evaluation

In terms of mentoring for pastoral formation, evaluation of a mentee in a particular ministry setting (e.g., conflict resolution, preaching, chairing a committee) is vitally important for her development and preparation for the pastorate. The mentee may have identified skills in her life that she wishes to develop, and it is your obligation as a mentor to contribute to her growth. Her involvement with a church or para-church ministry that enables her to preach, lead worship, or undertake hospital visitation may be an entirely new activity in her life. She may relish these newly assigned tasks or she may become quite anxious at the prospect. In either case, it is important for you to commit adequate time to support, encourage, and evaluate your mentee. Support outside of normal arranged meetings is an excellent way to see a fuller picture of the unfolding of the mentee's ministry. If that visit is unannounced, the mentee may feel that you are "checking up" on them. Thus it is wise to discuss ahead of time when it might be appropriate to observe the mentee in the course of her work, how you will record your observations, and when you will be able to meet to share your thoughts.

Firsthand Observation

Firsthand observation gives you the opportunity to observe the mentee in the midst of a situation rather than receiving a secondhand account through the mentee's recollection and reflection. Participating in a worship service led by the mentee, or listening to his sermon from the vantage of a pew, or sitting in on a lesson or planning session will enable you to offer faithful feedback to the mentee. You should observe the mentee's reactions and responses to others as well as others' reactions to the mentee. Most mentees will have had some previous experience receiving feedback on a sermon or lesson. Though not always comfortable, the experience usually proves beneficial, for ministry requires the pastor to shape the gospel for both public and private speech, and it is naïve to think that we do not need help learning how to do both well.

Audio / Video Recording

While it should be used sparingly, audio or video recording does allow both mentor and mentee to observe the event from a relatively objective point of view. The mentee can observe his or her own physical and non-verbal communication, and the tape can be stopped for discussion. The mentee can verify that not everyone in the room was sleeping or doing crossword puzzles, as he or she may have believed, and the mentor can suggest that the mentee's detailed exposition of Charles Williams's *Figure of Beatrice*, however brilliant, might not have actually clarified the youth group's understand of love and dating. Audio-visual recordings are more appropriate for public acts of ministry, though, with the permission of everyone involved, they could be used for intimate settings of ministry as well.

Verbal and Written Reports

Verbal and written reports can also be useful mediums for bringing a particular event or question to the mentor. These could be either informal descriptions and reflections, or more formal "verbatims" (extensively employed in Clinical Pastoral Education, or CPE), which reproduce as faithfully as possible the actual words and flow of a conversation. Usually, these will include the following: 1) some description of what the mentee knew about the person or situation beforehand, 2) how they anticipated the conversation would unfold, 3) a record of the conversation and the accompanying emotions, 4) a personal and theological evaluation of the situation, 5) deliberation about similar events in the future.

Regardless of the medium, as a mentor, you will need to be alert to four dynamics, any of which you may discuss with the mentee: a) the actual content of the sermon, lesson, or conversation; b) the medium or structure of a sermon or lesson, or the tone and disposition of a conversation; c) the emotions of the mentee, and her self-perception as person and pastor, and d) the responses of the listener or conversant, whether verbal, cognitive, behavioral, or affective. By discussing these dynamics with the mentee, you can help her gain a more accurate picture of the situation, or help her understand what others might have heard or understood. This can be particularly important if the mentee interprets her sermon as an unmitigated disaster, or regards those present as obstinate, unrepentant sinners. Perspective is hard to gain from inside the situation.

For an example of an evaluation, refer to **Appendix 2**.

Suggesting Further Study

It may occasionally be appropriate to suggest particular tasks or readings as "homework" for the mentee, with the aim of encouraging growth and facilitating further reflection on a particular ministerial, practical, or theological issue. You may want him to engage with the liturgy used for marriage or funeral services, so that he can begin to more fully understand the theological principles used in each rite. You may want him to convey his thoughts and feelings on a congregational issue to help him understand the intricacies involved in leading a congregation. You may ask him to read a particular article or listen to a particular sermon tape. However, be mindful of the mentee's other responsibilities and demands upon his time from school, church, or family.

Listen to Your Past and Recall Your Spiritual Landscape

> As supervisors we need to know where we are in our pilgrimage in life and in faith. We have a particular history, heritage and future. All of these affect what happens on the interface between our supervisees and ourselves. The supervisory relationship is shaped by how long we have been in the ministry, our dreams and whether they are being fulfilled or frustrated.[8]

Each of us is affected in one way or another by our past. One of the strengths you can offer as a mentor is insight and perspective born of your experience. This, however, will require you to reflect upon your own journey of pastoral formation and pastoral ministry. As a mentor, you are called to reflect upon God's work and guidance in your own life, which will serve as testimony to the grace of God at work in others' lives. Recalling the struggles, joys, failures, and successes in your own life and ministry, and then relating those to the experience of your mentee, will help to deepen the relationship by developing mutual identification and trust. For example, your mentee may question her chosen vocation and doubt whether this is where God has led her to serve. If you can identify with the same struggle, recalling your own doubt and fear and vocalising this to the mentee may in fact aid her through this difficult time of struggle, or at least lessen her anxiety. Therefore, be attentive to the life of the other and be willing to share your life as a means through which God can minister and his Holy Spirit can guide.

Questions for Consideration

1. Listen to the voices from your past—what impact have they had? In what ways did they guide/counsel you?

2. What circumstances in life did you find difficult or exhilerating? What did you learn that will add depth to your mentoring?

Confidentiality

Confidentiality is essential to pastoral mentoring, as it is in any aspect of pastoral ministry. We should give the same care to the words that someone confesses or reveals to us in speech as we give to that person, because that person is embodied in his or her speech. For this reason, nothing that the mentee shares with you should be divulged, even discriminately, to someone else unless you first discuss it with the mentee. However, there may be certain circumstances that warrant input from a counselor, doctor, or other qualified pastor. If you decide that this is necessary, you should first secure the mentee's permission to include this third person, regardless of whether this person ever attends one of the weekly meetings. The issues surrounding expectations of confidentiality should be discussed explicitly at the first meeting and perhaps even written into the covenant agreement. The care taken with regards to confidentiality can be a dignifying act of love to the mentee.

MENTEE

Choosing an Internship/Mentor

Whether you are seeking a mentoring relationship in order to fulfil an academic requirement for "supervised ministry" or simply for the sake of your pastoral formation, one of your initial questions will be how and where to find a mentor.

It would be easy to suggest that in choosing a place of ministry you simply accept the first available placement, or that in choosing a mentor you look for the most approachable or successful pastor. However, consider carefully how your particular interests and needs might match with a potential place of ministry and mentor. For this formative experience in your pastoral formation, be careful not to overlook either the small, the subtle, or the quiet places. You will spend a considerable amount of your time and energy in this place and with this person, and you may not have many other opportunities of this kind. Therefore, choose wisely, and in consultation with friends, family, and colleagues who know you well. Mentees will occasionally meet with two or three potential mentors before making a decision. Try to be as forthright as possible when you meet, sharing your interests, concerns, and reasons for considering them as mentors. However, be mindful that some pastors may not be able to devote the necessary time and space, given their other responsibilities. Find a mentor that has the time and energy to give to you. Below is a sampling of questions you may wish to consider as you prepare to choose your internship and mentor.

1. Describe your call to ministry. Include the role played by a community of faith as well as individuals who assisted you in naming your gifts for ministry.

2. What type of ministry do you see yourself doing after you graduate?

3. What time constraints do you have?

4. What are your strengths—personal and professional? Your weaknesses?

5. What are your developmental needs—personal and professional?

6. What are the reasons or factors that attract you to this internship?

7. Why do you think this is the right place for you?

8. What do you want to learn?

9. In a mentor or supervisor, what kind of leadership style do you dislike? What do you like?

10. Why do you want to be mentored by this particular person?

11. What do you want to learn from this person or internship?

12. How will this internship or relationship stretch you and help you to grow—personally, professionally, emotionally, socially, theologically and spiritually?

13. How will this internship and relationship with this mentor lead you to become a more effective pastoral minister?

Prepare

Mentoring and formation happen during the regular rhythm of meeting, sharing, thinking, and praying together. In order for this time to serve its purpose, both mentor and mentee need to prepare ahead of time. The need for preparation attends the mentoring meetings, just as it does the preaching of a sermon, the teaching of a lesson, or the visiting of parishioners. Our responsibility in these events is to do what we can to enable them to become swift conduits of the Spirit's work. It would be foolish irresponsibility to step up to preach or teach having given no thought before that moment as to what we should say. It is unloving to counsel a parishioner if we have not given his or her unique situation consideration before he or she stepped into our office. In order to do these things with integrity, insight, and understanding, we prepare.

As a mentee, you may want to prepare for the meeting by reviewing the past few weeks of work and ministry. What has happened? What have you experienced and learned? Were there times you were frustrated either with another person or with yourself? Was either your theology or your practice of ministry challenged? Out of all that happened, can you focus your thoughts on one or two significant events or questions. Without such preparation, the regular meetings may become casual chatting sessions. The quality of engagement between mentor and mentee—or the depth of friendship and formation—will in most instances be directly proportionate to the time spent in thoughtful preparation for the meetings.

There are various methods that can be used to record your ministry experience, such as verbatims, "experience-in-ministry reports," or even an audio or visual record, accompanied by your reflections after the event. Whatever vehicle you choose, consider reflection on the following:

• *Context* of the experience: What took place? When and where? Who was involved? How did they respond?

- *Analysis* of the experience: How do you consider it biblically? Theologically? Pastorally? Personally?
- *Evaluation* of the experience—Evaluate your acts and words. Did the experience confirm or challenge you? Would you say or do the same thing next time? Why or why not?
- *Interpretation* of the experience: What did it reveal about you personally? About your theology? About your understanding of ministry? About your skill set and competency?
- *Response* to the experience: What can you do in response? What will you do similarly or differently next time?

Retreat

This exercise should supplement regular mentoring meetings. We have already seen that in the life of Catherine of Siena, personal retreats alone with God apart from her sisters became central to her life and ministry. Indeed, time for this in the rhythm of daily living is vital for pastors long exercised in ministry. Days of retreat and sabbath should become regular practices for pastors early in their formation and preparation, as these will help to sustain them during their long years in pastoral ministry. This may mean a two-day respite in a retreat centre, or a weekend away in a cabin, or a day hiding out at a friend's empty house. Wherever and whatever that place is, time should be made for praying, reading Scripture, and seeking God's counsel, comfort, and challenge. This is the "day alone," which, as Bonhoeffer counseled, should accompany the "day together" with other pastors or believers—a day for being alone with the triune God away from the distractions of the outside world.

Journal

To facilitate regular and beneficial reflection and deliberation, and to supply material for discussion with the mentor, you might consider practicing the art and discipline of journaling. Like any art or skill, journaling requires the regular sequestering of time devoted solely to its pursuit. To journal is more than simply to maintain a diary. The journal is a commentary on one's journey—one's theological, personal, pastoral, spiritual journey through events both mundane and extraordinary. This discipline is a gifting to ourselves of time and space, set aside to help us understand who we are, where we are, what we are doing, and what the Triune God of grace is doing in, through, and with us. Journaling can be the means by which we enter into the felt absence and presence of God and begin to develop our theological and pastoral vision to see God's hands at work in our lives no matter how things appear to our physical eyes. Journaling is also a very tangible way to track our growth and formation, to recall how God has graced our lives, and to confirm that in fact the Spirit has been working in and through us.

This obviously does not mean that everything you write must be shared with your mentor. On the contrary, as you pour out your soul onto the written page, you may legitimately feel that such transparency should remain between you and God alone. However, journaling and sharing extracts from what you have written, particularly if you record your ministerial activity, will certainly add depth and focus to the time with your mentor.

On the other hand, some academic programs may require students to journal and to submit their journals to be read by a field supervisor or professor. Enormous risk and trust are required in these situations, which, presumably, will be honored by the person designated to read and respond to them. If this is the case, the following questions may be helpful:

1. What was the significant ministry-related event(s) of my days or week?

2. How did I interact with others, such as my mentor, other staff members, or the people of the church?

3. What has this event(s) helped me to understand about the church and the people among whom I am working, or about myself as a person, as a Christian, and as a minister?

4. Where was I most comfortable in the experience? Why? Where was I least comfortable? Why?

5. Where am I finding joy and inspiration in my ministry? What depresses, troubles, or unsettles me?

6. To what extent do the difficulties I am encountering lie within the ministry-situation itself or within me?

7. To what extent am I free to do acts of love for people, emotionally, spiritually, intellectually?

8. How is this ministry experience helping me to know God and to know who I am in relation to God?

Though not everyone will take up the art of journaling, this commonly practiced discipline is a useful tool, commended by countless generations of believers and pastors for increasing knowledge and understanding of yourself and of the God who has called you to be his child and his minister.

Group Meeting—Collegial Consultation

With Karl Barth and Eduard Thurneysen, with the Eclectic Society, and with the Finkenwalde seminarians, many know the benefit of candid conversations with friends and peers about a common vocation, common struggle, or a common interest. "There is nothing more enjoyable for me than to find a number of preachers, with able minds, meeting together to discuss various views in order to arrive at a common opinion," wrote John Newton.

Our joys are rarely greater and our burdens seldom lighter than when shared with another person who has known a similar experience. Like stories common to prairie-dwellers—whether Kansan, Saskatchewan, or Ukrainian—or city-dwellers—whether Hong Kong, New York, or Delhi—any two pastors, despite the differences in details between their situations, will usually find the other's experiences and concerns strangely familiar.

A practice that many mentees have found exceedingly beneficial is occasional conversation with a small group of other students, interns, or mentees also involved in ministry. Persons in the group are thus able to "mentor" each other and provide a web of support or a sympathetic ear. Each person will bring particular gifts and insights, strengths, and weakneses, and so each may learn from any of the others.

This kind of "collegial mentoring" requires trust, a willingness to listen, share, encourage, and challenge. The group may choose to leave each meeting open for any person to bring significant questions or ministry experiences, or it may choose to designate one or two persons to offer the subject matter for discussion, be it an experience, a challenge, or a question that has arisen in the course of their ministry. Prayer together and individual prayer for the other persons should become their common practice.

CONCLUSION

Each of these tools are potentially helpful means that the mentor and mentee may keep at hand. Building the relationship around a structured set of times and practices can be very helpful, especially in the world of ministry, where flexing and changing schedules are often the norm. Therefore, mentor and mentee may want to discuss each of the suggestions offered in this chapter in order to determine which ones may prove most beneficial for their relationship in their time and place.

CHAPTER 10

A BENEDICTION

Saint Jerome, one of the great doctors of the Western church and the translator of the Latin Vulgate, was for several years a student of Gregory of Nazianzus in Constantinople.[1] In his letters Jerome often referred to the wise counsel and instruction he received from Gregory, his mentor—that previously unwilling and hesitant young priest who fled from the ordination forced upon him. Saint Jerome, however, was not only mentee to Gregory, but in turn became mentor to many other priests and laypersons. Rather than give the final word to Gregory himself, we will listen to the counsel his mentee passed on to a newly ordained pastor in 394—counsel that closely resembles that which he had received from Gregory: "Read the divine scriptures constantly; never, indeed, let the sacred volume be out of your hand. Learn what you have to teach . . . Do not let your deeds belie your words . . . [for] in a priest of Christ mouth, mind, and hand should be at one."[2]

Here at the end we return to our opening questions: How may a man or a woman who is called to participate in the Trinitarian life of love between Father, Son, and Spirit, who is set in the midst of a local community of believers, and who faces an increasingly impersonal and intolerant culture—how may he or she be adequately prepared for a life of ministry in service to God, the church, and the world? How may he or she be adequately formed so that mouth, mind, and hand are one?

We have inquired of Scripture concerning the arduous and unglamorous nature of this work to which the Spirit has called generation after generation of sinful and disordered, yet created and loved, vessels of clay. We have asked these questions of many pastors and teachers of the church—Gregory of Nazianzus, Augustine, Catherine, Newton, Bonhoeffer, Thurneysen, and Barth. We have attempted to listen to their wisdom, to attend to their examples, and to heed their direction. Doing so we find them consistently pointing us to some version of the practice we have been considering throughout these pages—personal mentoring for the sake of a pastor's formation and preparation for faithful ministry. Thus it appears that "mentoring," in one form or another, has been commonly practiced and heartily commended by the church as a way that is faithful to Scripture, theology, and human experience.

Our guides have taught us that the congruence of mouth, mind, and hand—and, we may add, heart—is not possible outside of the care, counsel, exhortation, encouragement, and hopeful liberation freely offered to us by other persons—and in this case by the mentor, who has become a traveling companion on our journey of pastoral formation. Though Christ and the Spirit are our primary guides and teachers on this journey, as Bonhoeffer reminds us, Christ and the Spirit speak to us through the community of believers:

> Christian community means community through Jesus Christ and in Jesus Christ . . . What does that mean? It means, *first*, that a Christian needs others for the sake of Jesus Christ. It means, *second*, that a Christian comes to others only through Jesus Christ. It means, *third*, that from eternity we have been chosen in Jesus Christ, accepted in time, and united for eternity.[3]

As for how to foster community, Bonhoeffer does not offer a single new technique, but instead offers the traditional practices of the church: reading Scripture together, praying together, confessing together, sharing one another's burdens, encouraging one another, and, through all of these, loving one another. These practices are fundamental to the formation of a Christian community and to the practice of mentoring for pastoral formation and preparation. We might say that they, in fact, define Christian mentoring.

Openness to be mentored and to mentor, therefore, is not a vain pursuit but rather a glad acknowledgement of who we are as persons, created and redeemed. Only through being "in Christ" in community are we enabled to live open and transparent lives, sharing our joys, weaknesses, and struggles. In Christ in community, we may move, however haltingly, toward a truer and more joyful integration of the person we have been created to be with the ministry that we have been called to exercise.

Therefore, with a host of other pastors and theologians, poets, and priests, we invite you to pull on your boots, find a companion, and begin this journey of joyful camaraderie, trekking back and forth along trails many others have trod, but trails that need to be cut again and again by each one of us. As you have been hosted, so host others; as you have been pastored, so pastor others; and as the Master potter has used others to shape you, so offer yourself to be the potter's rib with which he may shape other vessels to carry the life-giving water of the gospel to a parched world.

APPENDIX 1

MENTORING COVENANT

Name of Student:

Name of Mentor

Agreed Time and Place:

Student — Consider your experience in the following areas:
1= None 2 = Little 3 = Considerable 4 = Extensive

PREACHING:

LEADING WORSHIP:

EVANGELISM:

SOCIAL JUSTICE:

AGE SPECIFIC MINISTRY (CHILDREN, YOUTH, ELDERLY):

PASTORAL VISITATION:

BBLE STUDY LEADERSHIP:

RECRUITMENT / TRAINING:

Student's learning goals / need for development in either a)
moral or spiritual formation; b) pastoral identity; c) theological
reflection and deliberation; d) practical pastoral skills:

Student's learning goals / need for development in either a) moral or spiritual formation; b) pastoral identity; c) theological reflection and deliberation; d) practical pastoral skills:

Specific ways to address my goals / need:

KNOWING:

BEING:

DOING:

RELATING:

To cultivate the mentoring friendship we will:

_____   _____
Signature of Student: Date

_____   _____
Signature of Mentor   Date

APPENDIX 2

MINISTRY EVALUATION REPORT

Name of Student:

Name of Mentor

Date:

Roles to consider and observable behaviour

Evaluation of Specified Area:

A = Exceptional
B = Good
C = Average
D = Weak
E = Poor
N/O = Not observed

PREACHING/LEADING WORSHIP SERVICE: Use of voice, communicates clearly, relevance, interprets text faithfully, leads service well

Rating:

ADMINISTRATION: can cope with time management, balances their work and life, oversees church meetings well, takes initiative in developing programs

Rating:

RELATIONSHIPS: can accept people different from themselves, responds with empathy, makes a point to complete visitation to the sick and elderly, makes a point of interacting with all Church staff

Rating:

EVANGELISM: identifies and cares for the needy persons within the community, can relate the Christian faith meaningfully with people outside the church

Rating:

CHURCH LEADERSHIP: involves learners, allows for views to be shared, encourages learning, understands when to lead and direct and when to allow others to lead and direct, remains humble in service

Rating:

WORK HABITS: is timely, keeps appointments, has smart appearance, is dependable

Rating:

CONTRIBUTION: what value has the student added to your Church or para-church ministry? Do you see their gifting aligned correctly with their chosen ministry path?

Rating:

Discussed with Student?   Y/N

_____   _____
Signature of Mentor   Date

NOTES

CHAPTER 1:
GREGORY OF NAZIANZUS AND THE FLIGHT OF PASTORS

[1] Gregory of Nazianzus, *In Defense of his Flight to Pontus, and His Return, After his Ordination to the Priesthood, with an Exposition of the Character of the Priestly Office* (trans. Charles Gordon Browne and James Edward Swallow; vol. 7 of *A Select Library of the Nicene and Post-Nicene Fathers of the Christian Church*, Second Series, ed. Philip Schaff and Henry Wace; Grand Rapids: Eerdmans, 1974). This "sermon" has traditionally been referred to as *Flight to Pontus*, or the *Second Oration*, and is cited as such: *Flight* 2.99.

[2] *Flight* 2.112.

[3] Athanasius was bishop of Alexandria at this time, though he was likely suffering one of his many periods of exile while Gregory was there.

[4] En route to Athens the as yet unbaptized Gregory found himself on a ship sinking in the midst of a violent storm off the coast of Cyprus. He raised his voice above the waves, and vowed to commit his life to Christian service were he spared from becoming, as he called it, a "sea-corpse." In an autobiographical poem he recalls his prayer: "To Thee I live, if I escape the waves, And gain baptismal dews; and Thou wilt lose A faithful servant if Thou cast me off, Even now Thine own disciple, in the deep." Quoted in "Prolegomena" to vol. 7 of *Nicene and Post-Nicene Fathers of the Christian Church*, Second Series, p. 189, fn. 4.

[5] Here he preached his famous *Five Orations on the Divinity of the Logos*, which earned him the title "Theologian of the Church."

[6] *Flight* 2.72–73.

[7] Augustine, "Letter 21: To My Lord Bishop Valerius," in *Augustine's Letters* (trans. Sister Wilfrid Parsons: Washington, D. C.: The Catholic University of America Press, 1981).

[8] *Flight* 2.108. On the subject of vocational holiness and Jonah's story, see Eugene II. Peterson's forthright book, *Under the Unpredictable Plant* (Grand Rapids: Eerdmans Publishing Company, 1992).

[9] John Chrysostom, *Treatise Concerning the Christian Priesthood*, III.16.

[10] John Newton, "Letter to a Young Minister," in *Curate of Souls, Being a Collection of Writings on the Nature and Work of a Priest from the first century after the Restoration 1660-1760* (ed. John R. H. Moorman: London: SPCK, 1958), 190-207.

[11] George Herbert, *Country Parson*, in *The English Complete Works* (ed. Ann Pasternak Slater: New York: Everyman's Library, 1995), II.

[12] Richard Baxter, *Reformed Pastor* (ed. William Brown; Edinburgh: Banner of Truth Trust, 1974), 54.

[13] St. Gregory the Great, *Pastoral Care* (trans. Henry Davis, S.J.: New York: Newman Press, 1978), I.1.

[14] Augustine "Letter 21: To Bishop Valerius," in *Augustine's Letters*.

[15] See Robert P. Meye's fine article, "Theological Education as Character Formation," *Theological Education*, Supplement I, (1988): 96-126.

[16] Cf. Eph 5:18 and Acts 2.

[17] Søren Kierkegaard, "Of the Difference between a Genius and an Apostle," in *The Present Age* (trans. Alexander Dru: London: Collins: 1969).

[18] Ibid.

[19] Ibid.

[20] Ray S. Anderson, *The Soul of Ministry* (Louisville: Westminster John Knox Press, 1997), 7.

[21] *Flight* 2.46.

[22] Bishops and priests in Spain, Gaul, Turkey, England, and Italy received Gregory the Great's *Book of Pastoral Rule* and translated it for the benefit of their fellow clergy. In the ninth century both King Alfred the Great in England, and Emperor Charlemagne made its study obligatory for all bishops in their lands.

[23] *Flight* 2.69.

[24] *Flight* 2.71.

[25] *Flight* 2.71.

[26] *Flight* 2.11.

[27] *Flight* 2.113.

[28] *Flight* 2.14.

[29] *Flight* 2.95.

[30] *Flight* 2.16.

[31] *Flight* 2.8.

[32] τεχνη τεχνων. *Flight* 2.16.

[33] *Flight* 2.22.

[34]Andrew Purves, *Pastoral Theology in the Classical Tradition* (Louisville: Westminster John Knox Press, 2001), 19.

[35] *Flight* 2.114-115.

[36] *Flight* 2.36.

[37] *Flight* 2.36.

[38] *Flight* 27.3

[39] *Flight* 2.40

[40] *Flight* 2.43

[41] *Flight* 2.41

[42] *Flight* 2.42

[43] *Flight* 2.45

[44] *Flight* 2.30

[45] *Flight* 2.35

[46] *Flight* 2.39

[47] *Flight* 2.54

[48] *Flight* 2.28

[49] *Flight* 2.30

[50] *Flight* 2.31

[51] *Flight* 2.33

CHAPTER 2:
PASTORAL *SAPIENCE* AND PASTORAL *HABITUS*

[1] *Flight* 2.50.

[2] Augustine, *The Soliloquies*, in *Augustine: Earlier Writings*; (trans. John H. S. Burleigh; The Library of Christian Classics; Philadelphia: The Westminister Press, 1953), I.ii.7.

[3] Augustine, *Confessions* (trans. Henry Chadwick; Oxford: Oxford University Press, 1998), X.i (1).

[4] John Calvin, *Institutes of the Christian Religion* (trans. Ford Lewis Battles; The Library of Christian Classics; ed. John T. McNeill; Philadelphia: The Westminster Press, 1960), I.i.1-2.

[5] Augustine, *On the Trinity,* (trans. Rev. Arthur West Haddan; vol. III of *A Select Library of the Nicene and Post-Nicene Fathers*, First Series, ed. Philip Schaff; Edinburgh: T & T Clark, 1998), XII.xv.25.

[6] Eugene Peterson and Marva Dawn, *The Unnecessary Pastor* (Grand Rapids: Eerdmans, 2000).

[7] Augustine, "Letter 73: To Jerome," in *Augustine's Letters*, 73.10.

[8] Ellen T. Charry, *By The Renewing of Your Minds. The Pastoral Function of Christian Doctrine* (New York: Oxford University Press, 1997), 19

[9] Jn 20:31

[10] Stanley Hauerwas, "Discipleship as a Craft, Church as a Disciplined Community." *The Christian Century* (October, 1991): 881-884.

[11] *Flight* 2.46.

[12] Quoted in Harold H. Rowden, "Theological Education in Historical Perspective" *Vox Evangelica* 7 (1971): 83.

CHAPTER 3:
MENTORING FOR PASTORAL FORMATION

[1] Ambrose, *Duties of the Clergy* (trans. Rev. H. De Romestin, with Rev. E. De Romestin and Rev. H. T. F. Duckworth; vol. 10 of *A Select Library of the Nicene and Post-Nicene Fathers*, Second Series. eds. Philip Schaff and Henry Wace; Grand Rapids: Eerdmans, 1998), bk. II.xx.97.

[2] Quoted in Eberhard Busch, *Karl Barth.* (trans. John Bowden; Philadelphia: SCM Press, 1976), 64.

[3] Richard Hooker, *Of the Laws of Ecclesiastical Polity* Book V, in *The Works of Mr. Richard Hooker* (ed. Rev. John Keble; Oxford: Clarendon Press: 1888), bk. V.lxxxi.2.

CHAPTER 4:
MENTORING AGAINST THE STREAM

[1] For a full characterization of these classical and modern options, see James Houston, *The Mentored Life* (Colorado Springs: Navpress, 2002).

[2] Walker Percy, *The Second Coming* (New York: Farrar, Strauss, Giroux, 1980), 15-16.

[3] Quoted by James Houston, *The Mentored Life*, 50.

[4] C. S. Lewis, *The Four Loves* (London: Geoffrey Bles, 1960), 73-78.

[5] St. Gregory the Great, "How to Admonish the Impatient and the Patient," in *Pastoral Care* (trans. Henry Davis, S.J.; New York: Newman Press, 1978), III.9.

[6] Houston, *Mentored Life*, 51.

[7] This is one reason Dante in his *Inferno* embedded Lucifer in a frozen lake at the center of hell, rather than a cauldron of fire. Whereas love and holiness blaze, and God is an active communion of three, its opposite, contemptuous disdain for others, leads to the immobile, "ungodlike isolation" of the solitary, frozen Lucifer.

[8] Augustine, *The City of God* (trans. Marcus Dods; New York: The Modern Library, 1993), XII.27.

[9] Augustine, *Soliloquies*, I.iii.8.

[10] Robert P. Meye, "Theological Education as Character Formation," *Theological Education*. Supplement I (1988): 100.

[11] *Flight* 2.21

[12] Thomas Merton, *Spiritual Direction* (Collegeville, MN: The Liturgical

Press, 1986), 22.

[13] Dietrich Bonhoeffer. *Life Together* (trans. Daniel W. Bloesch and James H. Burtness; *Life Together* and *Prayerbook of the Bible*, vol. V of *Dietrich Bonhoeffer Works*; English ed. Geffrey B. Kelly; German eds. Gerhard Ludwig **Muller and** Albrecht Schonherr; Minneapolis: Fortress Press, 1996), 95.

[14] Keith R. Anderson and Randy D. Reese, *Spiritual Mentoring. A Guide for Seeking and Giving Direction* (Downer's Grove, Il: IVP, 1999), 103.

[15] Alternatively, as Francis Kelly Nemeck and Marie Theresa Coombs, point out, "spiritually proud people ordinarily want to discern their spirit only with someone whom they think will praise them and be impressed by what they do. . . . They flee those who would change them." *The Way of Spiritual Direction.* (Collegeville, MN: The Liturgical Press), 34.

[16] Eugene Peterson. *The Contemplative Pastor* (Grand Rapids: Eerdmans, 1989), 119

[17] Bonhoeffer, *Life Together*, 108.

[18] Jacob Firet, *Dynamic in Pastoring* (Grand Rapids: Eerdmans, 1986), 282.

[19] Charles Spurgeon suggested that what people see when in this mindset is "no better than what they hear and see at the opera—not so good, perhaps, in point of aesthetic beauty, and not an atom more spiritual." "The Minister's Self-Watch," in *Lectures to My Students* (Grand Rapids: Zondervan Publishing, 1954), 11.

CHAPTER 5:
PASTOR AS MENTOR

[1] Lewis, *The Four Loves*, 104-5.

[2] George Herbert, "Love (3)." *The Complete English Works* (ed. Ann Pasternak Slater; New York: Everyman's Library, 1995).

[3] Karl Barth, "The Task of Ministry," in *The Word of God and the Word of Man* (trans. Douglas Horton; New York: Harper & Brothers Publishers, 1957), 168.

[4] Paulo Freire, *Mentoring the Mentor: A Critical Dialogue with PauloFreire* (ed. Paulo Freire; New York: Peter Lang Publishing 1997), 324.

[5] Parker J. Palmer, *To Know As We Are Known: A Spirituality of Education* (San Francisco: Harper & Row, 1983.)

[6] Flannery O'Connor, "The Nature and Aim of Fiction," in *Mystery and Manners* (eds. Sally and Robert Fitzgerald; New York: Farrar, Strauss & Giroux, 1969), 81.

[7] St. John of the Cross. *The Living Flame of Love* (trans. Kieran Kavanaugh, OCD and Otilio Rodriguez, OCD; ICS Publications, 1997), 3.46.

[8] John Linnan, CSV, "Spiritual Formation in the Roman Catholic Church: A

Historical Sketch," *Journal of Supervision and Training in Ministry* 15 (1994).

[9] Steve Turner, *In the Beginning* (Oxford: Lion Publishing, 1996).

[10] Augustine, "Sermon 6: On the Lord's Prayer in Matthew's Gospel, Chapter 6:9, etc. To the Competentes." (trans. Rev. R. G. MacMullen; vol. 6 of *A Select Library of The Nicene and Post-Nicene Fathers,* First Series. ed. Philip Schaff; Grand Rapids: Eerdmans, 1974). This is sermon LVI of the Benedictine Edition.

[11] Georges Bernanos, *The Diary of a Country Priest* (trans. Pamela Morris; New York: Carroll & Graf Publishers, Inc., 1986).

[12] Kenneth Pohly, *Transforming the Rough Places* (Tennessee: Providence House Publishers, 2001), 108.

[13] Karl Barth, *Church Dogmatics* IV/3 (trans. Geoffrey W. Bromiley; Edinburgh: T&T Clark), 885.

[14] The following recent and quite sobering books will help to alert and sensitize mentor and mentee to the gravity of this area, and likely, to their own vulnerability: Marie M. Fortune, *Is Nothing Sacred? When Sex Invades the Pastoral Relationship* (New York: Harper & Row, 1989); Stan Grenz and Roy Bell, *Betrayal of Trust: Confronting and Preventing Clergy Sexual Misconduct* (Grand Rapids: Baker Books, 2001).

[15] Eugene Peterson, *The Contemplative Pastor* (Grand Rapids: Eerdmans, 1989), 18.

[16] Ambrose, *Duties of the Clergy*, bk. II.xii.62.

[17] Many of the novels of George MacDonald, and all of the novels of Charles Williams show us indeed how thin is this scrim.

[18] Flannery O'Connor, "The Nature and Aim of Fiction," in *Mystery and Manners* (eds. Sally and Robert Fitzgerald; New York: Farrar, Strauss & Giroux, 1969), 68-71.

[19] 1 Cor 5:16.

[20] Charles Williams, *The Descent of the Dove* (London: Longmans, Green, 1939), 1.

[21] For a more nuanced and thick (!) development of some of these themes, see Oliver O'Donovan, *The Desire of the Nations* (Oxford: Oxford University Press, 2000); and Douglas Farrow, *Ascension and Ecclesia* (Edinburgh: T&T Clark, 1999).

[22] George Herbert. "Chapter XIV: The Parson in Circuit," in *The Country Parson.*

[23] Dietrich Bonhoeffer, *Christology* (trans. Edwin Robertson; Glasgow: Collins Fount Paperback, 1978), 27

[24] Bonhoeffer, *Life Together,* 98.

[25] Eph 4:29

[26] Nemeck and Coombs, *The Way of Spiritual Direction,* 73.

[27] Augustine, "Letter 231: To Darius" (trans. Rev. J. G. Pilkington; vol. 1 of *A Select Library of the Nicene and Post-Nicene Fathers,* First Series; ed. Philip

Schaff; Grand Rapids: Eerdmans, 1998), 231.6.

[28] Augustine, *Confessions*, X.i (1-2)

[29] They also received, of course, the Ten Commandments, Leviticus, the writings of the Prophets, and the Wisdom Literature, which obviously emerge from the history of Israel, and which communicate identity and purpose, but which are not themselves narratives.

[30] Quoted in Nicholas Berdyaev, *Dostoevsky* (trans. Donald Attwater; New York: Living Age Books, 1958), 31.

[31] Dietrich Bonhoeffer, *Spiritual Care* (trans. Jay C. Rochelle; Minneapolis: Fortress Press, USA, 1985), 69. Italics added.

[32] 1 Tim 1:4; 1 Cor 16:17; Rom 15:32; Rom 15:30; Phil 1:8

[33] 2 Cor 7:6

[34] Bonhoeffer, *Life Together*, 32.

[35] Augustine, *De Magistro. The Teacher* (trans. John H. S. Burleigh; in *Augustine: Earlier Writings*), 38, 46. Italics added.

[36] Margaret Guenthe, *Holy Listening: The Art of Spiritual Direction.* (Boston: Cowley Publications, 1992), 95.

[37] Jacob Firet, *Dynamics of Pastoring*, 68-82.

[38] Ibid, 70.

[39] See also 1 Thes 5:11; Heb 3:12-13

[40] Firet, *Dynamics of Pastoring*, 90.

[41] Henry Zylstra, "Why Read Novels?" in *Testament of Vision* (Grand Rapids: Eerdmans, 1958), 67.

[42] Phil 4:9; 3:17.

[43] Stanley Hauerwas, "Clerical Character: Reflecting on Ministerial Morality," *Word & World*, Luther Seminary 6, no. 2 (1986): 192.

[44] John Calvin, *Commentary on The Second Epistle of Paul the Apostle to the Corinthians.* (trans. T. A. Smail; in *Calvin's New Testament Commentaries*; eds. David W. Torrance and Thomas F. Torrance; Grand Rapids: Eerdmans), 152.

[45] Bonhoeffer, *Spiritual Care*, 95.

[46] My debt to two works in particular will be obvious to anyone familiar with them: Douglas B. Farrow. *Ascension and Ecclesia.* (Edinburgh: T&T Clark, 1999); and Oliver O'Donovan, *Resurrection and Moral Order,* Second Edition (Grand Rapids: Eerdmans Publishing Company, 1996). They, however, should not be held accountable for the substance of this chapter.

[47] Acts 1:6-11

[48] The argument of the book of Hebrews depends on this point.

[49] 1 Cor 15:42-50; cf. Rom 5.

[50] Popular culture may find it as hard to commercialize and capitalize on Ascension Day as it finds it with Good Friday, though I do not doubt its distorting creativity could find a way.

[51] Karl Barth, *Evangelical Theology: An Introduction* (trans. Grover Foley; New York: Holt, Rinehart, and Winston, 1963).

[52]Karl Barth, "The Humanity of God" (trans. John Newton Thomas; in *The Humanity of God*; Atlanta: John Knox Press, 1960), 37.

[53] Dietrich Bonhoeffer, *Sanctorum Communio. A Theological Study of the Sociology of the Church.* (trans. Reinhard Krauss and Nancy Lukens; vol. 1 of *Dietrich Bonhoeffer Works*; English ed. Clifford J. Green; German ed. Joachim von Soosten; Minneapolis: Fortress Press, 1998), 146.

[54] Though teachers—and computer grammar programs—discourage the use of the passive voice in composition, the sentence above cannot be written otherwise, for our passivity and Christ's activity is precisely the point.

[55] See 2 Cor 5:21; 8:9

[56] Farrow, *Ascension and Ecclesia*, 60.

[57] O'Donovan, *The Desire of the Nations*, 181-3.

[58] 1 Pet 1.

[59] For further on this, see, among other works, Bonhoeffer, *Sanctorum Communio*, especially chapter five.

[60] Dietrich Bonhoeffer, *Life Together*, 33.

[61] I recognize, of course, that the biblical data on the "image of God" is notoriously sparse and the range of characteristics that have been ascribed to it is notoriously broad.

[62] Eph 4:24

[63] Rom 8:29

[64] 1Cor 15:49

[65] Calvin, *Institutes* I.iv.4.

[66] As Stanley Grenz explains: "the traditional designations 'Father' and 'Son' are primarily intended to carry relational, rather than substantial (or, for that matter, masculine) connotations and therefore may be viewed as shortened references to the relationalities 'Father of the Son' and 'Son of the Father.'" *The Social God and the Relational Self* (Louisville: Westminster John Knox Press, 2001), 315.

[67] From Gregory of Nazianzus, *Oration* 40.41; quoted by Calvin, *Institutes* I.xii.17.

[68] Paul Fiddes, *Participating in God. A Pastoral Doctrine of the Trinity.* (Louisville: Westminster John Knox Press, 2000), 6.

[69] Eberhard Jungel, *God's Being is in Becoming.* (trans. John Webster; Grand Rapids: Eerdmans Publishing Company, 2001.)

[70] Calvin, *Institutes* I.xiii.2; cf. I.ii.2; I.iii.1; I.xiii.1. Calvin says to those who protest against the inclusion of non-biblical words like "trinity" and "person" into theology: "What wickedness to disapprove of words that explain nothing else than what is attested and sealed in Scripture!" *Institutes* I.xii.3.

[71] Calvin, *Institutes* I.xiii.5: "Say there is a Trinity of Person in the one Being of God, and you will have said in a word what the Scriptures say."

[72] Calvin, *Institutes* I.xix.19: "For in each hypostasis the whole divine nature is understood, with this qualification—that to each belongs his own peculiar

quality. The Father is wholly in the Son, the Son wholly in the Father, ever as he himself declares: 'I am in the Father, and the Father in me [John 14:10].'"

[73] Augustine, *On the Holy Trinity* (trans. S. McKenna; in *The Fathers of the Church*; Washington: Catholic University of America Press, 1963), V.6. Calvin argues as well that the relation between the persons marks their distinguishing "incommunicable qualities." *Institutes* I.XIII.6.

[74] Thus for you medieval scholastics, Aquinas affirms that "in God relation and essence do not differ from each other, but are one and the same . . . hence it does not follow that there exists in God anything besides relation in reality." *The Summa Theologica* (trans. Father Laurence Shapcote; vol. 17 of *Great Books of the Western World: Aquinas: I*; ed. Mortimer J. Adler; Chicago: Encyclopaedia Britannica, Inc., 1991), Q.28 A.2.

[75] "In the ancient Greek world for someone to be a person means that he has something added to his being." John Zizioulas, *Being as Communion* (Crestwood, NY: St. Vladimier's Seminary Press, 1985), 33. "He" is used intentionally here, as only men participated in the theatre.

[76] The patristic, medieval, Reformation, Protestant scholastic, and twentieth-century "Trinitarian theologians" appear united in their use of "person" to refer to a being's relational nature, rather than the colloquial modern use of the term to describe emotional individuality or rational consciousness. This was also part of Athanasius' defense against Sabellianism, which envisaged the one God taking on three faces or forms, like the common children's lesson that compares God to a person who is concurrently father, uncle, and brother, or daughter, sister, and mother.

[77] Colin Gunton, *The Promise of Trinitarian Theology* (Edinburgh: T&T Clark, 1997), 98.

[78] James Torrance, *Worship, Community, and the Triune God of Grace.* (Downers Grove, Illinois: Inter Varsity Press, 1996), 38.

[79] This excellent phrase is taken from Timothy J. Gorringe, *Karl Barth: Against Hegemony* (Oxford: Oxford University Press, 1999).

[80] John Zizioulas, "Human Capacity and Human Incapacity: A Theological Exploration of Personhood." *Scottish Journal of Philosophy* (1975): 401-448.

[81] An interesting development of this can be found in Charles Williams's works. Like Bonhoeffer, he learned much about personal relations from Kierkegaard and was responsible for the first translations of Kierkegaard's work into English. Williams, in fact, referred to his friends, including the other Inklings—C. S. Lewis, J. R. R. Tolkien, Warnie Lewis, Owen Barfield, etc.—as "the companions of the coinherence," to whom he dedicated his book, *Descent of the Dove.*

[82] cf. Jn 17 and 1 Jn 4. "The biblical imperative to love is an anticipated outworking of the principle that the ultimate foundation for human relationships resides in the eternal dynamic of the triune God. Thus, humans fulfil their purpose as destined to be the *imago dei* by loving after the manner of the triune

God." Stanley Grenz, *The Social God and the Relational Self,* 320.

[83] Karl Barth, *The Christian Life. Church Dogmatics IV/4. Lecture Fragments* (trans. Geoffrey W. Bromiley; Edinburgh: T&T Clark, 1981), 204.

[84] See O'Donovan, *Resurrection and Moral Order,* chapter 11, "The double aspect of the moral life," 226-244.

[85] David S. Cunningham, "Participation as a Trinitarian Virtue," *Toronto Journal of Theology* 14, no. 1 (Spring 1998): 10.

CHAPTER 6:
FOUR AREAS OF PASTORAL FORMATION RECONSIDERED

[1] Ambrose, *Duties of the Clergy,* dII.xii.60, 62.

[2] Baxter, *Reformed Pastor;* italics in original.

[3] See also p. 92-98 of this text.

[4] Karl Barth, "Speech on the Occasion of his Eightieth Birthday" (trans. Eric Mosbacher; in *Fragments Grave and Gray*; ed. Martin Rumscheidt; London: Collins The Fontana Library, 1971), 113.

[5] "Measure everything by the Word of God, the sole truth, which is our judge and our best teacher! You will understand me correctly if you allow what I say to lead you to what *he* says."

[6] Barth, "Speech on the Occasion of his Eightieth Birthday," in *Fragments Grave and Gray,* 116.

[7] Georges Casalis, *Portrait of Karl Barth* (trans. Robert McAfee Brown; Garden City, NY: Anchor Books, 1964), xiii.

[8] H. Richard Niebuhr, *The Purpose of the Church and its Ministry* (New York: Harper & Row, 1977), 64.

[9] Charles H. Spurgeon, "The Call to the Ministry," in *Lectures to my Students,* 22 - 41.

[10] *The Works of The Rev. John Newton. Complete in one Volume* (London: T. Nelson and Sons, 1853).

[11] See also p. 85 of this text.

[12] Cf. Ray S. Anderson, "A Theology for Ministry," in *Theological Foundations for Ministry* (Edinburgh: T&T Clark, 1979), 6-21.

[13] Kenneth Pohly, *Transforming the Rough Places: The Ministry of Supervision* (Franklin, TN: Providence House Publishers, 2001).

[14] Baxter, *Reformed Pastor,* 70.

[15] Saint Augustine, *Teaching Christianity / De Doctrina Christiana* (trans. Edmund Hill, O.P.; ed. John E. Rotelle, O.S.A.; Hyde Park, NY: New City Press, 1996), IV.59-60.

[16] See also p. 129, 259-261, and Appendix 2 of *The Potter's Rib.*

CHAPTER 7.
MENTORING FOR PASTORAL FORMATION IN SCRIPTURE

[1.] Joseph A. Grassi, *The Teacher In The Primitive Church and the Teacher Today* (Santa Clara, CA: University of Santa Clara Press, 1973), 3.

CHAPTER 8:
MENTORING FOR PASTORAL FORMATION
IN THE CHURCH

[1] Augustine, Letter 21: To Bishop Valerius, in *Augustine's Letters*.

[2] Among other more aggressive instances of suppression, apparently in Hippo, the Donatist leader, Faustinus, instructed the Donatist bakers not to sell bread to the Catholic minority. *In Answer to the Letters of Petilian, the Donatist, Bishop of Cirta*, 2.184.

[3] Augustine, Letter 21: To Valerius, in *Augustine's Letters*.

[4] More often than not, he says, he and other bishops had to find just the right moment to approach the local magistrate, only to "stand in line at the door, wait while the reputable and the disreputable alike are shown in, then get ourselves announced, be received at long last, and pour our heart out in pleading, bearing in silence the humiliations heaped upon us, and for all our pains succeed only sometimes, while other times we have to go away disgruntled." Sermon 302.17

[5] See "Sermon 339" and Letter 122: "To the well-beloved brethren the clergy, and the people of Hippo," in vol. 1 of *Nicene and Post-Nicene Fathers*, First Series.

[6] Possidius, *Life of Augustine*, 24.

[7] Letter 110.5: "It is exceptional if a few drops of time are allowed to fall for me." In vol. 1 of *Nicene and Post-Nicene Fathers*, First Series.

[8] Letter 211: "To the Nuns." Augustine wrote to the nuns of a monastery, where his sister had been prioress, to provide instruction for settling a contentious situation.

[9] Letter 10: To Nebridius. In vol. 1 of *Nicene and Post-Nicene Fathers*, First Series.

[10] Augustine, *Newly Discovered Sermons* (trans. Edmund Hill; Hyde Park, New York: New City Press, 1997).

[11] Frederic Van der Meer, *Augustine the Bishop: The Life and Work of a Father of the Church* (trans Brian Battershaw and G.R. Lamb; New York: Sheed & Ward, 1961), 200. See also Cardinal Michele Pellegrino, *The True Priest.* (trans. Arthur Gibson; New York: Philosophical Library, 1968); Lee Francis Bacchi, *The Theology of Ordained Ministry in the Letters of Augustine of Hippo* (Bethesda, MD: International Scholars Publications, 1988); Peter Brown, *Augustine of Hippo: A Biography, Reprinted with* Epilogue (London: Faber/ Berkeley: University of California Press, 2000); Peter Brown, "Augustine the

Bishop in Light of New Documents," *Reflections* 4 (2000).

[12] Van der Meer, *Augustine the Bishop*, 226.

[13] *Confessions* 4.7.

[14] Sister Marie Aquinas McNamara, O.P. *Friends and Friendship for Saint Augustine* (Staten Island, NY: Pauline Fathers and Brothers, Society of St. Paul, 1964), 220-1.

[15] Letter 143: To Marcellinus. In vol. 1 of *Nicene and Post-Nicene Fathers*, First Series.

[16] Letter 55: To Januarius. In vol. 1 of *Nicene and Post-Nicene Fathers*, First Series.

[17] Letter 67: To Jerome. In vol. 1 of *Nicene and Post-Nicene Fathers*, First Series.

[18] Letter 166: To Jerome. In vol. 1 of *Nicene and Post-Nicene Fathers*, First Series.

[19] Letter 258, in *Augustine's Letters*.

[20] Letter 258.1—2, in *Augustine's Letters*.

[21] *Teaching Christianity (De Doctrina Christiana)*, 1. 22.21.

[22] Letter 120.2.4. In vol. 1 of *Nicene and Post-Nicene Church Fathers*, First Series.

[23] Letter 73.10. In *Augustine's Letters*.

[24] Augustine, *On The Catechising of the Uninstructed in one Book*, 1.1-2,

[25] Quoted in McNamara

[26] Letter 54.

[27] Letter 69.2. In vol. 1 of *Nicene and Post-Nicene Church Fathers*, First Series.

[28] Letters 158-164. In vol. 1 of *Nicene and Post-Nicene Church Fathers*, First Series.

[29] Letter 85. In vol. 1 of *Nicene and Post-Nicene Church Fathers*, First Series.

[30] Letter 250. In vol. 1 of *Nicene and Post-Nicene Church Fathers*, First Series.

[31] Letter 228. In vol. 1 of *Nicene and Post-Nicene Church Fathers*, First Series. One thinks of the "whisky priest" in Graham Greene's novel, *The Power and the Glory*, who seems to have heeded Augustine's advice to Honoratus.

[32] Letter 22.

[33] Letter 41. In vol. 1 of *Nicene and Post-Nicene Church Fathers*, First Series.

[34] Ibid.

[35] Letter 91. In vol. 1 of *Nicene and Post-Nicene Church Fathers*, First Series.

[36] Letter 150.

[37] Letter 245. In vol. 1 of *Nicene and Post-Nicene Church Fathers*, First Series.

[38] In 393, only two years after his ordination, Valerius had Augustine teaching the pan-African assembly of bishops on "Faith and Creed" when they came to Hippo.

[39] He was ignorant at the time that this violated an important regulation of the Nicene Council.

[40] Letter 32.

[41] Quoted in Pellegrino, 62.

[42] Quoted in Pellegrino, *The True Priest*, 62.

[43] Letter 118.3.22. In vol. 1 of *Nicene and Post-Nicene Church Fathers*, First Series.

[44] Ibid.

[45] Letter 95.

[46] Sermon 140. Quoted in Pellegrino. *The True Priest*: 84.

[47] Letter 134.

[48] Augustine, *Contra Faustum* 22.56.

[49] Letter 65, in *The Letters of Catherine of Siena*, vol. I (trans. Suzanne Noffke; Tempe, AZ: Arizona Center for Medieval and Renaissance Studies, 2000), 207.

[50] Letter 63 to Pope Gregory XI, in *Letters*, 202.

[51] Letter 53, in *Letters*, 165.

[52] Letter 70, in *Letters*, 220.

[53] Suzanne Noffke, O.P. *Catherine of Siena—Visions Through A Distant Eye.* (Liturgical Press, 1996), 14.

[54] Letter 87, in *Letters*, 263.

[55] John H. Pratt, *Eclectic Notes; or, Notes of Discussions on Religious Topics at the Metings of the Eclectic Society, London during the years 1798—1814* (London: James Nisbet and Co., 1856), 1.

[56] Quoted in D. Bruce Hindmarsh, *John Newton and the Evangelical Tradition* (Grand Rapids: Eerdmans, 1996), 313.

[57] The same slave-trade Augustine had protested over 1300 years earlier!

[58] Letter "To the Hon. and Rev. W. B. Cadogan," in Josiah Bull, *John Newton of Olney and St. Mary Woolnoth. An Autobiography and Narrative, Compiled Chiefly from his Diary and Other Unpublished Documents* (London: The Religious Tract Society, 1868): 412.

[59] Recall Gregory of Nazianzus' similar prayer when despairing on the Mediterranean Sea in 360 A.D.

[60] John Newton, *An Authentic Narrative*, in *The Works of The Rev. John Newton. Complete in one Volume* (London: T. Nelson and Sons, 1853). See also Letter VIII.

[61] cf. Greg Schaefer, " "My Dear Friend . . . ": Concepts on Mentoring a Hymn Writer Based on Selected Correspondence of Rev. John Newton and William Cowper, 1767-1786." *The Hymn* 50, no. 1 (January 1999): 34-37.

[62] Like Gregory of Nazianzus, Newton compared his journey into the

pastorate to Jonah: "[Jonah] was the only one delivered after having been entombed in the belly of a fish, and I, perhaps, the only one ever brought forth from bondage and misery in Africa to preach 'Jesus Christ and him crucified.' " Letter to Mrs. Hannah Moore, May 24, 1800.

[63] Hindmarsh, *John Newton*, 169.

[64] Letter II, "Extract of a Letter to a Student in Divinity," in *The Works of The Rev. John Newton*.

[65] Letter from Newton to William Bull, April 17th, 1782. Josiah Bull, *Letters of John Newton of Olney and St. Mary Woolnoth* (London: The Religious Tract Society, 1869), 257.

[66] The following is from "A Plan of Academical Preparation for the Ministry," in *The Works of The Rev. John Newton*, 897-909.

[67] "Unless I can procure a proper tutor, I must give up my design."

[68] Along with this came the ability to select out for students worthy authors "from the surrounding rubbish in which they are almost buried"—wisdom needed even more so in our own day than in Newton's.

[69] Letter II, "Extract of a Letter to a Student in Divinity," in *The Works of The Rev. John Newton*, 39.

[70] Ibid.

[71] "A Plan of Academical Preparation for the Ministry" in *The Works of The Rev. John Newton*.

[72] Letter II, "Extract of a Letter to a Student in Divinity," in *The Works of The Rev. John Newton*

[73] Observation for the sake of learning by example was a regular practice of Newton's. He advised other pastors to it on numerous occasions, and in a letter to the Rev. Thomas Bowman in 1765, he commented that though he had only been in pastoral ministry a short eighteen months, he was greatly prepared for it through his increasing acquaintance and observation with believers and pastors of various offices and denominations over the previous twelve years. "I endeavor to avail myself of the examples, advice, and sentiments of my brethren, yet at the same time to guard against calling any man master." Letter I, "To the Rev. T. Bowman," in *Letters by the Rev. John Newton of Olney and St. Mary Woolnoth*, 120-3.

[74] Quoted in Josiah Bull, *John Newton of Olney and St. Mary Woolnoth*, 225.

[75] Letter V, "On the Snares and Difficulties Attending the Ministry of the Gospel," in *The Works of The Rev. John Newton. Complete in One Volume*, 45.

[76] "To the Hon. And Rev. W.B. Cadogan," Rev. Josiah Bull, *John Newton of Olney and St. Mary Woolnoth*, 416.

[77] Letter July 24, 1793; Ibid, 380.

[78] Letter to the Rev. Thomas Jones, in *Letters by the Rev. John Newton of Olney and St. Mary Woolnoth*, 112.

[79] Josiah Bull records someone at the time commented that as these six were

expelled for having too much religion, the proper response would be to inquire into the conduct of some who had too little. Ibid.

[80] Letter to the Rev. Thomas Jones (January 7, 1767), in *Letters by the Rev. John Newton of Olney and St. Mary Woolnoth,*

[81] Many of the following details come from Leonard G. Champion, "The Letters of John Newton to John Ryland," *The Baptist Quarterly* (1977): 157-163. Champion refers to many as yet unpublished letters between these two.

[82] Hindmarsh, *John Newton*, 49-50.

[83] Ibid, 142-168.

[84] Quoted by Champion, "The Letters of John Newton to John Ryland," 163.

[85] John H. Pratt, ed., *The Thought of the Evangelical Leaders. Notes of the Discussions of the Eclectic Society, London, during the years 1798-1814* (Carlisle, PA: Banner of Truth, 1978).

[86] Quoted in Bull, *John Newton of Olney and St. Mary Woolnoth*, 262.

[87] "Incomplete Draft from the Year 1942 of a Proclamation from the Pulpit after a Political Overthrow." Quoted by Gerhard Ludwig Muller and Albrecht Schonherr, "Editors' Afterword to the German Edition," in *Life Together; Prayerbook of the Bible*, 124.

[88] Thirty years after its publication, Karl Barth, in his own exposition of ecclesiology, confessed "I have misgivings whether I can even maintain the high level reached by Bonhoeffer, saying no less in my own words and context, and saying it no less forcefully, than did this young man so many years ago." *Church Dogmatics* IV/2 (Edinburgh: T & T Clark, 2000), 641.

[89] This experience was decisive for Bonhoeffer. He developed a close friendship with Franklin Fisher, an African-American student at Union who introduced him to the church, the writings, and the music of Harlem. Pastored by the dynamic Adam Clayton Powell, Sr., the vitality of this church, in spite of the caustic racism of the society, deeply impressed Bonhoeffer.

[90] It was during these years that Bonhoeffer became friends with the influential Anglican Bishop, George Bell, of Chichester, who relayed to the British government news from Bonhoeffer of German resistance to Hitler, and who secretly met with Bonhoeffer in Sweden, in 1942, to arrange a possible coup.

[91] Letter to Karl Barth, September 19, 1936. Quoted by Muller and Schonherr, "Editors' Afterword to the German Edition," *Life Together,* 121.

[92] Bethge, Eberhard *Dietrich Bonhoeffer A Biography*, Revised Edition. (Minneapolis: Fortress Press, 2000), 422.

[93] Some of these "underground" seminaries had to set watches in the street to look for Gestapo raiding parties. If alerted, students and professor would flee out window and door, only to regroup a few minutes later at a predetermined location and continue whatever lecture or exam had been interrupted.

[94] Bonhoeffer, *Spiritual Care*, 7.

[95] Ibid, page 155. During these times together, Bonhoeffer introduced his German seminarians to the "negro spirituals" for which he had developed a deep fondness in Harlem.

[96] Bonhoeffer, "Preface," *Life Together*, 25.

[97] Letter to Wolfgang Staemmler, June 27, 1936. Quoted by Geffrey B. Kelly, "Editor's Introduction," in *Life Together* and *Prayerbook of the Bible*, 19.

[98] Wolf-Dieter Zimmermann. *I Knew Dietrich Bonhoeffer (trans.* Kathe Gregor Smith; London: Collins, 1964), 109-110.

[99] Quoted by Gerhard Ludwig Muller and Albrecht Schonherr, "Editors' Afterword to the German Edition." *Life Together* and *Prayerbook of the Bible*, 120.

[100] Bonhoeffer, *Life Together*, 34.

[101] Bonhoeffer, *Sanctorum Communio*, 249.

[102] Ibid, 83.

[103] Hans-Werner Jensen, In Zimmerman, *I Knew Dietrich Bonhoeffer, 152.*

[104] Bonhoeffer, *Spiritual Care.*

[105] Dietrich Bonhoeffer, *Spiritual Care*, 66-67.

[106] Dietrich Bonhoeffer. *Life Together*, 95.

[107] Dietrich Bonhoeffer, *Sanctorum Communio*.

[108] Eberhard Busch, *Karl Barth*, 60.

[109] Quoted by Busch; ibid, 70.

[110] See Thurneysen's "Introduction" to Part I, and Barth's "Introduction" to Part II, in *Revolutionary Theology in the Making: Barth-Thurneysen Correspondence, 1914-1925* (trans. James D. Smart; Richmond: John Knox Press, 1964), 11-25, 65-73.

[111] Some of these early letters were published in English in the volume mentioned above. The Barth Archive in Basel is currently editing other volumes of letters. Volumes including letters up through 1938 have been published in German, though not yet in English.

[112] Busch, *Karl Barth,* p. 137. This reference is interesting also in light of the fact that Barth scrapped his first volume of a *Christian Dogmatics,* and started over on the *Church Dogmatics.* The adjective "Christian" claimed too much for the project; "Christian" was a much better noun than adjective, he thought. His project was to be a work of the Church for the Church. Douglas Horton, translator of Barth's *The Word of God and the Word of Man*, comments: "Parish ministers have found his utterances stimulating because, having been one of them himself, he speaks and writes from their standpoint." "Forward," in Karl Barth, *The Word of God and The Word of Man* (trans. Douglas Horton; New York: Harper and Brothers, 1957), 5.

[113] "Preface to the Second Edition," *The Epistle to the Romans* (trans. Edwyn C. Hoskyns; New York: Oxford University Press, 1977), 15.

[114] These were published in German as *God's Search for Man*, in 1917, and *Come, Holy Spirit,* in 1924. English Translations: *God's Search for Man* (trans.

George W. Richards, Elmer G. Homrighausen, Karl J. Ernst; New York: Round Table Press, 1935); *Come, Holy Spirit* (trans. George W. Richards, Elmer G. Homrighausen, Karl J. Ernst; New York: Round Table Press, 1933).

[115] Thurneysen to Barth, letter of May 9, 1922, in *Revolutionary Theology*.

[116] Quoted in Busch, *Karl Barth*, 74.

[117] Along with Barth, Thurneysen's references to the "Word of God" alludes not only to Scripture, the written word, but also and primarily to Christ, the incarnate Word, and to the Spirit, who carries on the work of Christ, the incarnate Word.

[118] *A Theology of Pastoral Care* (trans. Jack A. Worthington and Thomas Wieser; Richmond: John Knox Press, 1962), 113-4.

[119] Barth to Thurneysen, letter of June 8, 1922, in *Revolutionary Theology*.

[120] Barth to Thurneysen, letter of March 26, 1922, in *Revolutionary Theology*: "Oh! If only someone would give me time, time, time, to do everything *properly*, to read everything at *my own* tempo, to take it apart and put it together again."

[121] Karl Barth, "Introduction" to Part Two, in *Revolutionary Theology in the Making*.

[122] Thurneysen, *A Theology of Pastoral Care*, 10. Thurneysen and Martin Buber, the Jewish philosopher who introduced the "I-Thou" terminology, conversed on numerous occasions, and Thurneysen considered him a theological ally.

[123] Ibid., 108-9.

[124] This happens to be from the Anglican Book of Common Prayer, but could be illustrated from numerous liturgies.

[125] Barth and Thurneysen together established two theological journals during these years: *Between the Times*, and *Theological Existence Today*.

[126] Barth's phone was illegally tapped, his lectures were banned, and his publications were confiscated by the Swiss authorities 1941. They considered jailing him, as the Swiss ambassador Frolicher said, "to put a muzzle on Barth" because he was "disturbing a proper relationship with Germany"—and this in 1941.

[127] Busch, *Karl Barth*, 498. Forty years earlier Barth had written similar words: "As regards theology . . . we cannot be in the Church without taking as much responsibility for the theology of the past as for the theology of our present. Augustine, Aquinas, Luther, Schleiermacher, and all the rest are not dead but living. They still speak and demand a hearing as living voices." See his *Protestant Theology in the 19th Century*.

CHAPTER 9:
TOOLS FOR MENTORING

[1] Aelred of Rievaulx, *Spiritual Friendship*. (trans. Mary Eugenia Laker; Kalamazoo, Michigan: Cistercian Publications, 1977), 51.

[2] Nemeck & Coombs, *The Way Of Spiritual Direction*, 79.

[3] Søren Kierkegaard, *The Prayers of Kierkegaard* (ed. Perry D. Lefevre; Chicago: The University of Chicago Press, 1956).

[4] Thurneysen, *A Theology of Pastoral Care*, 343.

[5] Anderson & Reese, *Spiritual Mentoring*, 37.

[6] Zylstra, *Testament of Vision*, 66.

[7] Nemeck and Coombs, *The Way Of Spiritual Direction*, 94.

[8] Doran McCarty, *The Supervision of Ministry Students* (Atlanta: Home Mission Board SBC, 1978), 79.

CHAPTER 10:
A BENEDICTION

[1] This was from 379-382, during the time of the great Second Ecumenical Council, at Constantinople, for which Gregory's leadership was decisive, and at which the Nicene Creed was reaffirmed.

[2] Letter LII(7), To Nepotian, A.D. 394, in *Nicene and Post-Nicene Fathers. Second Series. Volume VI. St. Jerome: Letters* (trans. W.H. Fremantle, with Rev. G. Lewis, Rev. W.G. Martley; ed. Philip Schaff; Edinburgh: T & T Clark, 1998).

[3] Dietrich Bonhoeffer, *Life Together*, 31.

Printed in the United States
60733LVS00003B/199-222